SUBSTANCE AND FORM IN HISTORY

FOR W.H.WALSH

SUBSTANCE AND FORM
IN HISTORY

A Collection of Essays in
Philosophy of History

EDITED BY

L.POMPA AND W.H.DRAY

FOR THE UNIVERSITY OF
EDINBURGH
PRESS

© 1981
EDINBURGH UNIVERSITY PRESS
22 George Square, Edinburgh

ISBN 0 85224 413 4

Set in Monotype Plantin
and printed in Great Britain by
Clark Constable Ltd
Edinburgh

901
S941

Contents

List of Contributors

Sir Isaiah Berlin	All Souls College, Oxford
Professor R. F. Atkinson	University of Exeter
P. Gardiner	Magdalen College, Oxford
Professor L. J. Goldstein	State University of New York at Binghamton
Professor D. O'Brien	Bucknell University, Lewisburg, Pennsylvania
Professor N. Rotenstreich	The Hebrew University of Jerusalem
Professor R. Martin	The University of Kansas, Lawrence
Professor L. O. Mink	Wesleyan University, Middletown, Connecticut
J. L. Gorman	The Queen's University of Belfast
J. R. Lucas	Merton College, Oxford
Professor P. H. Nowell-Smith	York University, Ontario
Professor W. H. Dray	University of Ottawa, Ontario
Professor L. Pompa	University of Birmingham

Preface

This *Festschrift* is in honour of Professor W. H. Walsh. Its focus is philosophy of history, a field in which his eminence is internationally acknowledged, but so many are the areas of philosophy in which he has achieved equal renown that it could as appropriately have comprised a volume of essays on the thought of Kant or Hegel, or in ethics, metaphysics or the history of metaphysics. It is unusual for a scholar to attain genuine international recognition over such a wide range of subjects and almost impossible to do justice to it in a single volume. It is our hope, however, that while centred in philosophy of history, the volume will be seen to relate its problems to those of other areas of philosophy in the way in which its dedicatee has done with such distinction in his own work.

William Henry Walsh – Richard, as he is known to his friends – was born in 1913. Educated at Bradford and Leeds Grammar Schools, he gained a Classical Exhibition in 1932 at Merton College, Oxford, thus beginning a life-long connection with the College. His undergraduate career there was highly successful: having been awarded the Gaisford Greek Prize and a First in Honours Mods in 1934, he went on to take a First in Greats in 1936 and won a Junior Research Fellowship at the College in the same year. Although his equal facility in history and philosophy had left him at first undecided between these two subjects, by the time he took up his Research Fellowship it was clear that the formative influence of his distinguished tutor, G. R. G. Mure, had turned the focus of his interests towards philosophy, giving him a special feeling for the work of Kant, Hegel and the British Idealists, particularly that of Merton's own former Fellow, F. H. Bradley. In 1938 he married Trixie (neé Pearson) whom he met when she was studying French as an Exhibitioner at St Hilda's College. Her own passionate belief in academic values has afforded him constant support in his own research. Their three children, Catharine, Stephen and Polly, inherited their abilities and interests, going on themselves to study philosophy and modern languages at university. The outbreak of the Second World War interrupted the tenure of his fellowship, at a time when he was primarily engaged in a study of Kant. During the war he served first in the Signals Corps and then, from 1941–5, in the Foreign Office. Upon his return to Merton in 1946, his specialised research on Kant gave way to a more general concern with the various ways in which metaphysicians have sought to make sense of the notion of experience as a whole, resulting in his first book, *Reason and Experience*.

After a brief spell as Lecturer in Philosophy at the University of Dundee (1946–7), his connection with Merton was re-established when he was appointed Fellow and Tutor of the College and Lecturer in the University of Oxford. Thus began the first of the two main periods into which his teaching career has fallen. He remained at Merton continuously until 1960,

with the exception of the year 1957–8, when he was Visiting Professor at the
State University of Ohio. Despite heavy teaching commitments – often
around twenty hours a week – as well as administrative tasks for his College,
he produced an almost continuous stream of publications throughout these
years. It was in this period also that his earlier interest in history resurfaced,
leading first to a series of lectures in philosophy of history – Professor R. F.
Atkinson recalls, in a personal letter, that it was these that first aroused his
own interest in the subject, and there are many others who would say the
same – and then to the publication of *An Introduction to Philosophy of History*
in 1951. Thirty years and two editions later, not only is this still the standard
work of its kind in English, but it continues to stimulate more specialised
work in this field, many detailed monographs still reverting to and discussing
it.

The second period of his teaching career began in 1960, when he was
appointed Professor of Logic and Metaphysics at the University of Edinburgh. His tenure of this Chair coincided with the expansion of the sixties
and the retrenchment of the seventies. As Professor and rotating Head of a
large department, he found himself inevitably drawn heavily into administration. Apart from his periods as Head of the Department, he was also
Dean of the Faculty of Arts, Chairman of the University of Edinburgh Press
Committee (a circumstance that necessitated delaying the planning of this
volume until he had retired from the University), a member of the University Court, one of the Curators of Patronage – a body empowered to make
recommendations for the appointment to the Vice-Chancellorship – and,
from 1975–9, one of the University's three Vice-Principals. Despite these
and many other administrative tasks, he still found time to teach for an
average of twelve hours a week, while attending to the needs of his own
department and of his research.

When he first arrived in Edinburgh, the teaching of philosophy was
divided along traditional Scottish lines into two central areas, falling under
the supervision of the Professor of Moral Philosophy and the Professor of
Logic and Metaphysics. This division was academically too restricting and
one of his first undertakings was, in consultation with his friend, the then
Professor of Moral Philosophy, Winston H. Barnes, to modify it in favour of
a more flexible structure which enabled both staff and students to pursue
more easily the systematic connections that run across the divisions of
philosophy. Another important development was to strengthen the teaching
of logic, an area of philosophy previously relatively neglected in the University. A third was to alter the balance of teaching methods, hitherto con-
sisting largely of lectures and seminars, more towards the needs of individual
students, by placing much more emphasis upon tutorials. Finally, the
number of post-graduate students was much increased and new programmes
of graduate work introduced.

Teaching, administration, membership of the Editorial Boards of such
journals as *Kant-Studien* and *History and Theory*, and incessant *ad hoc*

advisory work, constituted in themselves a heavy enough load. Nevertheless his academic output was fully maintained in these years. Apart from a steady flow of articles and papers delivered to international conferences, three books, *Metaphysics, Hegelian Ethics* and *Kant's Criticism of Metaphysics* were published in 1963, 1969 and 1976, respectively, these reflecting three of the dominant themes with which he has continuously been concerned. *Metaphysics*, which continued to grapple with the problem posed in *Reason and Experience*, was written as a defence of that branch of philosophy, at a time when it was fashionable to question its very existence. *Hegelian Ethics*, apart from being a contribution to Hegelian studies, expresses his own view that a satisfactory understanding of the moral life must take into account the concrete social and historical context in which the agent finds himself, rather than seek to find an essence of morality which can be grasped in abstraction from it. With *Kant's Criticism of Metaphysics* a longstanding ambition was fulfilled: to present an account of Kant's doctrines which, while sensitive to the difficulties and obscurities of the text of the *Critique of Pure Reason*, would show, by critical discussion, the on-going philosophical worth of Kant's work.

Recognition of the academic value of his work was expressed in a series of honours conferred on him during these years. In 1963 he was the Dawes Hicks Lecturer in the British Academy. In 1964–5, he was President of the Aristotelian Society. In 1969 he was elected Fellow of the British Academy. In 1978 he became a Fellow of the Royal Society of Edinburgh and, in the same year, the University of Rochester conferred an Honorary Doctorate upon him. His standing in the U.S.A. was, indeed, such that he also spent periods of varying length there teaching, at Dartmouth College in 1965, at the University of Maryland, 1969–70, and, upon his retirement from Edinburgh, at the University of Kansas as the Rose Morgan Visiting Professor, 1979–80.

In 1979 he retired from Edinburgh University as Professor Emeritus and returned to Merton, where he is now Fellow Emeritus of the College. It is not, however, in his nature to be inactive and already in 1979 he had helped to found the Hegel Society of Great Britain, of whose Council he is now a member. In addition he has completed work on an anthology of selected essays, some of which are previously unpublished. He is now about to undertake a long-term project for which his background and abilities perfectly suit him: a study of the Oxford Idealists, particularly his own distinguished predecessor at Merton, F. H. Bradley. Its completion will be awaited with eager anticipation.

Richard Walsh has never been a fashionable philosopher in the sense of being prepared to allow his interests to be too much determined by current trends in philosophy. Although always well aware of what these were, he has nevertheless pursued his research according to his own evaluation of what is important in the subject. This has had the consequence that whereas, in the case of philosophy of history, his work has been the object of much attention because it has coincided with current interests, in the case of history of philosophy or metaphysics, due to their comparative neglect until recently, it has been studied largely by those who share his belief that most of the problems of philosophy are of perennial interest. For them, however, and their number is large, his work has served as an inspiring example and, when the prevailing philosophical climate has seemed unsympathetic, a constant support.

A *Festschrift* honours its subject. At the same time it affords pupils, friends and admirers of distinguished scholars the great pleasure of expressing their gratitude and admiration publicly. We offer these essays to Richard Walsh in the knowledge that in so doing we express the sentiments of countless others throughout the academic world.

L.P., Birmingham, *March* 1981

Acknowledgements

We wish to express our gratitude to Dr Jonathan L. Gorman and to Professor W.H.Walsh, who were responsible for compiling the Bibliography of Professor Walsh's writings. They were given very considerable help by the Librarian of the Queen's University of Belfast and the Editorial staff of *The Times Higher Educational Supplement*, to whom we are also most grateful. Our other main debt is to Mrs Shirley Shakespeare, Secretary to the Department of Philosophy of the University of Birmingham. It is not possible to express too fully our gratitude for the invaluable assistance she has given us throughout, in the editing of this volume. We are also grateful to the editors of *The British Journal of Eighteenth-Century Studies* for permission to print a revised version of Sir Isaiah Berlin's paper that appeared in their issue of Autumn 1980, Vol.3, No.2.

1. Note on Alleged Relativism in Eighteenth-century European Thought

ISAIAH BERLIN

It is an accepted truth, of which this audience certainly does not need to be reminded, that the central view of the French *philosophes* (whatever their, often very sharp, differences) is that (in the words of the eminent American anthropologist, Professor Clifford Geertz) 'Man is of a piece with nature: there is a human nature as invariant as Newton's world' (Geertz, 1973). The laws that govern it may be different, but they exist. Manners, fashions, tastes may differ, but the same passions which move men everywhere, at all times, cause the same behaviour. 'Only the general, the universal, the unchanging is real, and therefore only this is truly human' (Geertz, 1973). Only that is true which any rational observer, at any time, in any place, can, in principle, discover. Rational methods – hypothesis, observation, generalisation, deduction, where it is possible experimental verification – can solve social and individual problems, as they have triumphantly solved those of physics and astronomy, and are progressively solving those of chemistry, biology and economics; philosophy, that is, ethics, politics, aesthetics, logic, theory of knowledge, can and should be transformed into a general science of man – the natural science of anthropology; once knowledge of man's true nature is attained, men's real needs will be clear: the only remaining tasks are to discover how they may be satisfied, and to act upon this knowledge. The majority of human ills – hunger, disease, insecurity, poverty, misery, injustice, oppression – are due to ignorance, indolence and error, consciously or unconsciously fomented by those whose interests are served by this reign of darkness; the triumph of the scientific spirit will sweep away the forces of prejudice, superstition, stupidity and cruelty, too long concealed by the mumbo-jumbo of theologians and lawyers. Some *philosophes* were pessimistic about the prospects of universal enlightenment, at any rate in a foreseeable future; but none among them denied that it was in principle, if not in practice, attainable. They knew, of course, that there had always existed those who had been sceptical about the central thesis itself – that it was possible, even in principle, to discover such final solutions: relativists, such as the Greek sophists assailed by Plato, or those who agreed with Aristotle that 'fire burns both here and in Persia, but what is thought just changes before our very eyes' (Aristotle). There were sceptics from Aenesidemus, Carneades and Sextus Empiricus to their modern disciples – Montaigne and his followers – who had maintained that in the vast welter of diverse human beliefs and practices (described as early as Herodotus, and by Voltaire's time much added to by the great increase in the number of travellers' tales and historical investigations) no universal rules could possibly be found. There were Christian thinkers, whether Bossuet or Pascal, who held that man in his fallen state had no means of establishing the full truth, which only God possessed. The majority of the French *philosophes* reacted against this outlook: for them the Christian view of man was demonstrably false. As for the doubts of Montaigne or Charron or La Motte Le Vayer, these had been understandable in a confused, pre-scientific age, but could now be dissolved, as those of the old natural philosophers had been, by the application of Newtonian methods. Nor were such contemporary doubters as Montesquieu or Hume a source of danger; Montesquieu did not doubt the universality of ultimate human values, founded, as they were, unlike passing tastes or conventions, on eternal reason or nature; all men by nature sought security, justice, social stability, happiness; only means differed according to natural, environmental, and social conditions and the institutions, habits, tastes, conventions, resulting from them. In his *Spicilège* (no.517), after describing the plot of a Chinese play, the first he had come across, Montesquieu remarks 'elle m'a paru contre nos moeurs, mais non pas contre la raison'; so, too, in his *Pensées* (no.122) he distinguishes *moeurs*, which vary widely, from *la nature* which is immutable; accordingly (in pensée 817) he declares that modern comedies are at fault in seeking to ridicule human passions (which are natural and can never be ridiculous) as opposed to manners, which can be absurd. The limits of relativism are here firmly established: the context is aesthetic, but examples show that the principle extends to the whole of experience (Beyer, 1963, p.179). In morals and politics and even aesthetic judgments, Montesquieu is no less objectivist about men's central ends than Helvétius: he merely probed and analysed more and preached less. As for Hume, he did away with the notion of natural necessity, and thereby did, indeed, destroy the metaphysical cement which had hitherto held the objective world together as a system of logically linked relations within, and between, facts and events; but even he did not seek to disrupt the accepted patterns of these relations, but merely transposed them into the empirical mode, from *a priori* necessity to *de facto* probability. A man who, in a famous passage, said 'Human nature remains still the same in its principles and operations . . . ambition, avarice, self-love, vanity, friendship, generosity, public spirit', or again, that if a traveller brought us an account of men 'wholly different from any with whom we were ever acquainted' – far nicer than any we have met – 'we should immediately . . . detect the falsehood and prove him a liar with the same certainty as if he had stuffed his narration with stories of centaurs and dragons, miracles and prodigies' (Hume, 1748; Crocker, 1959, pp.186–7) – such a thinker offered no serious threat to the programme of the *philosophes, pace* Professor Becker's over-dramatised account of Hume's alleged subversion of the Heavenly City of the eighteenth century. Nor were Diderot's speculations on how the world of the blind and deaf would differ from that of the healthy, a form of relativism; for differences of climate, legislation, education, physique, only dictated different paths to the same goals, which nature and reason had set for all men, everywhere. Locke, despite his celebrated lists of societies which looked without disapproval on deicide, infanticide, cannibalism and other monstrous practices, nevertheless found the central universal human purpose in the 'absolute necessity' of 'holding society together', elaborated as a species of utilitarianism (Locke, 1690, Book 1, Ch.II, Book 2, Ch.XXVIII). Among eighteenth-century writers perhaps Sade and Deschamps uttered genuinely relativist opinions about ends as well as means, but they were marginal figures and disregarded. When Racine says (Racine, 1674; Geertz, 1973, p.35) 'the taste of Paris . . . conforms to that of Athens; my spectators have been moved by the same things which, in other times, brought tears to the most cultivated classes of Greece', he is echoed equally by Voltaire and Dr Johnson (Geertz, 1973). When cultural differences are stripped off, what remains, at least until Burke, is Rousseau's natural man. So, too, within every kind of civilised man there is Diderot's immutable natural man struggling to get out: the two are everywhere locked in a civil war that is the permanent condition of human culture everywhere.

This position, perhaps the deepest single assumption of Western thought, was attacked by two of the fathers of modern historicism, Vico and Herder (I use the term not in Karl Popper's sense, but in the more usual one employed by Meinecke, Troeltsch and Croce). We all know that these thinkers denied the possibility of establishing the final truth in all the provinces of human thought by the application of the laws of the natural sciences. Both Vico and Herder are sometimes described as relativists. In this connection one thing ought to be made clear. There are at least two types of relativism, that of judgments of fact, and that of judgments of values. The first, in its strongest form, denies the very possibility of objective knowledge of facts, since all belief is conditioned by the place in the social system, and therefore by the interests, conscious or not, of the theorist, or of the group or class to which he belongs. The weaker version (e.g. that of Karl Mannheim) exempts the natural sciences from this predicament, or identifies a privileged group (in Mannheim's view, the intelligentsia) as being, somewhat mysteriously, free from these distorting factors. Whether the first, or stronger, version is ultimately self-refuting (as I am inclined to believe) is a philosophical crux that cannot be discussed here. It is, however, only the second type of relativism, that of values or entire outlooks, that is in question here. No one, so far as I know, has ascribed relativism regarding factual knowledge to Vico or Herder. Their critique of the unhistorical approach which they attribute to the French *lumières* is confined to the interpretation and evaluation of past attitudes and cultures. I wonder how much *Wissenssoziologie* (radical sociology of knowledge) as we know it today is to be found before Marx and the Young Hegelians. This audience does not need to be reminded that Vico regarded each stage of the historical cycle of cultures (through which each gentile nation was bound to pass) as embodying its own autonomous values, its own vision of the world, in particular its own conception of the relations of men to one another and to the forces of nature; and that he believed that it was in terms of this alone that their culture, that is, the significance attached by these men themselves to what they did and what was done to them, could be understood by us, their descendants. He maintained that men at each stage of this process generated their own expressions and interpretations of their experience – indeed, that their experience *was* these expressions and interpretations, which took the form of words, images, myths, ritual, institutions, artistic creation, worship. Only the study of these could convey what the human past was like: and enable posterity not merely to record it, which could be accomplished by a mere description of the regularities of behaviour, but also to understand it, that is, to grasp what these men were at – not merely to describe the gestures, but to reveal the intention behind them – that is, tell us what their words, movements, gestures meant to themselves; only so could we avoid being totally at sea about them. To understand what our ancestors saw, felt, thought, it is not enough merely to record, and offer causal explanations for, observed human behaviour, as zoologists record the behaviour of animals, which, for example, Condorcet regarded as basically the correct approach to human societies. For Vico, each of these cultures, or stages of development, is not just a link in a causal chain or contingent sequence, but a phase in a providential plan governed by divine purpose. Each phase is incommensurable with the others, since each lives by its own light and can be understood only in its own terms, even though these terms form a single intelligible process, which is not wholly, or, perhaps, even largely, intelligible to us. If a civilisation is interpreted, or, worse still, evaluated, by the application of criteria that hold only for other civilisations, its character will be misunderstood – be a form of what is nowadays attacked as cultural imperialism; and the account presented will, at best, be a systematically misleading, at worst a scarcely coherent story, a haphazard succession of events, somewhat like Voltaire's entertaining parodies of the Dark Ages. Neither Vico nor Herder are Humean empiricists: human history for them is not a mere set of *de facto* regularities; the pattern – every section of it – serves God's purposes; the different characters of each culture are imposed by this pattern – a species of temporalised natural law. Hence the constant warnings by both against cultural egocentricity and anachronism: and their appeals (whether valid or not) to the use of a special imaginative faculty to enable historians to enter, with whatever difficulty, into outlooks which they perceive, even while understanding ('entering into') them, to be unlike our own. This doctrine, whether, as in the case of Vico, it is applied to the past stages of a recurrent cycle, or, as it was by Herder, to differences of national cultures, is wholly incompatible with that expressed in Racine's lines quoted above, or that of Voltaire, who seemed to be convinced that the central values of civilised men everywhere, and at all times, were, more or less, identical; it was still less compatible, if that is possible, with the position of those *Encyclopédistes* who believed in linear progress – a single upward movement of mankind from darkness to light, which, rising in ignorance, brutish savagery, superstition, delusion, after much stumbling, many detours and retrogressions, finally culminated in the ideal reign of knowledge, virtue, wisdom and happiness.

I come to my central point. Because of their conception of the cultural autonomy of different societies (whether divided by space or time) and the incommensurability of their systems of values, Vico's and Herder's opposition to the central tenets of the French Enlightenment have commonly been described as a form of relativism. This *idée reçue* seems to me now to be a widespread error, like the label of relativism attached to Hume and Montesquieu, an error which, I must admit, I have in the past perpetrated myself. In a recent review (New York Review of Books, 1976) a distinguished and learned critic wondered if I had fully appreciated the implications of the historical relativism of Vico and Herder which, unacknowledged by them, dominated the historical outlook of these Christian thinkers, and constituted a problem which has persisted to this day. If we grant the assumption that Vico and Herder were in fact relativists – that is, not merely historicists who hold that human thought and action are fully intelligible only in relation to their historical context, but upholders of a theory of ideology according to which the ideas and attitudes of individuals or groups are inescapably determined by varying conditioning factors, say, their place in the evolving social structures of their societies, or the relations of production, or genetic, psychological or other causes, or combinations of these – on an assumption of that kind, the point made by my critic was valid. But I now believe this to be a mistaken interpretation of Vico and Herder, although I have, in my time, inadvertently contributed to it myself. Doubts about the possibility of objective knowledge of the past, about changing perspectives of it determined by transient, culture-conditioned attitudes and values, such as are said to have oppressed Mommsen towards the end of his life, and troubled Wilamowitz in his prime, problems anxiously discussed principally by German thinkers – Max Weber, Troeltsch, Rickert, Simmel, and leading to the radical conclusions of Karl Mannheim and his school – these problems seem to me to have originated in the nineteenth century. When Voltaire said that history was a pack of tricks which we played upon the dead, that cynical witticism can hardly be regarded as contradicting his general moral and cultural objectivism. True relativism developed from other and later sources: German Romantic irrationalism, the metaphysics of Schopenhauer and Nietzsche, the growth of schools of social anthropology, the doctrines of William Graham Sumner and Edward Westermarck, above all the influence of thinkers who were not necessarily relativists themselves – Marx, for example, or Freud, whose analyses of appearance or illusion and reality entailed belief in the objectivity of their own disciplines, without, perhaps, awareness of, at any rate, some of their full implications.

I may be speaking in ignorance, and stand ready to be corrected, but I know of no consistent effort by any influential thinker in the eighteenth

B

century to put forward relativist views. Some leading French *philosophes* certainly declared that passions and 'interest' could unconsciously mould values and entire outlooks; but they also believed that critical reason could dissipate this and remove obstacles to objective knowledge both of fact and of value. So, too, Lessing, who believed that values alter as mankind progresses, was not troubled by relativist doubts, any more than the leading historians of the first half of the nineteenth century – Ranke, Macaulay, Carlyle, Guizot, Michelet (the self-confessed disciple of Vico), Taine, Fustel de Coulanges; not even the early nationalists influenced by Herder. There is, so far as I can see, no relativism in the best known attacks on the Enlightenment by reactionary thinkers – Hamann, Justus Möser, Burke, De Maistre. Relativism, in its modern form, tends to spring from the view that men's outlooks are unavoidably determined by forces of which they are often unaware – Schopenhauer's irrational cosmic force; Marx's class-bound morality; Freud's unconscious drives; the social anthropologists' panorama of the irreconcilable variety of customs and beliefs conditioned by circumstances largely uncontrolled by men.

Let me return to the alleged relativism of Vico and Herder. Perhaps I can make my point best by giving as an example their aesthetic views. When Vico speaks of the splendour of the Homeric poems and gives reasons why they could only have been produced in a society dominated by a violent, ambitious, cruel and avaricious élite of 'heroes', so that such epics could not be generated in his own 'enlightened' times; when Herder tells us that to understand the Bible we must try to enter the world of nomadic Judaean shepherds, or that men who have seen sailors struggling with the waters of the Skagerrak can better understand the stern beauty of the old Scandinavian sagas and songs; when both thinkers maintain that unless we succeed in doing this, we shall not understand what these earlier men lived by, spiritually as well as materially, they are not telling us that the values of these societies, dissimilar to ours, cast doubts on the objectivity of our own, or are undermined by them, because the existence of conflicting values or incompatible outlooks must mean that at most only one of these is valid, the rest being false; or, alternatively, that none belong to the kind of judgments that can be considered either valid or invalid. Rather, they are inviting us to look at societies different from our own, the ultimate values of which we can perceive to be wholly understandable ends of life for men who are different, indeed, from us, but human beings, *semblables*, into whose circumstances we can, by a great effort which we are commanded to make, find a way, 'enter', to use Vico's term. We are urged to look upon life as affording a plurality of values, equally genuine, equally ultimate, above all equally objective; incapable, therefore, of being ordered in a timeless hierarchy, or judged in terms of some one absolute standard. There is a finite variety of values and attitudes some of which one society, some another, have made their own, attitudes and values which members of other societies may admire or condemn (in the light of their own value systems) but can always, if they are sufficiently imaginative and try hard enough, contrive to understand – that is, see to be intelligible ends of life for human beings situated as these men were. In the house of human history there are many mansions; this view may be un-Christian; yet it appears to have been held by both these pious eighteenth-century thinkers.

This doctrine is called pluralism. There are many objective ends, ultimate values, some incompatible with others, pursued by different societies at various times, or by different groups in the same society, by entire classes or churches or races, or by particular individuals within them, any one of which may find itself subject to conflicting claims of uncombinable, yet equally ultimate and objective, ends. Incompatible these ends may be; but their variety cannot be unlimited, for the nature of men, however various and subject to change, must possess some generic character if it is to be called human at all. This holds, *a fortiori*, of differences between entire cultures. There is a limit beyond which we can no longer understand what a given creature is at; what kinds of rules it follows in its behaviour; what its gestures mean. In such situations, when the possibility of communication breaks down, we speak of derangement, of incomplete humanity. But within the limits of humanity, the variety of ends, finite though it is, can be extensive The fact that the values of one culture may be incompatible with those of another, or that they are in conflict within one culture or group or in a single human being at different times – or, for that matter, at one and the same time – does not entail relativism of values, only the notion of a plurality of values not structured hierarchically; which, of course, entails the permanent possibility of inescapable conflict between values, as well as incompatibility between the outlooks of different civilisations or of stages of the same civilisation.

Relativism is something different: I take it to mean a doctrine according to which the judgment of a man or a group, since it is the expression or statement of a taste, or emotional attitude or outlook, is simply what it is, with no objective correlate which determines its truth or falsehood. I like mountains, you do not; I love history, he thinks it is bunkum: it all depends on one's point of view. It follows that to speak of truth or falsehood on these assumptions is literally meaningless. But the values of each culture or phase of a culture are (for Vico or Herder or their disciples) not mere psychological, but objective, although not therefore necessarily commensurable facts, either within a culture or (still less) as between cultures. Let me offer an illustration of this view. The English critic Wyndham Lewis, in a work named *The Demon of Progress in the Arts*, pointed out that it is absurd to speak, as many have, and still do, of progress between one style of art and another. I cannot remember his actual examples, but his principal point was that it was absurd to range artists in a linear series – to think of, let us say, Dante as a more developed Homer, or of Shakespeare as an inferior Addison (as Voltaire thought), or of Phidias as a rudimentary Rodin. Are the paintings of Lascaux superior or inferior to those of Poussin? Is Mozart a less developed forerunner of *musique concrète?* The Quarrel of the Ancients and Moderns was based on the presupposition that such questions were answerable; perhaps even Montesquieu thought so. Vico and Herder did not. For them, values are many; some of the most fascinating come to light in the course of voyages, both in time and space; some among them cannot, in principle, be harmonised with one another. This leads to the conclusion, not explicitly formulated by either thinker, that the ancient ideal, common to many cultures and especially to that of the Enlightenment, of a perfect society in which all true human ends are reconciled, is conceptually incoherent. But this is not relativism. That doctrine, in all its versions, holds that there are no objective values; some varieties of it maintain that men's outlooks are so conditioned by natural or cultural factors as to render them incapable of seeing the values of other societies or epochs as no less worthy of pursuit than their own, if not by themselves then by others. The most extreme versions of cultural relativism, which stress the vast differences of cultures, hold that one culture can scarcely begin to understand what other civilisations lived by – can only describe their behaviour but not its purpose or meaning, as some early anthropologists described the behaviour of savage societies. If this were true (as, e.g., Spengler, and at some moments even Dilthey, seemed to say) the very idea of the history of civilisation becomes an insoluble puzzle.

At the heart of the best known type of modern historical relativism lies the conception of men wholly bound by tradition or culture or class or generation to particular attitudes or scales of value which cause other outlooks or ideals to seem strange and, at times, even unintelligible; if the existence of such outlooks is recognised, this inevitably leads to scepticism about objective standards, since it becomes meaningless to ask which of them is correct. This is not at all Vico's position; nor (despite one or two remarks, as when he says 'Mother Nature has created . . . limited horizons for various men beyond which they cannot see and scarcely speculate') (Herder, v, Sec.1; Barnard, 1969, p.186) is it in general that of Herder either. This would indeed have been, to say the least, a strange doctrine for Christian thinkers, however unorthodox, to hold; paradoxes are not unknown in the history of ideas; but no such oddity arises in this case. Both thinkers advocate the use of the historical imagination which can enable us to 'descend to' or 'enter' or 'feel oneself into' the mentality of remote societies; thereby we understand them, that is, grasp (or believe that we grasp, for we cannot ever be certain, even though Vico and Herder seem to speak as if we can) what the acts of the men in question, the sounds or marks on stone or papyrus that they make, or their bodily movements, mean: that is, what they are signs of, what part they play in the conceptions of their worlds held by these men and women themselves, how they interpret what goes on; we are urged to 'achieve familiarity' (to quote Professor Geertz, 1973, again) 'with the imaginative universe within which their acts are signs'. This is the goal, he tells us, of social anthropology; it is certainly the conception of historical understanding of the past held by both Vico and Herder. If the quest is successful, we shall see that the values of these remote peoples are such as human beings like ourselves – creatures capable of conscious intellectual and moral discrimination – could live by. These values may attract or repel us: but to understand a past culture is to understand how men like ourselves, in a particular natural or man-made environment, could embody them in their activities, and why; by dint of enough historical investigation and imaginative sympathy, to see how human (that is, intelligible) lives could be lived by pursuing them.

Pluralism in this sense actually ante-dates the new historicism of the eighteenth century. It is manifest in the polemics against Rome of the jurists among the Reformers in the sixteenth century. Men like the Chancelier Pasquin or Dumoulin or Hotman argued that while ancient Roman law or custom was relevant to Rome, ancient or modern, it would not do for the descendants of Franks or Gauls; they insisted on the equally objective validity of different sets of values for dissimilar societies and conditions; and believed that the appropriateness of a particular code to a particular society and form of life could be demonstrated by universally valid, i.e. non-relativist factual and logical considerations. This is Herder's (and Chairman Mao's) garden of many flowers. When Herder says 'Each nation' (and elsewhere 'each age') 'has its own centre of gravity' (Herder, v, Sec.1; Barnard, 1969, p.188), he recognises a single principle of 'gravitation': the anthropology which Herder wishes to develop is one which would enable one to tell what creates the happiness of what social whole, or of what kinds of individuals. 'General progressive improvement of the world . . .' is 'a fiction'. No 'true student of history or the human heart' could believe this. Each stage of development has its own value: 'the youth is not happier than the innocent, contented child; nor is the peaceful old man less happy than the energetic man in his prime.' There is an order, a growth, a dependence of each stage, each human group, on one another – but no progress towards an optimum (*ibid.*). But for Herder all the various peaks of human endeavour, based on differences in needs and circumstances, are equally objective and knowable. This is anything but relativism.

There are many kinds of happiness (or beauty or goodness or visions of life) and they are, at times, incommensurable: but all respond to the real needs and aspirations of normal human beings: each fits its circumstances, its country, its people; the relation of 'fitting' is the same in all these cases; and members of one culture can understand and enter the minds of, and sympathise with, those of another (Herder, v, 47). When Herder attacks Voltaire's dogmatic assumption that the values of civilised societies – his own – of a few selected cultures in the past – in Athens, Rome, Florence Paris – are alone true, he uses all his considerable creative gifts to bring to life the aims and outlooks of many cultures, Eastern and Western, and contrasts them with those of the Enlightenment: not simply as a matter of brute fact – of variety as such – of the prevalence of *sic volo, sic jubeo* – but as the ways of life which, no matter how different from our own, normal men could find it natural to pursue; such ways of life as we, armed as we are (for both Vico and Herder) with the capacity to perceive the (objectively) good, beautiful and just, in all their guises and transformations, should not find it too strange to pursue in similar conditions, even if we do not ourselves accept them. In his Journal of 1769 Herder wrote that there was not a man, a country, a people, a national history, a state, which resembled each other. Hence truth, goodness and beauty differed one from another. Yet they must all be recognisable as possible ends of beings whom we recognise to be men and women like ourselves (Herder, IV, 472). We are called upon to exercise our imaginative powers to the utmost; but not to go beyond them; not to accept as authentic values anything that we cannot understand, imaginatively 'enter' into.

Relativism is not the only alternative to universalism – what Lovejoy called 'uniformitarianism' – nor does incommensurability entail relativism. There are many worlds, some of which overlap. The world of the Greeks is not that of the Jews nor of eighteenth-century Germans or Italians; nor is the world of the rich the world of the poor, nor that of the happy the world of the unhappy; but all such values and ultimate ends are open to human pursuit, as the comparative study of history and literature and philosophy and *Völkerpsychologie* and religion reveals. This is what Vico and Herder mean when they tell us not to judge past cultures by the measuring rods of our own civilisation, not to perpetrate anachronisms under the influence of what Vico attacks as national or philosophical vanity. Both thinkers insist on our need and ability to transcend the values of our own culture or nation or class, or those of whatever other windowless boxes to which some cultural relativists wish to confine us. Herder's writings teem with contemporary examples of disdain for non-European cultures or the European Middle Ages (in some respects, he tells us, superior to our own), due to the tendency of the *lumières*, both French and English, to see the past through the distorting spectacles of what Vico, with similar irony, calls 'our own enlightened times'. Herder's theses are among the earliest – if not the earliest – antidotes to Gibbon's or Hume's or Macaulay's blindness to medieval civilisation, to Russell's dismissal of Byzantium, or Voltaire's antipathy to the Bible or Cromwell or learning for learning's sake. But, unlike later thinkers, neither Vico nor Herder attribute such attitudes to the influence of inescapable impersonal forces, but, like the sceptics of the sixteenth to seventeenth centuries, to bias or ignorance or lack of integrity, from which anyone can be saved by the use of the normal powers of the imagination, greater knowledge and closer regard for the truth – virtues open to all. There is nothing here about the mazes of false consciousness.

The fact that they are not cultural relativists of an insulated kind is shown by this alone. For it is idle to tell men to learn to see other worlds through the eyes of those whom they seek to understand, if they are prevented by the walls of their own culture from doing so. Unless we are able to escape from the ideological prisons of class or nation or doctrine, we shall not be able to avoid seeing alien institutions or customs as either too strange to make any sense to us, or as tissues of error, lying inventions of unscrupulous priests; the doors which, according to Vico, myth and fable and language open to us will remain romantic delusions. What are the alternatives to such ability to see beyond the bounds of one's own *Kulturkreis?* In the first place, attribution to members of other civilisation of motives, goals, values, ways of thinking prevalent in one's own; this is the anachronistic disregard of historical change against which our two thinkers warn us, and of which they offer us glaring examples intended to make us aware of its dangers. Secondly, an anthropology modelled on the biological sciences, an attempt to construct a science of man characterised by the neutral objectivity of other natural sciences, at the price of regarding mankind as being no more than a species of the animal kingdom; this, for Vico and Herder, is gratuitously to treat human beings as less than human; to pretend that we know less than we do, if only from our own experience, of what it is to be human and conscious of having purposes, of the differences between action and behaviour. The last possibility is an all pervasive scepticism: what is beyond the ken of our culture cannot be known nor speculated about; *ignoramus et ignorabimus;* history and anthropology may be pure culture-conditioned fictions. So, indeed, they may; but why should we attend to this wild piece of subjective idealism? The onus of proof is on the sceptics; to say that the past is completely unknowable robs the concept of the past of all meaning: it is thus a strictly self-annihilating notion.

So much for doubts about the possibility of understanding the past. But to understand is not to accept. Vico experiences no intellectual discomfort – nor need he do so – when he damns in absolute terms the social injustice and brutality of Homeric society. Herder is not being inconsistent when he denounces the great conquerors and destroyers of local cultures – Alexander, Caesar, Charlemagne, or glorifies Oriental literature or primitive song. This would not be consistent with conscious (or, shall I say, conscientious) relativism of values, but is compatible with pluralism, which merely denies that there is one, and only one, true morality or aesthetics or theology, and allows equally objective alternative values or systems of value. One can reject a culture because one finds it morally or aesthetically repellent, but, on this view, only if one can understand how and why it could, nevertheless, be acceptable to a recognisably human society. Only if its behaviour is not intelligible at all are we reduced to a mere 'physicalist' description and prediction of the gestures; the code, if there is one, which would yield their meaning, remains unbroken: such men are not fully human for us; we cannot imaginatively enter their worlds; we do not know what they are up to; they are not brothers to us (as Vico and Herder supposed that all human beings were), we can at most only dimly guess at what the point of their acts, if they are acts, may be; then truly do we have to confine ourselves to mere behaviourist reports of unexplained brute fact, or, at best, resort to the language of pure relativism to the extent that these men's ends, somehow grasped as ends, seem wholly unrelated to our own. I should like to say once again that pluralism – the incommensurability and, at times, incompatibility of objective ends – is *not* relativism; nor, *a fortiori*, subjectivism, nor the allegedly unbridgeable differences of emotional attitude on which some modern positivists, emotivists, existentialists, nationalists and, indeed, relativistic sociologists and anthropologists found their accounts. This is the relativism from which I hold Montesquieu, Vico and Herder to have been free. Plainly thinkers who, like those Renaissance critics who, by historical and philological analysis, exposed the forged Donation of Constantine, or like Vico, the fable of the Athenian origin of the Twelve Tables of early Rome, can scarcely be accused of the cruder forms of culture-bound misinterpretation. Indeed, the very formulation of the central principle of such relativism which claims to cover all possible assertions of fact leaves no possibility of determining the status of the principle itself, since it must fall outside all the categories which it regards as together being exhaustive of all that can be asserted. This is no less true of other, more reactionary, critics of the Enlightenment: of Justus Möser, for example, in his polemic against Voltaire's disparaging references to the absurd variety of laws and customs in the various little German principalities; or Burke, in his indictment of Warren Hastings, for trampling on the traditional ways of life of the natives of India. I am not attempting to judge the validity of their objectivism or their pluralism, only to report it. *Je ne suppose rien, je ne propose rien, je n'impose rien, j'expose.*

If these fathers of cultural history are not relativists in the sphere of values and action, they are not even pluralists in that of knowledge. Vico nowhere supposes that we cannot reach even certainty (*certum* – let alone *verum*, demonstrable truth) in some sphere, because our categories and conceptions and methods of investigation are hopelessly culture-bound, as are those of other cultures, and therefore neither more nor less valid than theirs. This is equally true of Herder. For all their erudition, they were philosophers of history rather than historical researchers; they did not possess the latest critical weapons of even their own time – they were not meticulous scholars like Muratori in Vico's day, or Michaelis, Schlözer and Heyne in Herder's. They neither used nor questioned the latest methods of scientific reconstruction of their own day. Vico conceded that Herodotus was full of fables and legends (which, of course, provided wonderful grist to the decoding mill of the *Scienza Nuova*), whereas Thucydides was far more accurate and reliable. Herder was not concerned with the factual truth of the Bible or the Eddas, only with the kind of social and spiritual experience of which they were the natural expression. There is no suggestion of *Wissenssoziologie* in the writings of either. On the issue of factual truth they are at one with the Enlightenment: there is only one truth, not many, the same for all men universally, and it is what rational men affirm it to be, that which their critical methods uncover; fable, legends, poetry, ritual, formulae, doors to past cultures, are therefore not literally (as opposed to poetically) true, and there is no more pluralism in the ideas of either thinker, let alone relativism, so far as the realms of facts and events are concerned than in those of the most doctrinaire *Encyclopédiste*. The idea that the concept of fact is itself problematic, that all facts embody theories (as enunciated by, for example, Goethe) or socially conditioned, ideological attitudes, seems as remote from them as it is from the outlook of Ranke. His view that every age is equal in the sight of God could have been uttered by Herder: for it is an undeniably pluralist sentiment.

For the full development of the ideas of false consciousness, of ideological or psychological distortion of the nature of objective truth, of the complex relationships between fact and interpretation, reality and myth, theory and practice, for the distinction between the unbreakable laws of nature and the 'reified' but breakable man-made laws and rules which govern conduct, one has to wait for Hegel and his Left-wing disciples, including the early Marx. It may seem odd to us, who live after Marx and Max Weber, that the issue of the relativism of the knowledge of the past should not have occurred to the historicist critics of the French Enlightenment: but such surprise is itself anachronistic. Categories of knowledge may have been distinguished earlier: but not varieties of knowledge as resembling styles of life and thought wholly or partially determined by climate, race, class, or any other social or psychological formation.

I return to my original thesis: relativism is not the only alternative to what Lovejoy called uniformitarianism. The attribution of relativism to the critics who charged the *philosophes* of Paris with anachronism seems to me to be itself anachronistic. The relativism which has so deeply troubled historians, sociologists, anthropologists and philosophers of history during the last hundred years is, in the main, if not entirely, a legacy of the schools of thought which look upon human activity as being largely caused by occult and inescapable forces of which explicit social beliefs and theories are rationalisations – disguises to be penetrated and exposed. This is the heritage of Marxism, of depth psychology, of the sociology of Pareto or Simmel or Mannheim – ideas of which, even in their embryonic form, the leading thinkers of the eighteenth century, in Paris and London and their cultural dependencies, as well as their critics in Italy and Germany, seem to have showed scarcely any systematic awareness.

John Stuart Mill once observed (in his *Principles of Political Economy*) 'It is hardly possible to over-rate the value, in this low state of human improvement, of placing human beings in contact with persons dissimilar to themselves, and with modes of thought and action unlike those with which they are familiar . . . Such communication has always been, and is peculiarly in the present age, one of the primary sources of progress'. This amounts to a thesis, particularly if for 'progress' we substitute 'knowledge', with which some critics of the thinkers of the Enlightenment (and perhaps a good many of us here) might not disagree.

REFERENCES

Aristotle, *Nicomachaean Ethics*, 1134b 26.
Barnard, F. M. (1969) *Herder on Social and Political Culture.*
    Cambridge, Cambridge University Press.
Beyer, C. (1963) Montesquieu et le relativisme ésthétique, *Studies
    on Voltaire and the XVIIIth Century*, XXIV.
Crocker, L. G. (1959) *An Age of Crisis.* Baltimore, Johns Hopkins
    University Press.
Geertz, C. (1973) *The Interpretation of Cultures.* New York, Basic
    Books.
Herder, J. G. *Sämmtliche Werke* (ed. Suphan 1877–1913).
Herder, J. G. (1769) *Journal.*
Hume, D. (1748) *An Enquiry Concerning Human Understanding.*
Locke, J. (1690) *An Essay Concerning Human Understanding.*
Montesquieu, C. de S. *Oeuvres Complètes de Montesquieu* (ed. A. Masson
    1950–5).
New York Review of Books (1976) 11 November.
Racine, J. (1674) Preface to *Iphigénie.*

2. Kant's Philosophy of History

R.F.ATKINSON

I

Professor Walsh, in his continuingly influential *An Introduction to Philosophy of History* (1951,1957), commends Kant's *Idea for a Universal History* at least as a conveniently small-scale, sharply outlined, example of a speculative theory, which is therefore a good starting point for the consideration of more luxuriant specimens. The piece really does have the virtues attributed to it. It is short – the whole of what Kant has to say directly about history fills only a small volume – and the author is notably clear headed about the nature of his undertaking. Such rather faint praise does, however, leave open the question whether the exercise is important either within the Kantian scheme of things or for the philosophy of history generally. The tendency of recent commentary, so far as it is known to me, is to rate the writings on history rather high from the former point of view. With this I am inclined to agree; but with regard to the latter point of view I am less sanguine. Kant has next to nothing to say about historical method and, though it is interesting to have speculation from the arch-critic of speculation, he is less innovatory than Rousseau or Herder, while the line of development he supposes mankind to follow is so general as scarcely to engage with the course of history at all.

In what follows I shall first outline the Kantian view and then go on to comment and criticism. The texts I shall be most concerned with, in addition to the *Universal History* (1784) itself, are *The Conjectural Beginning of Human History* (1786) and *Perpetual Peace* (1795), though there are other relevant works in the Beck collection (see References, Section 1). Also important, for the assessment of the teleological argumentation which is prominent in Kant's writings on history, is the *Critique of Judgment* (1790). Since his philosophy of history originates within the period of the Critiques, the presumption must be that, to an extent despite appearances, it is relateable to the main critical programme (cf. Fackenheim, 1957, p.382).

II

In the *Universal History* nine theses are formulated and briefly supported. There are also a few introductory paragraphs and a conclusion stating what the author thinks he has been about and the status of his claims. A footnote at the beginning indicates that Kant is expanding a view that had been attributed to him, namely that the ultimate purpose of history is the attainment of a perfect civil constitution (it will emerge that this is less than the whole story) and that a philosophical history of humanity might be written from this point of view.

Although he is committed to the belief that phenomenal human actions are subject to causal law, Kant begins with the thought that individual human behaviour presents itself as pretty random. He is, however, like others of his day, impressed by the stability of such statistical aggregates as birth and marriage rates, from which he draws the general moral that there may be regularities in human behaviour taken in the gross. If we look at the human race as a whole, we may hope to discern a progressive, if slow, actualisation of its potential. Few or no individuals are conscious of any line of development; but it is open to the philosopher to try to discover a natural purpose or plan in the apparently senseless course of human affairs. Kant himself is offering no more than a clue to the pattern: the Kepler who might discover definite laws and the Newton who might explain them are yet to come.

After these preliminaries comes the first thesis, that all the natural capacities of a creature are destined to evolve completely to their natural end – an important and dubious claim which is scarcely argued here. We are simply told that 'An organ that is of no use, an arrangement that does not achieve its purpose are contradictions in the teleological theory of nature' (p.18). Without teleology we can make no sense of the course of nature generally or human behaviour in particular.

The second thesis is that the rational faculties, which are unique to man, can attain full development only in the human race, not in an individual. An individual life is too short for anyone to get very far. The capacity and knowledge suitable to nature's (presumed) purpose for humanity can be attained only over many generations, each passing its own 'enlightenment' on to its successors. It is unfortunate, in view of the difference of status accorded to inner and outer teleology in the third Critique, that Kant does not clearly distinquish between enlightenment as an individual capacity, fully developed only late in history, and enlightenment as a possible collective attainment or possession. Nevertheless, it is plain enough that enlightenment will not be present at or near the beginning of history; there is consequently scope for trying to specify the principal conditions that are organisationally necessary for its subsequent development

The third thesis in effect identifies enlightenment as nature's end for man. Nature has willed that everything that 'goes beyond the mere mechanical ordering of his animal existence' (p.19) should be produced by man's rational, non-instinctual activity. This seems to mean that characteristically human arrangements are cultural or conventional rather than biological. (There is a similar emphasis in Herder, 1784–91, chapter 1.) Since nature withheld that larger endowment of instinct which would have made man happier, it must be supposed that it aims at his rational self-esteem rather than his mere well-being. It may seem strange and hard that earlier generations should suffer and labour for results they will not live to see, but 'it is necessary if one assumes that a species of animals should have reason, and, as a class of rational beings each of whom dies while the species is immortal, should develop their capacities to perfection' (p.20). Galston (1975, p.230) comments that the problem would not have arisen had Kant been willing to consider mankind as a single developing entity or totality; but I do not think that Kant is genuinely perplexed. He is not interested in contending that things by nature work out for the good of every individual, but only that the rational faculties he so highly values will ultimately leave their mark on history.

The fourth thesis contains the central claims of the essay: that nature's means for developing human capacities is men's mutual antagonism, and that this (paradoxically) is the cause of lawful order among men, which is itself the necessary condition of all rational progress. Men are propelled by vainglory, lust for power, avarice – their passions, not their reason (though the emphasis is different in the *Conjectural Beginning*) – propelled to try to surpass their fellows whom they can neither tolerate nor avoid. These unamiable qualities enforce the first steps from barbarism to culture. 'Man wishes concord; but Nature knows better what is good for the race; she wills discord . . . that [man] should be plunged from sloth and passive contentment into labour and trouble, in order that he may find means of extricating himself from them' (p.21). Man's 'unsocial sociability' is not, therefore, dysfunctional, but is conceivable as the means chosen by a wise creator for developing the capacities with which he has endowed mankind.

The fifth and seventh theses set out the two sorts of lawful order that are necessary for progress. The former is organisation into states, ideally 'republican' states, with liberal constitutions, separation of powers and the rule of law (more on this, of course, in the *Theory of Law*, *Perpetual Peace* and *Theory and Practice*); but, though this is more emphasised elsewhere than in the *Universal History*, any form of state is better than none. The competitive, destructive energies, which make the pre-political condition intolerable, once channelled and disciplined by a republican constitution, are the source of all culture.   Kant's sixth thesis emphasises both the importance and the difficulty of the task of establishing civil society. Man is an animal who needs a master (*pace* the soft-minded Herder – see Kant's review, p.64); but the master can only be a man, himself susceptible to the corruption of power, even if he be a philosopher (*Perpetual Peace*, p.369). The problem of setting up 'a magistracy which can maintain public justice and which is itself just' can never be completely solved – 'From the crooked timber of humanity no straight thing is to be made' (p.23). The solution (in so far as it is humanly achievable, since the republican constitution is an idea of reason to which no phenomenal situation is entirely adequate) depends on correct political conceptions, great experience *and* good will. In *Perpetual Peace*, however, it is said that good will is not a pre-requisite and can only result from a good constitution (p.366). There are differences of emphasis, but (despite Galston, 1975, p.241), I do not think that Kant argues circularly that morality both presupposes and is presupposed by the state. The former seems to be the dominant view. His Lutheran conviction of the radical evil in human nature inclines him to Hobbism; and the polemical stance of the later writings, in which he has to defend himself against charges of naive utopianism, precludes his assuming an already moral, pre-political human nature.

It is in his seventh thesis that Kant moves beyond Hobbes. A perfect civil constitution cannot be securely achieved in advance of the establishment of lawful external relations among states, i.e., a league of nations. Practical reason, both prudential and moral, clearly requires this; and it is not simply a utopian dream, for nature, by means of the horrors of international warfare, will in the end force men to establish an international order. From this point of view even war is functional; wars being attempts, on the part of nature rather than man, to adjust the relation of states towards a confederal end. Kant hesitates to claim that this consummation is inevitable. It might come about gradually; but he is prepared to contemplate the possibility of the annihilation of 'civilisation and all cultural progress through barbarous devastation' (p.25). Nevertheless, he seems to feel – to a degree that will not be sanctioned by the third Critique – that, if purposiveness is recognised in the part, it must also be recognised in the whole. The union of states is the halfway mark in the development of mankind. Until it is passed humanity has to suffer the cruellest hardships. Rousseau, with whom Kant is determined to agree as far as he can, was hardly wrong to suppose the lot of savages superior to that of political but pre-cosmopolitical man. Though civilised, man is a long way from a perfectly moral condition. The goods of civilisation, so far as they are not based on a moral disposition, are merely 'glittering misery' (p.26).

Everything so far has been very general, just the setting up of a certain model of human nature and society. The eighth thesis, however, assures us that 'the history of mankind can be seen, in the large, as the realisation of nature's secret plan to bring forth a perfectly constituted state . . . and . . . external relation among states' (p.27). The route to the final goal cannot be determined with much certainty. Competition between states makes it impossible for them to neglect their internal cultural development. For the growth of wealth economic freedom proves to be necessary, and this tends to bring with it freedom of individual action and religious belief. 'Enlightenment . . . must step by step ascend the throne and influence the principles of government' (p.28). Commercial linkages between the European states will prepare the way for world government.

There is still no close connexion with the actual course even of European history, though the discussion following the ninth thesis maintains that this can be presented from Kant's point of view, which reduces to system what would otherwise be a pointless conglomeration of human actions. There then follows the outline story of Greece and Rome, the barbarian invasions, and the development of the European states, which will probably give law to others. It is no doubt possible to see here the groundplan of Hegel's philosophy of history (cf.,e.g., Galston, 1975, p.262, though I think the more important precursor may be Herder). There is here a guiding thread, which clarifies the past, is a basis for prediction, and a source of consolation. It is as reasonable to see providence in history as it is in nature.

Kant concludes by disclaiming any desire to supplant the work of empirical historians, He has simply made a suggestion, up to a point based on an *a priori* teleological principle, as to how history might be written by a philosophical mind well versed in history. Such a history would appeal to future world citizens, if there are any, and in a small way would tend to bring world citizenship about. Plainly everything depends on Kant's *a priori* teleology, which has yet to pass the test of criticism.

III

Kant's second essay on history, the *Conjectural Beginning* (1786), is ostensibly a demythologising reinterpretation of *Genesis*, an imaginative exercise no doubt offered as an improvement on those of Herder. It affords further evidence concerning Kant's pessimism about the individual and optimism for the species, his interpretation of and relation to Rousseau, and of his Mandevillean insistence that the private vices causing inequality and war promote public benefits.

Kant's conjectural 'pleasure trip' through pre-history sketches the development of man, assumed to be already possessed of speech and thought but associating only in reproductive twosomes, into a social and moral being. The original guide is instinct, 'that voice of God' (p.111); but reason begins to stir and, aided by imagination, creates artificial desires which may run contrary to instinct. Hence the first choice – the Fall, in fact, but still not wholly for the bad. Hunger, and sexual desire too, as evidenced by the fig leaf, move away from the purely instinctual level. A sense of beauty develops and a sense of decency, the first hint of morality. Awareness of the future and of the power of choice comes in, and with them the anxieties that led the first couple to curse the use of reason which had cost them their primal innocence. On the brighter side, man comes to recognise that he is the end of nature and that the other animals exist simply for his use. It is a further step in the direction of morality when it is realised that all men are equally ends.

It may be asked whether the role here assigned to reason is inconsistent with the *Universal History*'s ascription of human development to nature working by the passions. I think not, partly because the *Conjectural Beginning* concerns an earlier stage of development than does the other work, and more because the passions that energise man's subsequent development are *human* passions and as such informed by reason in the shape of knowledge, imagination and self-awareness.

The transition from animality to humanity – 'from a stupid and limited animal to a moral being and a man' (*Social Contract*, I,viii) – is unquestionably a gain from the point of view of the destiny of the species, since it is the pre-condition of the perfection of characteristically human capacities. But it is less clearly for the good of the individual. With the birth of reason came vices. Morally the transition was a fall, a loss of innocence, and physically it was a punishment because of the host of new ills that follow from it. 'The history of nature therefore begins with good, for it is the work of God, while the history of freedom begins with wickedness, for it is the work of man' (p.115). The individual, says Kant with extraordinary severity, has to put down to his own fault the evil he suffers as well as the evil he does; but as a member of the species he can only admire the arrangements made for its development. Thus is it possible to reconcile, on the one hand, Rousseau's *Arts and Sciences* and *Origins of Inequality* with their conflict between culture and humanity *qua* natural species and, on the other, his *Emile* and *Social Contract* with their conception of the development of man as a moral species. Painful conflict between natural impulse and culture will persist until the moral end of the species is attained and culture becomes second nature.

After bringing man to the threshold of humanity and society Kant moves quickly through the long period of development from hunting and gathering via herding to agriculture, which last begins to disperse men all over the earth. It is the farmer who first resorts to violence in order to curb the herdsman. For security families have to band together in villages, which makes trade possible and public administration necessary. Inequality develops, 'that rich source of so many evils but also of everything good' (p.119). Cities grow, with consequent vice and threats to liberty; dangers that are, however, offset by inter-city warfare, which has the progressive consequences noted in the *Universal History*. War and the preparation for it are the greatest evils of civilised nations; but without war and the fear of it things would be much worse. Only in a state of perfect culture would perpetual peace be beneficial or possible – a conclusion presumably inadvertently at odds with the work to be considered next.

IV

Perpetual Peace (1795) is primarily relevant for its note of caution about the legitimacy of the teleological considerations employed in Kant's philosophy of history – it, of course, post-dates the *Critique of Judgment*. It makes clear too that it is passion and prudence rather than moral reason which fuel the drive to perpetual peace and that morality comes only after the establishment of juridical society.

In the work the nations are imagined coming together in a convention in order to bring about permanent peace. Certain articles are proposed for agreement: there are to be no standing armies or national debts for war purposes, no interference in the internal affairs of other states; there are to be republican constitutions all round and a federal union of free states. The question then supposed to arise is how to guarantee that the treaty will be kept. The answer is that the guarantor is nature herself – sometimes, indeed, it is said to be providence, but the more modest term 'nature' is preferred.

Nature's aim 'in her mechanical course is to produce harmony among men, against their will and indeed through their discord' (p.360). 'Nature [thus] guarantees perpetual peace by the mechanism of human passions' (p.368). Still involved here is the teleological idea of there being an end or goal for nature and mankind. That this is so, however, it is now emphasised, can neither be observed nor inferred from observational evidence regarding the line of development followed by human affairs. The teleological idea comes from our own minds. From a purely theoretical point of view it is transcendent (metaphysical in the pejorative sense). This is the easier of Kant's claims to understand. The other, that from the moral point of view it is dogmatic, is much harder. He is evidently following the line of the third Critique. There teleology, in contradistinction to, for example, substance and causation which are constitutive principles of the understanding, is held to be no more than a regulative principle for reflective judgment. Without substance and causation nothing could be an object for us (there could be no objective knowledge); but teleology comes in only so that we can discern non-mechanical forms of order in objects. Living organisms, even the humble blade of grass, cannot be made sufficient sense of on mechanical principles alone (*Critique of Judgment*, p.400). This is intrinsic or internal purposiveness. External purposiveness, where one thing contributes to the existence or flourishing of another (absolute extrinsic purposiveness where the other is conceived as an ultimate end) – and this is the sort of purposiveness involved in the philosophy of history – is unhappily less securely grounded. So far as theory is concerned we are entirely in the realm of 'as if', and merely may, not must, view man as appointed by God to be the end of nature. If we elect to do so, we can present apparently dysfunctional discord and war as contributing to the perfection of the human species in the way already described (*op. cit.*, section 83).

All this, however, is only hypothetical, and I have to confess that I cannot see how an ultimate end can be categorically designated (how the moral dogmatism can come in) without the question being begged. We are told (*op.cit.*, section 84) that man *qua* physical being cannot be the end of nature, while man *qua* moral being can, because it does not make sense to ask why the latter exists. But the reason why not is precisely that, without man as the end of nature, the chain of mutually subordinated ends would have no point of attachment! There is the additional difficulty that, if we need morality to set up our teleology, we cannot without circularity employ our teleology to bridge the gulf between morality and nature. Despland (1973, p.26) is surely mistaken in praising Kant for the control which his moral philosophy exercises over his teleological thinking. More generally, it seems to me that virtually everything Kant offers in support of external teleology in the third Critique he also takes back.

But to revert to *Perpetual Peace*. There follows a schematic account of the preparatory arrangements made by nature for peace among mankind. In every region she has made it possible for people to live – Kant is recurrently

C

impressed by the way driftwood enables people to live in the treeless arctic. By war nature has driven peoples far apart, as witnessed by linguistic affinities between widely separated nations, and into even the most inhospitable regions. War additionally forces people into political organisation (strictly war presupposes it, but Kant's meaning is clear enough). He attaches considerable importance, as he did in the *Conjectural Beginning*, to the change from hunting, fishing and herding to agricultural society. Thus is completed the first stage of human progress, the establishment of the state, which – Kant is here quite explicit – can be attained even by devils so long as they are practically intelligent (p.366). Morality presupposes law, not vice versa. 'A good constitution is not to be expected from morality, but, conversely, a good moral condition of a people is to be expected only under a good constitution' (*ibid.* and cf. *An Old Question*, p. 92).

With regard to the second stage of human progress we are told that nature prevents peoples uniting into soulless despotism, using (*sic*) differences of faith and scripture to keep them apart. At first this leads to war, but nations thus divided tend to move closer together again as the spirit of commerce gets the upper hand. While the actual achievement of perpetual peace cannot be predicted theoretically, it is sufficiently certain from a practical point of view, and it is our duty to work towards it. I have already suggested that morality gets no support from teleology if teleology cannot stand without morality. Sometimes 'being sufficiently certain from a practical point of view' seems to mean no more than 'it is our duty to work towards it'. Witness the passage at the end of the *Theory of Law* (p.354) where it is said that perpetual peace is less a probability than an idea in accordance with which we must act, i.e. it is something we must seek to promote so long as its theoretical impossibility cannot be demonstrated – a surely vacuous proviso (see section v below). There are, however, passages which are predictive, e.g., in *An Old Question* (pp.91–2) and *Theory and Practice* (section III).

Perpetual Peace concludes with a defence of the adoption of its apparently utopian objective against the scepticism and cynicism of the practising politician. (The theme of *Theory and Practice* is similar.) Kant argues that, since it must be possible to do our duty, there can properly speaking be no conflict between morals and politics. Practical men think morality never achieves anything, and it is true that civil societies are normally established by force; but it is still possible to entertain the idea of a 'moral politician' i.e. one who restricts himself to policies compatible with morality. The converse idea of 'political morality', i.e., adapting morality to political ends, does not make sense – Kant presumably does not seriously think that this makes it impossible to pursue political ends regardless of morality. The case for the practicality of moral politics seems to be twofold. Firstly, contrary to popular belief, it does not require foolish extremism or utopianism and, secondly, morality (or at least its external condition, perpetual peace) will ultimately prevail. Kant makes such observations as that moral politicians are entitled prudently to delay introducing reforms; and that, although neither revolution not counter-revolution is legitimate, it is acceptable, if not mandatory, to build on good results that have been obtained by unjust means. It is even said that the maxim *fiat justitia* should not be interpreted as requiring rigorous moralism of individuals, but simply as enjoining those in authority not to allow arbitrary exceptions to their laws. For the rest, politics, uninformed by morality, is very chancy. It is beyond the wit of man to calculate what to do for the best. But the solution to the problem of political wisdom (the problem of the moral politician) is very clear: 'Seek ye first the kingdom of pure practical reason and its righteousness, and your end (the blessing of perpetual peace) will necessarily follow' (p.378).

V

By way of conclusion I shall consider and defend Kant against two sorts of criticism, and then try to assess the importance of his work on history both inside the critical philosophy and generally.

Both criticisms in effect allege a contradiction between the recognition of developmental patterns in history and the autonomy of the individual, on which Kant himself notoriously sets such store. A version of the former is to be found in Collingwood's complaint (1946, p.93) that Kant, as a true representative of the Enlightenment, sees history as a spectacle of human irrationality, from which he looks forward to a truly rational age. Doubtless Kant was unduly dismissive of some periods in the past and he was certainly proud to belong to the century of enlightenment; though it is equally certain that he was not content slavishly to follow the ideas of his day, but developed them in the light of his own philosophy (cf. Despland, 1973, pp.76–83). Collingwood's main charge is that Kant looked at the past from an external point of view, seeing past actions simply as phenomena, and not regarding their authors as rational agents like himself. This I consider unjustified. Although, as we have noted, Kant was prepared to imagine a pre-history before the development of reason, I am sure that he regarded the deeds of the historical past as rational actions. That he did not emphasise this is only because he took it entirely for granted, and saw no incompatibility between it and the existence of large-scale patterns in human affairs, which are not reflected in the consciousness of the people involved. The legitimacy of an interest in such patterns can surely not be denied. For Collingwood it might, with some show of reason, be said that it is not an interest in history as ordinarily understood. But then Kant went out of his way at the end of the *Universal History* to distinguish his concerns from those of the practising historian.

It is true that Kant ascribes the large-scale patterning to nature or even to providence; but, apart from occasional misleading pronouncements, he is far from seriously regarding these as occult forces in whose grip people are helpless. In the interests of making sense of history we are entitled or obliged to see patterns in it, but there is no suggestion that individuals are constrained by them. No more is required than that intentional actions may have unforseen consequences. It may be that Kant encourages misunderstanding by his (usual) insistence that it is passion rather than reason, which is the 'motor of history'. But is it evident from the *Conjectural Beginning* that for Kant human passion is instinct and appetite informed by reason and imagination. Moreover, in *Perpetual Peace* it is rational egoism which directs people towards national and international organisation. And in the *Anthropology* he actually asserts that moves towards political organisation may be consciously rational (p.330). Kant does, indeed, often insist on a radical discontinuity between reason in the service of desire, which he allots to nature, and moral reason, which alone belongs to freedom. Consciousness of this may lead one to suppose that Kant regarded phenomenal human action as less rational (in the ordinary sense) than he did or than it is – though I do not claim that Collingwood himself was specially influenced in this way.

The other sort of criticism is to the effect that Kant is too narrowly political or juridical in his conception of culture, Herder and Hegel both being held to be superior in this respect (Delbos, 1926, p.290 note; but see Hassner, 1962, p.92). Moreover, morality – autonomous morality as conceived by Kant – is not something for which there could be natural causes in the shape of national and international organisation (Kelly, 1969, p.117; Fackenheim, 1957, pp.396–7). There is doubtless truth in the former part of the criticism; but it is very wide of the mark to suppose that Kant considered political organisation the whole of culture. In fact he sees it only as a *necessary* condition for cultural development, including therein the development of the phenomenal manifestations of morality, i.e., a good moral condition of mankind, which is possible (not inevitable) only within an established juridical order. Phenomenally sufficient conditions may well be incompatible with moral autonomy, but phenomenally necessary conditions are not. That Kant is so emphatic that they must obtain shows, incidentally, how mistaken is the common conception of him as a totally unworldly absolutist in moral philosophy (cf. Philonenko, 1972, pp.59–60). And, if he is right in holding that there is a natural tendency that they should obtain, then he has done something to show that the phenomenal world (nature) is such that morality is not necessarily futile within it.

It is in this regard that the philosophy of history is important in Kant's practical philosophy. It provides a context in which specific moral imperatives and indeed morality generally make phenomenal sense.

Take Kant's notorious total opposition to revolution and his alternative policy of reformist gradualism. There is so much that is exceptionable in the derivation of the absolute prohibition (as in the other notorious case of the ban on lying) that one is tempted to suppose that Kant is merely indulging arbitrary prejudices. Among other things, he unquestionably loads the dice against revolution when he claims (*Perpetual Peace*, p.382) that the publicity version of his universalisation test excludes rebellion but not repression. And he very likely allows himself to be bewitched by the truism that unconstitutional resistance cannot be constitutional. All the same, it remains the case that Kant's philosophy of history provides a framework within which his opposition to revolution is intelligible in the light of possible long-term outcomes. It may at least be hoped that a universal political order will one day come about. The moral politician, though he is offered no guarantee of phenomenal progress in the short term, is at least not cutting against the grain of history.

In regard to the general problem, of bridging the gulf between freedom (morality) and nature, whilst Kant goes out of his way not to represent morality as good policy for the individual, his philosophy of history does enable him to maintain that morality is not absurd (cf. Galston, 1975, p.23). The social world may be hoped to be progressing towards a condition in which morality can flourish. There is hope for the species, if not for the phenomenal individual.

There here arises the difficult question of how Kant's philosophy of history is to be related to his philosophy of religion, particularly that of the second Critique, where the emphasis is on *individual* hopes of immortality and God, rather than that of the *Religion*, where there is some social reference. Are the philosophies of history and religion complementary or in tension? It is hard to give a firm answer. The difficulty is that the philosophy of history is less fully integrated with Kant's general philosophical position than is the doctrine of the postulates of practical reason at least, if not that of the *Religion*. The centrifugal forces are very strong outside the three Critiques. One may speculate how Kant might have balanced them, or even how a rejuvenated Kant, beginning again at the beginning, might have fitted everything together in an historical account of developing human nature. But the actual Kant never did.

There remains the question whether Kant's opinions on history have any importance outside his own scheme of things. Few are likely to accept his claims for teleology generally; and, if such a mode of thinking be acceptable anywhere, it is presumably in biology rather than history (cf. Fackenheim, 1957, p.397), as Kant himself in effect recognises in holding intrinsic teleology more securely based than extrinsic. It can, however, hardly be disputed that historical studies are commonly structured by points of view brought to rather than found in history. Accordingly it is *possible* to present history on the lines favoured by Kant. But this is to say very little, for as much can be said for many other points of view. The question must be what makes a structuring point of view better or worse, and the likeliest answer is that it is the extent to which it engages with the facts of history by suggesting fruitful lines of enquiry and being falsifiable in the light of their results. It follows that extreme generality is not a merit in an historical point of view. Kant, it is true, does occasionally write as if he intended to present his view as falsifiable, namely, when he insists that we are entitled to hope that universal peace may come about *so long as it is not shown to be impossible*, which presumably could only be shown by reference to the actual course of history. Appearances are, however, deceptive. Given the indefinitely prolonged time scale envisaged, it is doubtful whether any state of affairs could count as demonstrating the impossibility of universal peace. To be sure, as we have seen, Kant is largely practical in his motivation: he preaches hope, lest despair might lead us to neglect our duties, not primarily to help with the organisation of historical data. What I cannot see, however, is how we can obtain any support at all from a hope so insecurely rooted in the actual course of history as is Kant's.

REFERENCES

1. *Kantian texts*

I give below date of first publication, English title, and volume number of the Academy edition. Page references in my text are to the volumes of this edition, of which the page numbers are given in most translations, though not in Reiss. Translations of Kant's writings on history are collected in Beck, L. W. (ed.) *Kant on History*, Bobbs-Merrill, 1963; and some of them appear as well in Reiss, H. (ed.) *Kant's Political Writings*, Cambridge U.P., 1970. I indicate below when a work appears in one or other of these collections.

(1784) *Idea for a Universal History from the Cosmopolitan Point of View*, VIII, in Beck and Reiss.

(1845–5) *Reviews of Herder*, VIII, in Beck.

(1786) *The Conjectural Beginning of Human History*, VIII, in Beck.

(1790) *The Critique of Judgment*, V, trans. Meredith, Oxford, 1928.

(1793) *On the common Saying: 'This may be true in theory, but it does not apply in practice'*, VIII, in Reiss.

(1795) *Perpetual Peace*, VIII, in Beck and Reiss.

(1797) *Metaphysic of Ethics: Theory of Law*, VI, trans, Ladd, Bobbs-Merrill, 1965.

(1798) *The Strife of the Faculties: Part II. Is the Human Race constantly progressing?*, VII, in Beck and Reiss.

2. *Other works*

Collingwood, R. G. (1946) *The Idea of History*. Oxford, Clarendon Press.

Delbos, V. (1926) *La Philosophie pratique de Kant*. Paris, F. Alcan.

Despland, M. (1973) *Kant on History and Religion*. Montreal and London, McGill–Queen's University Press.

Fackenheim, E. L. (1957) Kant's concept of history. *Kant-Studien* 48, 1956–7.

Galston, W. A. (1975) *Kant and the Problem of History*. Chicago and London, University of Chicago Press.

Hassner, P. (1962) Situation de la philosophie politique chez Kant. In *La Philosophie politique de Kant*. Paris, Presses Universitaire de France.

Herder, J. G. von (1784–91) *Reflections for a Philosophy of the History of Mankind*, abridged by Manuel, F. M. (ed.), 1968. Chicago, University of Chicago Press.

Kelly, G. A. (1969) *Idealism, Politics and History*. London, Cambridge University Press.

Philonenko, A. (1972) *L'Oeuvre de Kant: Tome II Morale et Politique*. Paris, J. Vrin.

Walsh, W. H. (1951, 1967) *An Introduction to Philosophy of History*. London, Hutchinson.

3. History and Morality in Hegel's Philosophy of History

PATRICK GARDINER

Among the various doctrines propounded by Hegel in his *Lectures on the Philosophy of World History* there are perhaps none that have aroused sharper criticism than those which concern the relevance of moral considerations to historical action and judgment. Here his views have often been felt to carry implications that extend beyond the sphere of purely theoretical speculation and to impinge upon the realms of practical policy and decision-making as well; consequently it is noticeable that, with the experience of twentieth-century atrocities freshly in mind, even his more sympathetic commentators have tended to approach what he said with a certain suspicion and disquiet, while those less charitably inclined have on occasions resorted to outright denunciation. It has been claimed, for instance, that Hegel, in the name of a historical theory which was itself highly questionable, was prepared not merely to excuse but to justify the commission of acts that were grossly wrong or immoral by ordinary standards. It has been held, moreover, that he was ready to do so in cases where the agent's own motives were admitted to be wholly self-seeking or even wicked; in this respect he has been compared unfavourably to Machiavelli, on the grounds that the latter never went so far as to give unqualified approval to criminal misdeeds. Hegel's attitude towards the conduct of public affairs in history amounted, in other words, to 'success-worship'; the criterion he proposed for judging what had been done in the past was solely one of whether the agents involved succeeded in pro-moting ends which they themselves desired or – alternatively – in contribu-ting in essential ways to the furtherance of tendencies and developments whose significance they did not envisage but which nonetheless could be seen in retrospect to have been historically dominant or enduring. In addition to this, it has also sometimes been urged that Hegel himself was obsessively fascinated by the phenomenon of power, appearing at times to take an unconcealed satisfaction in the fashion in which those exercising it had flouted the commonly accepted constraints of justice and humanity. Hence his theoretical endorsement of the overriding claims of political expediency and long-term historical success was accompanied and reinforced by a strong temperamental attraction to the ruthlessness characteristically dis-played by the great political and military leaders of the past.

There are certainly sections in the text of Hegel's *Lectures*, especially in the Introduction, which appear to lend support to such portrayals of his position. In general, it is difficult to overlook the dismissive or derisory tone

in which he frequently refers to those who seek to introduce 'moral reflections' into their historical accounts; a foretaste of this occurs, indeed, at a
very early stage of the work, when he criticises 'moralising' historians for
attacking 'events and individuals in their flank' with moral onslaughts and
when he claims that, while 'examples of virtue elevate the soul', the fact
remains that such things as the interests and destinies of nations are 'of a
different order from that of morality'. It might be suggested that in passages
like these Hegel should be understood as trying to make no more than a
methodological point: he was merely insisting that the aspects of human life
and behaviour which interest the moralist should be clearly distinguished
from those that properly fall within the province of written history, and that
it is simply not the historian's business to interlard his narratives with moral
comments or reproofs. But even if this is allowed to be correct so far as
Hegel's approach to 'ordinary history' was concerned, the impression given
by what he subsequently went on to say about moral considerations in the
context of 'philosophical history' is that here, at any rate, it was by no means
all that he had in mind. For there, notoriously, the task was one of interpreting the historical process as a whole and of showing it to be directed towards
the realisation of an 'absolute' goal or aim. Within this teleological perspective the deeds of individual human beings could certainly be seen to have
their place and to perform an essential role; it was, however, only in terms
of an overarching purpose that transcended their own limited objectives that
the true significance of what they did could be ascertained. In the light of
such considerations Hegel seems often to imply, not merely that the historical
import of what men have thought and done is distinguishable from its moral
import, but that in the final analysis it is the former that must take precedence
in any overall evaluation of actions and events. There is, for example, his
claim that world history moves on a 'higher plane' than that occupied by
morality; as the expression of a spiritual principle whose ultimate objective
is the realisation of universal freedom, its requirements can be said to rise
above 'the obligations, liability, and responsibility which attach to individuality by virtue of its ethical existence' (Hegel, 1975, p. 141).Again, when
speaking of 'world-historical deeds and those who perform them', Hegel
contends that 'the litany of private virtues . . . must not be raised against
them', and that 'world history might well disregard completely the sphere to
which morality and the much discussed and misunderstood dichotomy
between morality and politics belong' (*ibid.*). The spirit with which such
remarks are imbued may indeed be felt to have already been epitomised in
his earlier description of the role played by 'world-historical' figures, a
description whose chilling quality has disconcerted many of his modern
readers:

> Such . . . individuals, in furthering their own momentous interests,
> did indeed treat other intrinsically admirable interests and sacred
> rights in a carefree, cursory, hasty, and heedless manner, thereby
> exposing themselves to moral censure. But their position should be

seen in an altogether different light. A mighty figure must trample many an innocent flower underfoot, and destroy much that lies in its path. (*ibid.*, p.89)

What lay behind these seemingly uncompromising pronouncements and how, in particular, were they related to other departments of Hegel's thought? In the chapter on Hegel in his *An Introduction to Philosophy of History* Professor Walsh refers to the 'apparently cynical nature' of some of Hegel's historical doctrines, saying that they 'provoke the question of whether a philosophy of history conceived on these lines can commend itself to moral reason' (Walsh, 1951, p.146). He himself does not attempt to give a detailed answer to the question he has raised, his main problem being the more general one of trying to determine the epistemological status of the kind of speculative enquiry upon which Hegel considered himself to be engaged. He does, however, suggest that an important clue to what is at issue may lie in certain features of Hegel's own moral theory, especially those that concern the notion that the conscience of the individual necessarily represents 'the highest court of appeal' in matters of conduct. This suggestion seems to me a valuable one, and in what follows I should like to explore some of its implications. As Walsh indicates, Hegel had from an early stage in his philosophical career become increasingly dissatisfied with views which accorded exclusive authority to the subjective will and inner convictions of the moral agent and which entailed a corresponding neglect of the social or public aspects of what was involved; he had come to regard them, moreover, as expressive of a widespread contemporary outlook that was closely associated in his mind with ideas propounded by Kant. The possibility, therefore, presents itself that part at any rate of what he had to say about morality in the context of his philosophy of history reflects such preoccupations and that it may take on an altered significance when set against the background of his general discontent with current approaches to ethics, of which the Kantian was the most pervasive and influential. If this does not make what he wrote finally acceptable, it may at least have the effect of showing his position to have been more complex and less crude than has sometimes been supposed, while at the same time helping to exhibit its continuities with themes previously developed in the *Phenomenology of Spirit* and the *Philosophy of Right*. For it is of course in the latter works that the alleged limitations and inadequacies of individualistic 'moralities of conscience' are to be found most fully discussed.

Hegel's objections to moral theories of the Kantian type vary widely in character, ranging from charges of internal incoherence to more general criticisms that seem often to depend on empirical rather than formal considerations. Further, in the course of examining them he gives the impression on occasions of sliding almost imperceptibly from one version of the position in question to another. As a result it is not always clear whether it is Kant's own views which are under consideration or those of one of his followers (e.g., Fichte), or again whether he has not in mind some more comprehensive standpoint to which analogies can be discerned in earlier periods of thought: names are seldom dropped and their absence is at best confusing, while at worst it may be felt to raise doubts about Hegel's accuracy and fairmindedness as a critic of particular philosophical doctrines. Such complaints about his procedure need not concern us here, however. Instead it is necessary for present purposes to look briefly at the salient characteristics which he ascribed to the kind of approach that preoccupied him and which he believed could be seen to exemplify a distinctive overall pattern.

One feature of the Kantian outlook on morality that Hegel repeatedly emphasised was its 'abstract' quality. Those who subscribe to it are prone to isolate the moral point of view from other dimensions of thought and consciousness, according it a uniquely privileged status and treating it as something that can be identified and fully understood without specific reference to the varied natural and social contexts in which moral choice and judgment typically occur. Thus it tends to be assumed that moral conceptions derive from a capacity with which every individual is innately endowed at the outset and that they do so in a way that renders them essentially immune to the contingencies of time and circumstance. Indeed, at the extreme of this position – adopted by Kant in his own account – such conceptions are held to originate in a rational faculty which does not belong to the empirical sphere at all and which is therefore in no sense subject to the laws that operate at the level of our ordinary experience of the world. In consequence the moral consciousness is not regarded as changing or developing in any fundamental manner from one historical period to another: it is portrayed as set apart from the realms of natural fact and social convention alike, an autonomous and invariant agency whose principles take precedence over all others and whose edicts cannot justifiably be overridden by appeals to any institutional authority, whether religious, political or legal. Enclosed within the circle of its self-imposed commands, it is forever destined to confront an external reality whose character it does not share and which stands before it as something inherently alien and recalcitrant.

According to Hegel, the tendencies towards dualism and abstraction which underlie the Kantian conception of the position of the moral subject in the world manifest themselves at other crucial points of the doctrine being considered. Thus one effect of centring morality upon the individual, to the exclusion of the forms of social life in which it is normally to be found embedded, was to deprive it of all objective content. By prising it apart from these forms, and by presenting the moral consciousness as confined within the sphere of its own ungrounded claims and injunctions, any possibility of providing a non-arbitrary external criterion according to which the acceptability of particular moral judgments could be determined appeared to have been removed. It was, of course, true that Kant himself had attempted to meet this difficulty by invoking the requirement of logical consistency as a means of distinguishing legitimate from illegitimate principles of action. In

Hegel's opinion, however, such an expedient was ultimately inadequate for the purpose proposed; a wholly abstract criterion of this sort was by itself quite empty and could only be put to substantial use on the prior condition that certain objectives or rules of conduct were already presupposed. But that left the question of how the validity of the latter was to be ascertained still unanswered. Hence the distinction between subjective certainty and objective truth seemed to collapse once more, the task of differentiating between moral right and wrong being again returned to the rarefied sphere of the individual's private judgment. And this, Hegel maintained, was tantamount to allowing any course of conduct to be justified provided only that it was sealed with the approval of inner conviction, or of what he sometimes referred to as 'formal' conscience: conscience in this purely subjective sense can be said to elevate itself above the realm of specific laws and determinate duties and to put 'whatever content it pleases into its knowing and willing' (Hegel, 1977, p.397), no more being demanded of the solitary self than that it should be inwardly assured of its essential righteousness and self-sufficiency. In fact – as he made clear in the fascinating studies in moral pathology which abound in the *Phenomenology* – Hegel thought that the adoption of such a standpoint opened the way to a series of perverted attitudes, ranging from an arrogant high-mindedness that rode roughshod over the divergent views and interests of others to the narcissistic self-regard of 'the beautiful soul', which 'lives in dread of besmirching the splendour of its own inner being' and which tended in consequence to withdraw from all practical contact with reality into a wholly passive condition of 'self-willed impotence' (*ibid.*, p.400). Hegel is to be discovered, indeed, reserving some of his most sardonic comments for persons who, while careful not to undertake anything of moment themselves for fear of staining the blank surface of their inward perfection, at the same time consider that this entitles them to seek out and denigrate the motives of those who are prepared to risk their reputations by intervening positively in the world.

It may be felt (reasonably enough) that direct responsibility for promoting attitudes of the latter kind can hardly be laid at Kant's door, and Hegel himself did not go so far as to assert that it could; what he had in mind was in any case seen by him as possessing an altogether wider historical significance. Nevertheless, he seems to have regarded such moral postures as emerging only too easily from an ethos in which purity of intention – the goodness of the Kantian rational will – was accorded supreme value and where the subjective motivation of actions was stressed at the expense of the social aspects and consequences of the deeds themselves as these were carried out in reality. The agent does not subsist – whether in a 'noumenal' or some other sense – outside the world but in it, and a true estimate of his worth cannot be detached from a recognition of what he actually achieves or brings about within the objective sphere of publicly observable events; from this standpoint it appeared that an obsessive prying into motives, either one's own or another's, was bound in the end to encourage the prevalence of distorted or lop-sided views of what was ultimately at issue. Nor was this all. In Hegel's opinion there were elements intrinsic to Kant's own moral psychology that also contributed to such a result.

When insisting upon the role of reason in ethics, Kant had drawn a picture which presented the rational and the passional sides of our make-up as being fundamentally separate and opposed. The status of the human agent as a creature determined by instinct and impulse was thus to be sharply distinguished from his character as a self-determining being capable of making his behaviour accord with rational principles; it was, moreover, only when he acted in the latter capacity, suppressing his natural inclinations in order to conform to the behests of pure reason, that he was entitled to moral approbation. In Hegel's eyes, this picture revealed once more the dualistic pattern that had pervaded Kantian portrayals of the relation in which the moral subject stands to the natural and social world he inhabits : here, however, it had been transposed to another setting, re-emerging in the relation posited between the subject and his own nature as a particular human being. And here again Hegel discerned difficulties; the account offered was both morally restrictive and at the same time psychologically unrealistic. To seek to confine moral worth to actions done from considerations of duty alone was intolerably narrow, as was the notion – suggested by certain of Kant's formulations – that morality is 'nothing but a bitter unending struggle against self-satisfaction' (Hegel, 1952, p.82). Quite apart from the reservations previously mentioned, Hegel felt that it was contrary to ordinary practice and sentiment, as well as being unjustifiable in principle, to maintain that conduct springing from, say, love or compassion was undeserving of moral praise; in his antipathy to this position (forcefully expressed in his early writings and reiterated later in the *Philosophy of Right*) he closely followed Schiller, whose *Aesthetic Letters* in particular he had read and admired. But he further believed that the psychological framework, in terms of which that position was stated and upon which it finally depended, was itself profoundly unsatisfactory. By postulating so sharp a division between the disinterested demands of reason and the selfish promptings of passion and inclination Kant had presented a grotesquely artificial model of human behaviour, thereby obscuring from view the complexities that characterise thought and action at every level of concrete experience.

It must be admitted – as Professor Walsh has himself pointed out in his perceptive study of the subject (Walsh, 1969, p.59) – that Hegel's own treatment of these topics is by no means as clear or explicit as might be wished. Without, however, entering into the various exegetical problems it raises, I think that one central point can be seen to emerge with some distinctness from what he wrote. This is the contention that it is wrong to think that a regard for general or publicly significant ends and the pursuit of personal satisfaction must always exclude one another, let alone that they must be involved in perpetual rivalry or conflict. To do so is to be governed, on the one hand, by an excessively primitive notion of human desire and, on the other, by a too limited conception of the ways in which conduct can be rationally determined. The various wants and needs that typically move men to act – at any rate within a developed community life – cannot be identified with bare natural appetites or isolated impulses; on the contrary, they are normally to be found interrelated and interwoven, and they take shape within a network of shared norms and conventions. Thus to interpret them properly it is essential to see them as fitting together within larger purposes, social as well as individual, and to comprehend the values or ideas which inform them and constitute their nature. To appreciate such things, however, is to realise that what is done may often be directed towards goals and objectives that transcend the agent's own personal good or satisfaction without in any way excluding these – the latter may, indeed, be part and parcel of what is aimed at; as Hegel observes at one point, 'the view that, in willing, objective and subjective ends are mutually exclusive is an empty dogmatism of the abstract Understanding' (Hegel, 1952, p.83). Yet in his opinion it was just such a dogmatism that encouraged 'psychological pedants' to disparage those who achieved something substantial in the world on the assumption that, since their actions were unquestionably influenced by self-interested desires and passions, they could have no other conceivable aspect. Generally speaking, it was as misguided to suppose that a concern for personal satisfaction was necessarily incompatible with a concern for the realisation of wider aims as it was to imagine that most of the worthwhile things achieved by individuals in the public realm could have been accomplished solely on the basis of a dispassionate respect for universal principles. To promulgate a standard according to which praiseworthy conduct rigidly precluded any regard by the agent for his own satisfaction was, amongst other things, to betray a conspicuous absence of realism. Although he never rejected as such the possibility of wholly disinterested behaviour, Hegel was deeply suspicious of many of the forms in which it was commonly held to manifest itself: he believed that the human character must be taken as it is, not as we might ideally wish it to be, and he exhibited at all times a particularly sharp sensitivity to the subtle ways in which egotism, seemingly banished from the scene, was apt to re-appear in novel shapes and unnatural guises. Proud appeals to the sovereignty of conscience only too often acted as a pretext for ruthless displays of self-assertion. And if, at the extreme of a fetishistic preoccupation with abstract virtue, an attempt was made to purify action of every trace of personal advantage or concern the chances were, not that conduct of supreme value would result, but that nothing of import would be done at all; in the end we should be left with no more than the sterile self-regarding passivity of the 'beautiful soul'.

Here, then, are some of the points that Hegel singled out as being central to what – for want of a better general label – may be called the Kantian outlook on morality. This could be said, in summary form, to comprise the following features, all of which – as has been seen – he viewed as closely connected. In the first place, it presented the moral consciousness as being in some sense 'outside' the world of everyday experience, occupying a privileged vantage-point that set it apart from and above all other aspects of human life and development. Secondly, it treated moral ideals and principles as deriving from an internal source and as being justifiable by reference to an absolute subjective criterion which necessarily took precedence over whatever social practices might be enshrined in a particular historical or cultural milieu. Thirdly, so far as the appraisal of individual agents was concerned it concentrated attention upon questions of inner motivation, thereby neglecting the public and consequential significance that attaches to conduct when it is viewed from an external standpoint. Finally, it was wedded to a dualistic psychology which invited over-simplified interpretations of such motivation and which led to a corresponding failure to appreciate the conditions generally requisite for effective intervention in the course of events.

Let us now take up the question of how far Hegel's palpable dissatisfaction with these elements in the Kantian position can be seen to bear upon some of the controversial claims about morality that occur in his lectures on the philosophy of history. It is worth noticing at the outset that one theme – implicit in much that has already been said – is to be found strongly emphasised in the *Lectures*. This was Hegel's opposition to all attempts to draw a hard and fast line between moral thought or practice and the various other activities in which human beings typically engage as members of a society. Morality, far from being the product of some supposedly self-sufficient rational faculty grounded in the individual ego, was essentially an institution that could only function properly in a social setting. As such it constituted an integral component in the life of any community, contributing in vital ways to the welfare of the society as a whole; to try, in conformity to the requirements of abstract theory, to sever it from these connections was to deprive it of whatever in the ordinary way gave it point and significance. For it was from existing customs and traditions, the mores of an actual living society, that it ultimately derived its objective content; in this sense what Hegel termed the 'ethical community' (*sittliches Gemeinwesen*) represented the true source and justification of the courses a man should follow in his capacity as a moral agent, a point that was persistently obscured by those who sought to trace everything back to edicts originating in 'private' or 'subjective' conscience alone. Moral duties, in other words, are rooted in 'the soil of civil life'; so far as the contingencies of everyday behaviour are concerned, conceptions of 'what is good and bad or right and wrong are supplied by the laws and customs of each state, and there is no great difficulty in recognising them' (Hegel, 1975, p.80).

One apparent consequence of this view is the claim that accounts of morality which portray it as comprising certain general precepts, universally recognised and presumed to be applicable to men at all times and places, must be misconceived. For Hegel in fact envisaged it as being a historical phenomenon that underwent radical variations over time and manifested itself in distinguishable forms at different stages of social and cultural development. It would hence seem illegitimate to criticise men belonging to earlier periods for doing or thinking things that might appear strange or unacceptable in the light of ideas which were specific to a later social milieu. Hegel reiterates in his *Lectures* the contention – previously stated in the Preface to the *Philosophy of Right* – that every person is a child of his society at a particular moment of its history, sharing its pervasive mental climate (*ibid.*, p.81). He may thereby be understood to imply that, if a historical agent is open to moral judgment at all, it can only be in relation to standards which he himself could have appreciated as a concrete human individual inhabiting a certain social environment; it is not as if he were the embodiment of a pure rational consciousness which, transcending the empirical sphere, was subject to a set of timeless principles in the Kantian sense. Hegel does not deny that it is possible to pick out, in an abstract fashion, various sentiments and attitudes as being fundamental to any moral outlook worthy of the name; he insists nonetheless that these remain empty when considered by themselves and that, once given determinate content, they can be seen to display wide and significant divergences from one historical period to another.

The incipient relativism implicit in some of Hegel's pronouncements on morality has not gone unnoticed by commentators and it is certainly plausible to regard part of his characteristic impatience with moralistic approaches to the past as stemming from this. Even so, such considerations can hardly be supposed to account for all that he wished to say on the subject. Whatever may have been his views about the dangers of anachronistic judgment in the case of historical individuals, he did not adopt a full-blooded relativist position in the sense of maintaining that no moral system can finally be judged to be objectively better or worse than another. On the contrary, his entire conception of moral variation and diversity was set within the framework of a progressivist theory of historical change, the successive forms of social and cultural life that manifested themselves in the course of history representing determinate stages of a necessary advance towards the realisation of what he referred to as 'freedom'. From this standpoint, it was indeed perfectly legitimate to portray morality as something that was inherently subject to progressive evolution; its development was integrally involved in a continuing process that must eventually culminate in the creation of a rationally ordered community with whose internal arrangements each member could inwardly identify himself as a conscientious agent and in which the human spirit would finally come to a full recognition of its potentialities. But, in subscribing to such a thesis, Hegel was far from wishing to maintain that the various historical embodiments achieved by ethical life could be treated as if they were the consciously willed products of human contrivance, conceived and planned in advance by individuals supposedly endowed with superior theoretical understanding and foresight. Rather, he tended expressly to dissociate himself from views of this description. It was not merely that an empirical survey of history suggested that things happened otherwise, though he generally held that to be so. Given his insistence upon the overall dependence of moral principles or beliefs on existing social practices and customs, he also seems to have felt that there were difficulties in principle in seeing how conceptions capable of serving as the model of a radically new social order could originate and gain acceptance in the proposed manner, let alone how they could be put forward with any sort of claim to objective validity. And he implies that, if we are correctly to identify the true sources of the kinds of change in question, we must look altogether elsewhere.

What were these sources? Throughout the *Lectures* Hegel repeatedly returns to the point that it is the needs, passions and interests of men that constitute the effective motive forces of history, contrasting the latter with what he describes as 'the fancies of isolated individuals' which cannot 'become binding upon reality at large' and which are constantly doomed to dissolve into nothingness. Much that he says on this theme in fact closely corresponds to related discussions in the *Phenomenology*, and especially to the passages dealing with those who – whether as putative agents or as critically minded spectators – adopted quixotic or utopian attitudes to the conduct of public affairs. Thus he contends that there is a widespread disposition among all too many of his intellectual contemporaries to suppose that matters of social policy should be governed by high-flown ideals of their own choosing, the world itself being regarded by them as either morally unworthy or rationally askew and in any case as constantly falling short of their personal notions of what it should look like; they typically 'contrast existence as it is with their own view of how by rights it *ought* to be', bitterly withdrawing into a condition of rebellious discontent when their ideas of how it might be transformed appear continually to be frustrated by events (*ibid.*, p.91). In Hegel's opinion, however, such outlooks – which recalled the Kantian divide between the imperious demands of the moral consciousness and the brute contingencies of empirical life – reflected fundamental misconceptions about the structure of social reality and its relation to reason. Rationality was not something that could, so to speak, be brought to bear upon reality from 'without' in the shape of abstract schemes or perfectionist blueprints, the sole authority for which derived from the subjective convictions of people who felt themselves to be in some manner set apart from the mundane concerns of ordinary men. Instead, it must be conceived as emerging within the forms and limits of what Hegel called 'the course of the world' and as finding expression objectively through the agency of persons who primarily thought of themselves as pursuing no more than their specific callings or their limited and largely self-interested projects and ambitions. It was motives and aspirations of this type that provided the principal springs of effective action in the historical sphere, and censorious theorists who sought to disparage the pervasive significance of such factors did so at the cost of living in a fantasy realm of dream and self-delusion.

It is in terms of these general considerations that Hegel's often quoted and much criticised references to the role of 'world-historical' figures have, I think, to be understood. Such figures are presented by him as being men who, above all others, may be regarded as responsible for large-scale social changes or upheavals of the kind mentioned earlier, appearing on the scene at times when some particular society has run its course and is either stagnant or in a state of dissolution; social reality has consequently become 'unstable and fragmentary', the established ethical order it embodied having lost its pervasive hold on the community. Hegel does not deny that, during such critical periods, individuals who feel alienated from their social and moral environment may – as he puts it elsewhere – 'try to find in the ideal world of the inner life alone the harmony which actuality has lost'. He nevertheless disputes the notion that it is through intuitions of the contemplative consciousness that the transition to a higher stage of development is achieved. His position seems rather to be that we must look, not to the ideas and conceptions of inwardly reflective individuals, but to overall social transformations of the kind to which 'heroic' leaders, historical agents on the scale of an Alexander or a Caesar, essentially contributed. Such men (he is prone to insist) are not to be thought of as guided by 'abstract reason' or universal principles; they do not even possess an articulate picture of the historical import of their actions or a clear vision of the different order of things these are destined to produce. They are described as 'practical men', not men of theory, and as being moved by what is termed 'passion', the word denoting the dedication of a man's entire energy and force of character to the pursuit of 'particular interests, special aims, or, if you will, selfish intentions'; in this sense, it can be affirmed that 'nothing great in the world has been accomplished without passion' (*ibid.*, pp.72–3). From all of which one might gather that Hegel considers such people to be centrally concerned – at least at the level of conscious intention – with the advancement of their own personal ends and to be prepared, in their single-minded quest after the objectives they set themselves, to override accepted moral constraints when circumstances require it.

Now it is, of course, precisely in this connection that Hegel famously refers to what he calls 'the cunning of reason', the latter being spoken of as operating through the passions of men in the process of realising the wider purposes of world history. And here, whatever may have been his divergences from Kant on the matter of morality, it might appear that Hegel's views at least displayed continuities with another aspect of Kant's thinking to which he himself (oddly enough) never explicitly alluded in the present context. For Kant, in his own philosophical treatment of history, had also written of there being a sense in which the egotistical activities of human beings could be regarded as affording the principal means whereby progress in the sphere of human affairs was achieved; moreover, again like Hegel, he had presented his interpretation of the historical process in teleological terms. Even so, there remain crucial differences between their respective

D

approaches. In a general way, Hegel's historical philosophy is integrally related to other departments of his system; in Kant's case, on the other hand, it is arguable that the contributions he made to the field of historical theory are comparatively peripheral to the complex epistemological and ethical doctrines he developed elsewhere. More specifically, there exists no real analogue in Kant's major philosophical works to Hegel's conception of the human mind as something that evolves in a social setting, or to the historically orientated interpretation of morality which was a corollary of this. Further, and so far as the status of historical agents is concerned, there is nothing in Kant's own writings on the subject to suggest that he wished to treat the behaviour of his self-interested individuals as possessing more than a purely functional value from the point of view of subsequent progress and social advancement. He may have argued that good overall consequences often flowed from selfish and even evil actions, but this was very different from seeking to defend historical figures against their detractors on the ground that their deeds happened, through no intention of their own, to issue in consequences that turned out to be beneficial; nor, again, did it involve awarding them credit for what they had unwittingly helped to produce. Given, indeed, his characteristic standpoint towards the appraisal of conduct, such attempts at justification could scarcely have appealed to him.

Hegel's position – at any rate with regard to the agents he identified as responsible for major historical changes – was altogether less straightforward. Thus in passage after passage he is to be found attacking the 'psychological approach' of those who seek to belittle or denigrate the activities of such persons by fastening upon their self-interested intentions or motives and subjecting them to cynical comment; conformably to a purely 'subjective' interpretation, it is made to look as if 'they have done everything because of some greater or lesser passion or *lust*' – 'lust for fame, lust for conquest, and the like' (*ibid.*, p.87). Hegel opposed these 'schoolmasterly' attitudes on more than one count. As was noticed earlier on, he was profoundly hostile to outlooks which laid exclusive emphasis upon the subjective promptings of behaviour. There was a sense in which a person was 'the series of his actions'; it was essential therefore to consider what people actually carried out and effected in the public sphere – the inner motivation of their acts was not the whole story, or even the most important part of it. Moreover, and as we also saw, he held that when motives and intentions were taken into account, it was illegitimate to treat self-regarding aims as necessarily precluding the operation of ones of a more general kind. And this, it would seem, had an important bearing upon his own interpretation of the conduct and mentality of 'world-historical' figures. It was undeniable that, by and large, such men were activated by self-interested considerations of the sort typically ascribed to them – Hegel himself had gone out of his way to stress the significance of these. He does, however, suggest in a number of places that there is a further dimension of their behaviour which their carping critics, influenced by a too narrow and unimaginative set of psychological assumptions, have tended to ignore. For he frequently implies that they also possess an intimation of what is demanded by their times or, again, of what in some manner corresponds to 'the inner will of mankind'. In putting forward such ideas, Hegel need not be understood to be retreating from his original claim that large-scale historical advances do not conform to anything explicitly envisaged or conceptually prefigured in the minds of those instrumental in bringing them about. Although on occasions he appears to equivocate, the predominant impression given is that he is referring to something of which they are only obscurely aware, and here I think that Charles Taylor is right in taking him broadly to mean that 'world-historical individuals have a sense of the higher truth they serve, but they see it through a glass darkly' (Taylor, 1975, p.393). Hence it will be true to say of them that, while at the level of articulate consciousness they are certainly preoccupied with their immediate personal ends, there exists nonetheless a wider perspective in which what they do can be seen to display an underlying insight and intent that transcends these, making it proper to appreciate their achievements in a more generous spirit than is sometimes shown. Such considerations, and not merely a vulgar and ultimately indefensible appeal to historical consequences alone, may thus be claimed to represent a vital part of what Hegel had in mind when he sought to vindicate them against their detractors.

An interpretation along these lines, according to which a concern with personal advantage is held to coincide with a valid if unformulated sense of historical mission, seems at least to be consonant with a good deal that Hegel wrote elsewhere when stressing the complexities involved in the evaluation of human behaviour. Moreover, and despite reservations suggested by certain notorious examples, it might even – at a pinch – appear to reflect some aspects of our ordinary thinking on the subject of historical 'great men'; it is not, after all, as if such personages were cast in a single mould. Whether Hegel himself sufficiently allowed for the latter point in the context of his overall theory is, however, another matter; and in this connection the general problem raised at the beginning of the present essay may be felt to return. For it is not, of course, just the self-seeking ambitions imputed to leading historical figures that have customarily attracted criticism: they are also apt to be accused of having violated moral norms and of having perpetrated crimes. How should Hegel's attitude to such charges be understood? And how far, for instance, was John Plamenatz correct when he argued that Hegel was prepared even to justify the actions of 'great criminals' provided only that in the long run they issued in good consequences (Plamenatz, 1963, p.267)?

To answer such questions adequately would involve considering issues in Hegel's historical metaphysics upon which there is not space to enter now. In the light of what has already been said, however, it is at least arguable that here again Hegel's outlook was rather less clear-cut and crude than has sometimes been alleged. That he held world-historical individuals to have been in some fashion justified in overriding the claims of accepted morality is beyond dispute; nor can it be denied that the tone he adopted when discussing the topic was frequently disagreeable. Even so, it is worth reminding ourselves of the context in which he tended to do so. Consistently with his views concerning the diversity of moral systems, he typically described the situation as being one in which the agents in question infringed rules and standards that were specific to the particular milieus or periods to which they belonged. Furthermore, he maintained that they came to the fore at moments of historical crisis when – as he put it – 'we encounter those great collisions between established and acknowledged duties, laws and rights, on the one hand, and new possibilities which conflict with the existing system and . . . destroy its very foundations and continued existence, on the other' (Hegel, 1975, p.82). Now it was, of course, such 'new possibilities' which these men were said to 'seize upon' and help to realise; their role was one of assisting in the creation of a different social order and *ipso facto* a different ethical one. Hence, given – as Hegel often suggests – that they had some (admittedly obscure) intimation of this, he may be interpreted as implying that they were entitled to disregard the existing moral ethos when it seemed to them that their role, and not merely their own personal ambitions, required them to do so. A contention of this kind no doubt raises difficulties on other counts; but it is at least distinguishable from the bare assertion – ascribed to Hegel by Plamenatz – that historical agents were justified in disregarding moral constraints provided only that their doing so happened to promote historical advance and quite irrespectively of how they themselves may have viewed their conduct.

Even if what has just been said in extenuation of Hegel's position is accepted, however, further problems remain. Among other things, it might be enquired what, if anything, entitled his world-historical figures to treat the future social order which they felt themselves in some sense called upon to realise as superior to the one that was being superseded. To what standards could they validly appeal? Hegel might argue that in retrospect, and by invoking considerations supplied by his own metaphysical system, he himself could justifiably draw such a distinction. But it is far from clear from his own account that the historical agents he has in mind were in a position to do so. It was perhaps partly with this in view that he showed himself sensitive to the situation of those who, in circumstances like the ones described above, continued to uphold the established moral order; thus he writes sympathetically of persons who are prepared to stand by its precepts on 'ethical grounds' and 'hence with a noble intention', comparing them favourably from this standpoint with the more ruthless agents of historical progress. Where he appears to be conspicuously less sympathetic is in his attitude to individuals who (he maintained) treated their private or 'subjective' convictions as morally authoritative and who pontificated about the conduct of public affairs in the name of absolutes to which they claimed to have privileged access. Individuals of this sort, who figure in sections of the

Phenomenology, reappear – as has been observed – in the Introduction to the lectures on history. Not only are they portrayed as exhibiting a persistent lack of realism about the possibilities and methods open to politicians in their dealings with the actual world; they are also habitually charged with judging and criticising others while not venturing to do anything themselves for fear of soiling the purity of their consciences. After reading Hegel on the subject one is, I think, left with an uneasy feeling that he was liable at times to confuse genuine moral integrity with hypocritical forms of vanity and self-regard, or at least that he provided no clear criterion for distinguishing between the two. This may be due to limitations inherent in his own moral philosophy as well as in his philosophy of history. But, whatever the reasons, he can hardly be said to stand alone in saying puzzling and provocative things about what has come to be known in the literature as 'the problem of dirty hands'.

REFERENCES

Hegel, G. W. F. (1975) *Lectures on the Philosophy of World History: Introduction*, trans. H. B. Nisbet. Cambridge, Cambridge University Press.

Hegel, G. W. F, (1977) *Phenomenology of Spirit*, trans. A. V. Miller. Oxford, Clarendon Press.

Hegel, G. W. F. (1952) *Philosophy of Right*, trans. T. M. Knox. Oxford, Clarendon Press.

Plamenatz, J. (1963) *Man and Society*, Vol.2. London, Longman.

Taylor, C. (1975) *Hegel*. Cambridge, Cambridge University Press.

Walsh, W. H. (1951) *An Introduction to Philosophy of History*. London, Hutchinson.

Walsh, W. H. (1969) *Hegelian Ethics*. London, Macmillan.

4. Dialectic and Necessity in
Hegel's Philosophy of History

LEON J. GOLDSTEIN

There are those for whom the very title of this essay would create problems, for it cannot be doubted that 'dialectic' and 'necessity' are crucial terms in Hegel's philosophy altogether, not simply in one or another of his works. Indeed, I have been told explicitly – during the discussion of some views on this subject that I presented to the philosophy department at the State University of New York College at Potsdam, 14 April, 1980 – that the issues involved in the understanding of these terms as Hegelian can be explored properly only from within the context of Hegel's philosophy taken as a whole. And it is obvious that the proper place to begin a systematic account of what Hegel intends by these ideas is the *Science of Logic*. But I must confess that I have still not made my peace with Hegel's *Logic*, and there is no way to know at this point if ever I shall. In addition, I have never been motivated during years of reading and teaching Hegel by a desire to contribute to Hegel scholarship for its own sake, though I certainly respect such scholarship and am in awe at the high level of its accomplishments and the extraordinary speed of its growth when I consider that during my own student days the field was virtually non-existent, at least in the English-speaking world. What has brought me over and over again to Hegel's writings is their relevance to interests of my own in the spheres of philosophy of history and social science, and the extraordinary insight into such matters that one may find in what Hegel says. If there are those who think that one can accept Hegelian insights only if one is prepared to make a major intellectual commitment to the whole of his thought, I am not one of them. It seems to me that there are important ideas which may be dealt with in terms of 'dialectic' and 'necessity' lurking within Hegel's *Philosophy of History*, and these may prove to be of worth even to scholars who cannot take the system as a whole.

I

One's view of dialectic and necessity in the *Philosophy of History* must depend, surely, on whether one takes Hegel's point of departure to be the beginning of the course of history he purports to be presenting in the lectures or the end, and what one takes the end to be. B. T. Wilkins observes, correctly, that Hegelian dialectic is 'retrospective' in its application (Wilkins, 1974, pp.74, 80, 81), yet his belief that it was 'logically' open to Hegel to make predictions about future states of historical affairs (*ibid.*, pp.77f.), suggests to me that he does not grasp fully the character of Hegel's retrospective method. The interpretation of Hegel offered in Wilkins' book is further complicated by the suggestion (*ibid.*, p.84) that Hegel's *Philosophy of History* is teleological and is intended to permit us to discern the end – in the purposive sense of the word – of human history. A similar view is to be found in G. D. O'Brien's recent work on the subject, O'Brien identifying Hegelian teleology explicitly with that of Aristotle (O'Brien, 1975).

A proper teleology would maintain that the end – in the sense of final stage or mature state – is contained in the beginning. During the course of the development to which attention is being paid, that end state comes into being, and the problem one presumes is to trace the course of development from beginning to end. If the one doing the tracing is Hegel, one presumes that the development being traced is dialectical in character – whatever that proves to mean. Must not this mean that an Hegelian intelligence situated at the beginning of the historical course traced in the *Philosophy of History*, i.e., sometime in ancient China, and equipped with a full mastery of the dialectical method, should be able to produce an equivalent of Hegel's lectures in advance? I confess that I find such a prospect unintelligible. It is true that there are any number of places in Hegel's writings in which he compares the particular development that interests him at the moment with the sort of organic growth of interest to botanists and horticulturalists, and this presumably is what lies back of those interpretations that evoke Aristotelian teleology as well as the bizarre prospect I have just suggested. Yet, for all that, an Hegelian reconstruction given in advance makes no sense at all, not least of all because it is totally foreign to the procedure of the *Philosophy of History*.

R. J. Siebert is essentially right when he says that for Hegel, 'world history is nothing more than the development of the *notion* of freedom' (Siebert, 1979, p.104, italics added), and while its stages 'contain the fundamental principles of its universal process' each particular stage 'constitutes the realization of one particular freedom principle' (*ibid.*, p.102). But there is one important element to which Siebert, among a great many others, fails to pay adequate attention, and though his own text (*ibid.*, p.104, near the top) does contain an indication of its significance he fails to attend to its consequences. And that is the importance of the contingent to the development traced in Hegel's lectures. If contingency has some determinate impact on the course being traced, then clearly the end cannot be contained in the beginning. There are at least two ways in which an end is contained in the beginning. One is the way of deductive inference, the conclusion, it may be said, being contained in the premises, with the only way for genuine novelty to emerge being for the reasoner to make a mistake. The other is the way in which seeds of whatever sort – *logoi spermatikoi* – are said to contain from the beginning the course of development which follows from their initial states. It is sometimes thought that plant life provides examples of such seeds, and we are told that the mature oak is contained in the acorn, that the former will emerge from the latter if there are no natural disasters that prevent it.

This is presumed by some – even, it sometimes appears, by Hegel himself – to be the model of Hegelian development. Both of these ways carry the suggestion of the necessity of the outcome given the character of the starting point, and while it may be presumed that the two kinds of necessity are different from one another, they are similar in that once the starting point is given the conclusion or end state is contained in it.

Many will think that some such view must be correct, and it is seemingly supported by any number of passages in Hegel's work in which we are told that the task of philosophy is to overcome contingency. This would seem to suggest that contingency is only apparent, and that in overcoming the appearance of it we show the necessity of the course we are tracing. The method of tracing is dialectical, clearly not deductive, hence we may presume that in Hegelian development we are dealing with the second of the two ways mentioned above. But in my opinion, what is important to an understanding of Hegel's project is not the use of this or that phrase, it is what he actually manages to do. It is what he manages to do which must, surely, provide the context in terms of which the phrases are to be interpreted. There are writers for whom overcoming contingency would mean showing the necessity of things, and these are likely to be writers on whose views it would be very hard to take seriously human freedom. For Hegel, however, overcoming contingency is not to establish necessity in the given way, but, rather, to render what happens intelligible. The well-known complaint that the transitions in Hegel's work are arbitrary is based on a failure to appreciate this and the expectation that a move from one moment to the next may be justified only if one can show that the latter *must* follow from the former. Hegel thinks that the course he depicts which begins in ancient China and culminates in what was in Hegel's day the modern world is a rational and intelligible course, but surely he was not so strange as to believe that any sense can be given to the possible claim that the latter was contained in the former or that given the former the latter was inevitable. Whatever 'necessity' can mean in Hegel's *Philosophy of History*, it cannot mean anything along lines such as these.

II

I said that one's view on the matters we are considering here must depend on where one locates Hegel's point of departure. And I agree that Hegel's method is retrospective, though simply to read through the lectures must give the reader the opposite opinion. The reason for this, clearly, is that Hegel seems to begin from the beginning. He does not begin with the modern world, and then, having completed his account of the modern Spirit, move back in time to the age and Spirit which preceded it. It may be recalled that Karl Löwith wrote his well-known historical study of the philosophy of history in that way, and it is worth presenting part of the justification that he offers for it:

> An adequate approach to history and its interpretation is necessarily

regressive for the very reason that history is moving forward, leaving behind the historical foundations of the more recent and contemporary elaborations. The historical consciousness cannot but start with itself, though its aim is to know the thought of other times and other men, different from our times and ourselves. History has time and again to be recovered and rediscovered by the living generations. We understand – and misunderstand – ancient authors, but always in the light of contemporary thought, reading the book of history backward from the last to the first page. This inversion of the customary way of historical presentation is actually practiced even by those who proceed from past ages to modern times, without being conscious of their contemporary motivations. (Löwith, 1949, p.2f.)

Hegel's lectures are like that 'customary' body of historical writing that seems to start from the beginning but actually finds its point of departure in the present. Indeed, it is only because of the character of the relevant present that one is able to discern what the beginning is.

It is clearly possible to charge Hegel with no small degree of arbitrariness. Much has happened in the course of human events, and many peoples have lived and acted on the stage of history, yet not everything of interest and importance finds a place in Hegel's account. To be sure, Hegel allows that some peoples who have no place in the account he offers may yet play some role in time to come, but the suggestion that the Slavic peoples have 'not appeared as an independent element in the series of phases that reason has assumed in the world' (Hegel, 1944, p.350), seems to be asserted rather dogmatically with no obvious basis. In addition, it had long seemed to me that the project of Hegel's lectures was irremediably flawed owing to the fact that Hegel could not know about all manner of things which have come to light in the century and a half since his death. Presumably, he believed that the Hittites were a small Canaanite people of whom we learn from the Bible; he could have had no knowledge of the mighty Hittite empire, the existence of which only became known decades after his death. Other examples could be cited, but the point is clear enough. The structure of Hegel's account seems to suggest that what he is doing is tracing a certain course the stages of which are connected dialectically and which moves geographically from east to west. To omit the Hittites – and the Hurrians, the Kassites, and who knows whom else – would seem to be to skip over stages of the process. Might it not be simply arbitrary to say that stage Y follows stage X in some determinate dialectical way when there may perhaps be a still not known stage that belongs between them? Dialectical transitions have, to begin with, the appearance of arbitrariness to those for whom only deductive moves are justified, and that Hegel seems to satisfy himself that Y does indeed follow dialectically from X may be only the mark of his own ingenuity. The Hittites were there, but Hegel could not know about them. The Russians were there, but Hegel simply omits them. How can we ever justify such a project as this?

The arbitrariness is merely apparent. It seems to be so because it seems as if Hegel begins at the beginning and then pushes forward – or, perhaps, is pushed forward by the necessities of the dialectic. But Hegel does not begin at the beginning. He begins at the end. The end, however, is not a completed Absolute from which nothing further can follow. It is, rather, simply the present, Hegel's present, not, of course, our own, that historical moment which is 'the point which consciousness has attained' (Hegel, 1944, p.456). It is from a determinate perspective – which is still to be clarified yet is clearly a perspective of Hegel's present – that Hegel is able to decide upon the starting point and to determine what is to be included and what not.

I do not intend to sketch the elements of Hegel's present here. Anyone can find them in the lectures themselves, and there is nothing about the details of it that I require to use here. Scholars may wish to disagree with the ways in which Hegel characterises this or that aspect of his present, or, for that matter, with the whole of his account of it. Our concern here is less with those details than with the nature of his enterprise in the *Philosophy of History* and, in the end, with 'dialectic' and 'necessity' in an enterprise of that sort. Whatever one wants to say about the details, what Hegel attempts to depict in presenting them is what it means to be free in the modern world. In an earlier paper, I noted that the *Philosophy of History* is 'an attempt to offer an account of the progressive evolution of culture which, in Hegelian terms, is at the same time an account of the development of the forms of freedom', and I go on to say that there is 'a form of freedom proper to each stage of the development of freedom' (Goldstein, 1962, pp.71–2). The language of 'development' or 'progressive development' may suggest a beginning at the beginning, but that early paper was written long before I came to recognise the retrospective character of Hegel's method. The point to be emphasised is that what Hegel presents in each of the sketches he offers of world-historical peoples is an account of what 'freedom' means for the people in question: in his own terms, the lectures present the 'principle phases of that form in which the principle of Freedom has realized itself' (Hegel, 1944, p.456). It is from the perspective of what freedom had become by Hegel's own time – obviously, Hegel's own conception of that – that the inquiry which is taken up in Hegel's lectures proceeds. Hegel's problem is to make sense of the state of affairs which is freedom in the modern world. There is no suggestion in Hegel's lectures that with Hegel's present, the course of history comes to an end, but the problematic of freedom for generations-to-come is not – cannot be – his concern. The perspective of freedom-to-be will provide those whose perspective it is with a standpoint from which to trace the course of freedom in their own terms. That, presumably, is the sense of Löwith's remark that 'History has time and again to be recovered and rediscovered by the generations'. But the particular problem that Hegel has to contend with is to make sense of what freedom has become in the modern world. On the one hand, that means to account for its institutional underpinnings. On the other, it means to provide an analysis of the concept of 'freedom'. In the end, these will prove to be one and the same problem.

III

Whatever freedom is, whatever form it takes in this or that period of history, its possibility is supported by ideas and institutions. In Europe, both ideas and institutions are affected in major ways by the history of Christianity, and much of Hegel's discussion of material in the lectures is concerned with the history of Christianity – the Church and its theology. To my mind, one of the most striking aspects of Hegel's treatment of the emergence of Christianity is where he locates it, namely in the context of his account of the Roman world. To be sure, the matters dealt with in the Gospels take place in Roman times and in a territory which was then a part of the Roman Empire. Nonetheless, it seems more natural to present the rise of Christianity – the very earliest emergence of it, not its subsequent history – in the context of Jewish messianism and apocalyptic. Yet, curiously, there is hardly a suggestion here that Christianity has historical roots in Judaism, and the character of the subjectivity to which Christianity is said to lead is rather unlike what Hegel ascribes to Judaism. But given what Hegel's project and procedure actually are, I have come to conclude that Hegel's way of presenting the material is reasonable. I would, however, not agree that Hegel's order of presentation is the only one that is reasonable, and I think that this is so for reasons which I take to be Hegelian.

For history written from the beginning, the order presented in Hegel's lectures is problematic. There can be no question that, for the most part, the elements of the most primitive Christianity betray its Jewish origins, and the emergence of Christianity ought to be shown to be the outcome of certain currents of first-century Jewish life. But Hegel's account is a retrospective one from the perspective of his present. There is an obvious sense in which the Roman world is ancestral to Hegel's modern world, and the forms of Christianity which contribute to the formation of the latter are transformed and affected by the Roman context into which they enter whatever their origin, Jewish or other. Christian scholars who write about the time of the Gospels will refer to the Judaism of the first century as *spätjudentums*. Thoughtful Jews are right in rejecting that designation and in being particularly sensitive to the potentialities it has for antisemitic mischief. And it is absurd to say that the Judaism of almost two millennia ago is 'late Judaism' given the course of Jewish history in the intervening centuries. But for a history of Christianity which is retrospective, Old Testament Judaism is early Judaism; the Judaism contemporary with Jesus and the Apostles is *spätjudentums*, and then comes Christianity proper. What happens to Judaism in the ages which follow is taken to be irrelevant to Christianity itself. To be sure, there never ceased to be contacts between Jews and Christians, but the history of Judaism is taken to be external and irrelevant to Christianity; nothing subsequent to the first century is seen to matter, and such perspectives as Christianity develops *vis à vis* Judaism is essentially from a perspective which takes it that Judaism has nothing to add to history since giving birth to Christianity.

In historical fact, the way in which this point is expressed is full of hostility to Jews and Judaism, and while Hegel was not himself an antisemite – indeed, had rather a contemptuous view of antisemitism (Hegel, 1942, footnote to Para.270 *zusatz*) – his reference to Judaism, in the lectures and elsewhere, are rooted in little, if anything, more than the simple appropriation of traditional Christian attitudes (See Fackenheim, 1973, and Rotenstreich, 1963). That there should have been hostility between Christianity and Judaism is not difficult to understand. Both claimed to be heirs of the same scriptural tradition which each interpreted in ways radically different from the other, and the stakes of the controversy, particularly on the Christian side, given its conception of the salvation of souls, were very high indeed (see Parkes, 1938, 1961). Not irrelevant to the character of the controversy is that it proceeds with an historical naivety which precludes those who participate in it from recognising that each side appropriates, hence interprets, the Hebrew scriptural writings from its own developing historical perspective, and that each appropriation is retrospective in a rather Hegelian way (see Rawidowicz, 1974). It is, however, precisely the mark of historical naivety that it fails to recognise its own perspective as a perspective. Judaism having led to Christianity, there is nothing left for it to do. It has exhausted its historical role (Hegel, 1944, p.321), and its own historical individuality has come to an end (*ibid.*, p.322). For anyone raised in the Jewish tradition, or whose sense of history is rather more lively than that of those who formed the Christian perspective, this is utter and complete nonsense. Yet one can understand how it emerges; it is largely a failure to recognise that one's perspective is a perspective. It is interesting to note that in the twentieth century there has been all manner of interest expressed in dialogue between representatives of Jewish and Christian traditions, and this, clearly, requires that the old Christian view that Judaism ran out its course almost two thousand years ago be given up. And this in turn, requires changes in the perspective out of which Christianity becomes open to such encounters: it requires recognition that there is a Jewish point to Hebrew scripture and a sense of toleration not compatible with the older conception of the stakes of the controversy. One may suspect that the historical sensitivity which emerged from the conflict over historicism – in the way participants such as Troeltsch, not Popper, use the term – may have made such openness possible.

The last paragraphs may seem somewhat digressive, and I should like to put their point more sharply. My claim with respect to Hegelian dialectic – at least insofar as it is a method for dealing with the socio-historical realm of human activity – is that it is retrospective in its application, and that there is no way to apply it from the beginning forward. If one could be so confident of the techniques of social description which are now available to us as to think it reasonable to produce a 'state description' of some identifiable human society, there could be no way to apply dialectical analysis to that description so as to produce a predictive description of the next stage, much less an entire sequence of stages. In fact, I cannot believe that the idea of such a thing has any intelligibility. Hegel's problem in the *Philosophy of History* is set by his attempt to render intelligible the character of his modern world with its attendant form of freedom. That provides the perspective from which he turns retrospectively to the course of human history in order to organise those of its elements he discerns to be relevant to the emergence of the modern world. Once the retrospective reconstruction is completed, it is presumed that we can see that each stage follows from its predecessor from a form of necessity which is neither deductive nor organic, but, rather, dialectical.

One important element – perhaps in Hegel's view the most important element – of the modern world is Christianity. I have found it striking that, for Hegel, Christianity emerges from the Roman world, but given the enterprise for which the emergence of Christianity is important, as it leads to the modern world, Hegel's treatment of it is entirely intelligible. But it has also been striking to note that in his appropriation of the Christian standpoint, Hegel swallows it whole, at least so far as its totally unperspectival attitude toward Judaism is concerned. Which means, of course, that he simply takes over Christianity's un-Hegelian way of relating to Judaism, a bit of naivety in what is essentially a very sophisticated orientation toward history.

IV

To think of historical reconstruction as retrospective requires a rethinking of the view that Hegel's philosophy is developmental. On its face, it is hard to gainsay that Hegel's lectures present a course of development. First there was China, then India, and, in due course, the modern world. And each of the moments of philosophical history has its own integrity, is capable of standing alone. In addition, there is the strong suggestion that the form of each succeeding moment is affected – to settle for only a mild term – by the character of its predecessor. Surely, then, the account presented in the lectures is developmental in some rather obvious sense of the word.

It has long been my opinion that, with the exception of the *Philosophy of Right*, Hegel's writings, to the extent that I knew them, tended always to be developmental. There are writers who do not make the exception just indicated, and, rather, see the *Philosophy of Right* as developmental too. Thus, Siebert writes of civil society as if it were a stage in a sequence of stages (Siebert, 1979, pp.92,95), and he can talk of something or other being the case 'as long as Civil society continues to exist'. He can even add post-Hegel stages as when he writes that 'early socialistic society is not yet sufficiently differentiated from late Civil society as to warrant the abandonment of Hegel's philosophy of history (Siebert, p.96, but cf.p.100, where he seems to have it right: 'For Hegel the state presupposes and contains the family and civil society'; this would seem to mean, not that civil society is a stage in a sequence of stages, but, rather something contained by any state). But if this view of the *Philosophy of Right* were correct, then it would be hard to see how abstract right, the moment with which the *Philosophy of Right* begins, could fail to be a stage, indeed the first stage of the sequence. Given, however, the way in which Hegel thinks about the relation of individual and society, that cannot be the case. If it were the case, there would be a stage in human history – or in the history of each human society – concerning which the state-of-nature theorists would be right, that the social world would in fact be only a sum of individuals. The standpoint of abstract right is the standpoint of the idiosyncratic individual conscience of his right as his own. In Hegel's view, that an individual may possess right *qua* individual makes no sense. The individual's right is his only because it may be located within a system of right which assumes that all who participate in it share in the rights in question. The dialectic of the *Philosophy of Right* does not move along to the next moment because of determinate historical factors which move it along, in the way that each step in the course of some history is determined by specifiable conditions allowing us to think of each step as a stage in a sequence of stages. Rather, the movement in the *Philosophy of Right* is conceptual; the idea of abstract right is, in the end, intrinsically unintelligible. There cannot be an actual human situation in which it is realised, hence it cannot be a stage in a sequence of stages. The *Philosophy of Right* is a conceptual reconstruction along the dialectical lines – whatever they prove to be – of the idea of the state. In the course of the work, Hegel, having started at what must surely seem to many to be the most reasonable starting point, the individual and his right as he is aware of it, moves forward, step by step, until the concept of the state is fully worked out. The steps are conceptual moments, not socio-historical stages.

But what shall we say about the *Phenomenology of Spirit?* – as apparently we are now to call it in English, Miller having triumphed over Baillie. It would be desirable to present in some detail an analysis or two from among the several well-known accounts of the different things that Hegel presents in the *Phenomenology*, but that would not serve the more immediate purposes of the present paper. I shall, instead, confine my observations to rather an overview of the early chapters of that work, limiting my remarks to the general purpose of those chapters. What, indeed, is the overall purpose of that part of the work? It might be possible to argue that what we find here is an early version of what is later to be called developmental psychology, and such a reading of the *Phenomenology* is not implausible. Consciousness develops in a series of stages and the succession of these stages may be taken to reflect the course of the increase of the subject's maturity. At first, it would seem, that the world of the knower – presumably an infant knower, though it must be added that there seems no reason to believe that Hegel had much interest in such matters – is determined by the buzzing confusion of pure sensation, but in the course of time and the subject's growing sophistication, the subject *acquires* concepts and the capacity to use them. If the moments of the *Phenomenology* are actual stages, then there is one stage, the first of the sequence, with respect to which sense-data empiricism would be the true epistemology. There is no reason to think that Hegel could accept such a view. In addition, attention to the actual character of the transitions – they are remarkably clear in the earliest parts of the discussion – shows that we are not dealing with stages of psychological development which are capable of persistence until such time as the subject's maturation leads one stage to be succeeded by the next. The very first moment of the discussion of consciousness, sense-certainty, has it that the 'I' which knows and the pure content which it knows is each a 'pure "This"'. The transition is then effected, not because the subject comes in time to be able to experience the contents of its experiences in new ways which may be said to reflect psychological growth, but, rather, because the 'pure "This"' cannot stand by itself, it is inherently incapable of any sort of persistence. One could hardly say this about a real stage of any sort, and what Hegel is in effect saying is that the moment of sense-certainty is conceptually incoherent.

Since the idea with which the *Phenomenology* begins proves to be incoherent – though not logically inconsistent – either one stops altogether or finds some way to move beyond it. I do not wish to discuss the actual character of the moving beyond sense-certainty in Hegel's first chapter, except to say that the move to the next step does not follow deductively from sense-certainty. Then how can it be justified? To my mind, it is not plausible that Hegel could have decided that sense-certainty was an obvious point of departure and then proceeded to follow it to see where it would lead. Rather, the starting point is suggested by some sense of the outcome, and, then, given the starting point and the method of dialectical analysis, Hegel moves forward to cover the domain of his inquiry.

V

Our discussion in the section just completed hardly proves the claims that I have made about the *Philosophy of Right* and the *Phenomenology of Spirit*. Nothing less than detailed treatment of these works with very close attention to the character of the transitions within them could accomplish that. But taken together with what I had said previously about the *Philosophy of History*, it surely creates a strong suggestion about the nature of Hegel's procedure, for each of the three seems to be retrospective reconstruction of its chosen domain beginning from a starting point determined by Hegel's sense of the conclusion, or a retrospective reconstruction which is itself a form of conceptual analysis. (Parenthetically it is worth noting that, for Hegel, the examination of a domain and the analysis of concepts go hand in hand. Cf. the opening statement of the 'Introduction' to the *Philosophy of Right*: 'The subject-matter of the philosophical science of right is the Idea of right; i.e., the concept of right together with the actualisation of that concept'.

Merold Westphal [1980, p.103] adds: 'The adequate conceptual grasp of any content can never be reached by conceptual analysis alone. Yet a prior understanding of the concept is needed to guide the discovery of that actualisation of freedom which alone can provide us with an adequate conceptual grasp'. Westphal takes it that that prior understanding is provided by the *Logic*. I find it difficult to see how the *Logic* can provide the prior understanding required for each of the domains of knowledge in which Hegel was interested and incline to suppose that the prior understanding comes from increasingly adequate knowledge of each domain itself.) In any event, that Hegel's procedure is a retrospective reconstruction of the sort just mentioned tells us something important about Hegelian dialectic and points us in the direction of the kind of necessity that such a dialectic involves. In order to be able to be more explicit about this, I think that attention must be paid to the character of the context within which transitions develop, and for this we may return to the *Philosophy of History*.

My talk of a 'context within which transitions develop' has a strange ring to it. What can 'context' and 'develop' mean if dialect is a form of conceptual analysis? 'Develop' suggests time, yet conceptual analysis is supposed to suggest something timeless. To be sure, to perform a piece of such analysis is to carry on an activity of a certain sort, and that is done in time. But the activity itself is supposed to draw out of the concept being analysed what might be said to be contained in it, not what might be said to be developing in it. But how, on this view, would one set about analysing the idea of freedom, the subject of Hegel's lectures? Can it be claimed seriously that the sense of the idea of freedom is fixed once and for all, and that the application of the tools of analysis may lead to its definitive explication? It has been thought that this must be the case if the concept of freedom is a concept at all, and we have Frege's word for it that 'A concept that is not sharply defined is wrongly termed a concept' (quoted in Weitz, 1977, p.xi). Increasingly, there has been developing a sensitivity to concepts which are not – cannot be – sharply defined, and they are being discussed under the rubric 'open concepts' (see Weitz, 1977; also Kovesi, 1967, and Brennan, 1976). The ideas that Hegel deals with in the writings to which our attention has been directed in this paper are certainly open concepts, and I take it that dialectical analysis of the sort he produced was intended to be a method for dealing with concepts open in the requisite sense. I do not, however, wish to involve myself here with the recent literature on the subject. Rather, I wish to continue to attend to what Hegel, himself, tried to do.

The question implicit in Hegel's procedure seems to be, not 'How shall we explicate concepts which are not sharply defined?' – to use Frege's expression – but, rather, 'What are the elements which enter into a concept's having the shape it has?' Some may wish to argue that a concept's history is not to be confused with what the concept means, and it is the latter which is to be extracted by a proper explication of it. I do not wish to take up the issue in a systematic way, and perhaps there are open concepts for which their histories are not relevant to their meanings. I have my doubts, however, that this could be the case for all concepts which are not sharply defined, and I should suppose that if one were to know all of the regulations concerning the election and operation of the British Parliament one could still not claim to understand the concept of parliamentary government if one were not acquainted with the history that gives shape to that idea. And that is clearly what Hegel seems to be saying about the idea of freedom to the exploration of which the *Philosophy of History* is devoted. We have seen, in my parenthetical observation above, that the analysis of a concept is not possible, in Hegel's view, without our attending to the actualisation of the concept. In the case before us, that actualisation is a course of historical development. Thus to say, as I did earlier in this paragraph, that Hegel's implicit question is 'What are the elements which enter into a concept's having the shape it has?', is to set oneself the task of tracing the course of development in question.

How is this done? Again, we may say what is not done. Hegel does not begin with some ancient idea of freedom, and then proceed to work out its implicit consequences, as if the history of ideas is simply the unpacking of what is already contained in the idea. It is because this is not what he does – nor is it anything that he can do, since the history of the idea of freedom is not such an unfolding – that some critics complain about the transitions. Likewise, Hegel does not trace the development of the idea on the 'model' of the oak's emerging from the acorn and proceeding along the path of its organic development. I know that there are passages in Hegel which suggest this, yet, for all that, I cannot imagine what such a procedure would be like, and, more important, it is not what Hegel actually does. To read the *Philosophy of History*, particularly the detailed, presumably factual, accounts which follows its famous Introduction, is to read what purports to be a sequence of cultural-historical descriptions. Hegel's point, surely, is that the character of the determinate history that he presents is what determined the shape or character of the concept he is seeking to elucidate. That means that what happens to the concept is affected/determined by the contingencies of its history. It is for that reason that no account of what Hegel does which sees the end contained in the beginning can be right, for there is no way that sense can be given to the suggestion – were anyone foolish enough to make it – that the logically contingent historical facts – and relative to the concept they are logically contingent – are already contained in the beginning. And even if Hegel's general procedure is deemed to be mistaken, if he is right in thinking that a concept reflects its history in some way, then it would necessarily follow that the working out of a concept or idea in the course of time could never be a deductive process.

The difficulty with Hegel's account of the idea of freedom is that it is presented as involving a number of cultures which do not really seem to participate in a common history. Should, at some future time, the human race over the entire globe come to form a common polity, that circumstance

E

would constitute a perspective from which to write its history. One may suppose that a pressing problem that would confront historians at such a time would be to account for how the unified polity came itself into being, and from the perspective of its existence efforts would be made – retrospectively – to trace its emergence in the course of human affairs. Events having no significance, or, perhaps some other significance, before the emergence of the perspective which defines the problem, would be seen, retrospectively, to have a new significance entirely. It can certainly not be claimed that such a perspective is one which defines historical problems in our time, and it is not easy to see that China, India, Persia, Egypt and others all participate in a common history. It would be plausible to be told that modern European conceptions of freedom may be traced back through the Renaissance and the Middle Ages to antiquity, and that elements have been taken up into that history from the classical cultures of Greece and Rome and from Biblical Israel. Should it be possible to show that elements relevant to the history of the idea of freedom which have been received from Greece have to some specifiable extent been affected by the Greek encounters with Persia and Egypt, then these cultures, too, could be understood to have contributed to the historical stream being traced. Beyond that, I suspect that most of us would find it hard to believe that ancient China and India have to be taken into account. For whatever reason, Hegel takes it that the experiences of those oriental peoples have, indeed, contributed to the history of the idea of freedom he is intent upon tracing, and, for the purpose of the present discussion, I see no advantage in arguing with him. What I want to do is to attend to the sorts of things Hegel talks about when he wants to discover how the historical cultures in question contributed to the shaping of the modern idea of freedom as he understood it a century and a half ago.

In China, Hegel tells us, only one – the Emperor – is free. But he is not satisfied to explicate the Chinese idea of freedom as if that were a task of a logical-analytic sort. Rather, he proceeds to tell about the relevant elements of the Chinese state or culture. Hegel discusses the totality of the Chinese spirit, which, for him, means that attention is paid to philosophy, religion and the nature of the socio-political aspect of Chinese life. Most important for Hegel in all this is the conception of subjectivity which prevails, for the idea of subjectivity plays a central role in every stage of the history of freedom (cf. Goldstein, 1962). The character that the idea of freedom takes on is, in some way, a reflection of these. The idea of freedom is not a political abstraction or an ungrounded ideal; rather, it is intimately a part of the total fabric of culture. It is in the context of Chinese culture that the first phase of the history of the idea of freedom takes form. When we move on to the next phase – India – elements of the same kind have to be taken into account. We have seen that Hegel takes it that there is an historical continuity between these phases, and I have already stated that I do not wish to raise difficulties in connection with that. It would seem that the idea of freedom that emerges from the Chinese experience is in some way taken up in India – I cannot quite say how – where it is reshaped by the culture of that world-historical people. The same kinds of consideration which entered into the discussion of freedom in China enter into the discussion of freedom in India. And explicit comparisons are made of the relevant element of the two cultures – say, Chinese unity in contrast to Indian diversity (Hegel, 1944, p.166) – in order that the reasons/causes for the change in the idea of freedom to which our attention is being called be understood.

To read through Hegel's lectures is to see the same pattern of analysis repeated stage by stage. There is, obviously a principle of unity which binds the stages together, for Hegel is attempting to trace one determinate course. But each step of that course is markedly different from what preceded it; the movement from one step to the next is one of change. And the change, as we have seen, is affected by elements of culture which are logically contingent with respect to the concept which is being analysed, yet for all their logical contingency these elements of culture do have an impact upon the history of the idea. What I have been saying is, of course, my own attempt to understand what Hegel is doing in the *Philosophy of History* because he is rarely explicit about it. There is, however, a discussion in which Hegel does come as close to a statement of his procedure as one could like. Hegel tells us about the innovations of Socrates concerning the principle of subjectivity and the corrupting influence it had upon the traditional moral life in Athens (Hegel, 1944, p.269f.). In the Athenian context, with the demise of social life to which it contributes, the higher principle of Socrates' morality is itself doomed. In Sparta, on the other hand, this same corrupting principle takes an entirely different turn: 'there we have merely the isolated side of particular subjectivity – corruption in its undisguised form, blank immorality, vulgar selfishness and venality' (Hegel, 1944, p.271). Nothing could be clearer. The course of conceptual development is not contained in the concept. The potentiality – if that is what it should be called – of the concept for development is affected variously by different cultural contexts, and no reading of Hegel which takes it that the unfolding of the concept makes explicit what is already contained in it makes the least bit of sense of what Hegel does in the lectures – assuming it makes any kind of sense at all.

VI

Hegelian dialectic turns out to be a method of retrospective conceptual analysis which takes seriously the way in which concepts are the outcome of their histories. Yet what can be meant by 'necessity' given what has been said? Given the importance of the logically contingent to the development of the concept, it is quite difficult to see what sort of necessity can be imputed to the course of development. One could, of course, collect all the uses of the term in Hegel's lectures, and so discover what he means by 'necessity' by attending to how he uses the word. One would certainly discover various uses, but for the most part I doubt that they would be relevant to understanding the sort of analysis to which we have been attending and the necessity which may be ascribed to it. Thus, for example, there is a necessity which is the absence of the spiritual (Hegel, 1944, p.246), and the suggestion seems to be that without the spiritual the necessities of nature would be imposed directly upon us in a manner which would be experienced as oppressive. But that has nothing obvious to do with the modern idea of freedom and its historical emergence.

If Hegel is right, and the character of the concept is owing to the historical course through which it has passed, then in the one sense we are not dealing with necessities at all. Nothing in the account contained in the lectures points to the necessity that the concept pass through the world historical peoples it does, or that they have the determinate historical cultures they had. On the contrary, there is no gainsaying the presence of the contingent. But we must take one more look at the matter. Hegel had always taken it to be a task of philosophy to overcome contingency. On the face of it, this appears to suggest that philosophy shows that what seems to be contingent merely seems so, that in reality what happens must happen. This would be rather like Spinoza's view that the accidental only appears to be accidental relative to our lack of knowledge. But it is not necessary to seek such an interpretation in Hegel's lectures, not least of all because such a view of necessity cannot but subvert any serious idea of freedom – which is, after all, the subject of the lectures. One must keep in mind that Hegel's approach is retrospective and that what he wants to do is to explicate and to make sense of the, for him, modern idea of freedom. The modern idea turns out not to be just any idea. It could not be just any idea. Hegel presumes to suggest that when we have completed our retrospective reconstruction we see what it is and why it *must* be what it is. The same would be so for the idea of freedom in any of its previous forms. When we have attended to the historical course which led to its formation, then we have seen why it must be what it was. Were any of its stages different from what they were in actual fact, Hegel's modern idea of freedom would have had to be different from what it was. What from one viewpoint is merely the outcome of contingencies is, from another, something which had to be what it came to be. And we seem to have a necessity which is entirely compatible with taking freedom seriously.

REFERENCES

Brennan, J. M. (1976) *The Open-Texture of Moral Concepts*. New York, Barnes and Noble.

Fackenheim, E. L. (1973) Moses and the Hegelians: Jewish Existence in the Modern World, in *Encounters Between Judaism and Modern Philosophy*. Philadelphia, Jewish Publication Society of America.

Goldstein, L. J. (1962) The Meaning of 'State' in Hegel's *Philosophy of History*, *Philosophical Quarterly*, 12, 60–72.

Hegel, G. W. F. (1942) *Philosophy of Right*, trans. with notes by T. M. Knox. Oxford, Clarendon Press.

Hegel, G. W. F. (1944 or any edition of 457 pages) *The Philosophy of History*. New York, Willey Book Company.

Kovesi, J. (1967) *Moral Notions*. London, Routledge & Kegan Paul.

Löwith, K. (1949) *Meaning in History*. Chicago, University of Chicago Press.

O'Brien, G. D. (1975) *Hegel on Reason and History*. Chicago and London, University of Chicago Press.

Parkes, J. (1938) *The Jew in the Medieval Community*. London, The Soncino Press.

Parkes, J. (1961) *The Conflict of the Church and the Synagogue*. Cleveland and New York, Meridian Books.

Rawidowicz, S. (1974) On Interpretation, in *Studies in Jewish Thought*. Philadelphia, Jewish Publication Society of America.

Rotenstreich, N. (1963) Man and the Estranged God, in *The Recurring Pattern: Studies in Anti-Judaism in Modern Thought*. London, Weidenfeld and Nicolson.

Siebert, R. J. (1979) *Hegel's Philosophy of History*. Washington, D.C., University Press of America.

Weitz, M. (1977) *The Opening Mind*. Chicago and London, University of Chicago Press.

Westphal, M. (1980) Hegel's Theory of the Concept. In Steinkraus, W. E. and Schmitz, K. L. (eds.) *Art and Logic in Hegel's Philosophy*. Atlantic Highlands, N.J., Humantics Press.

Wilkins, B. T. (1974) *Hegel's Philosophy of History*. Ithaca and London, Cornell University Press.

5. *Psyche* and *Geist* in History

DENNIS O'BRIEN

This essay presents a comparative account of two thinkers whose influence goes well beyond the philosopher's seminar room. G.W.F. Hegel, either in his own right or in his Marxist inversion, could well be said to be the most influential philosopher in the contemporary world arena. Sigmund Freud's influence on the treatment of mental disorder is, of course, profound but his work has been no less influential in the creative arts, literary criticism and historical research. No thinker is likely to have broad public effect unless he presents some striking and highly perspicuous picture of human life. Freud's view of the human psyche as the battleground for the conflicting forces of sexual libido, moral super-ego and the realistic ego is relatively easy to grasp and appears to offer deep insights into formerly incomprehensible behaviour. Hegel's dialectic of history which posits great civilisations in inner conflict also can be understood in outline without undue effort. Philosophical complexity and vital nuances of argument are often lost in the adaptation of such dense theorists as Freud and Hegel to public perception. Much of what passes as Freudianism, Hegelianism (or Marxism) may even run counter to the mainstream of the founder's thought. Yet the public image, however distorted, usually relates to strong currents within the more carefully stated body of theory.

My presentation is written with an eye toward the public character of Freud and Hegel. It is not, therefore, intended to dive deeply into the intricacies of Hegel's *Phenomenology* or Freud's 'Project for a Scientific Psychology' (Bonaparte *et al.*,1954). I wish to examine the 'philosophy of history' of each man since it is through their respective 'myths' of human origin that much of the broad public effect has occurred. I am not, however, interested in a mere historical presentation of two contrasting ideologies; I hope to deepen the understanding of these theories by examining fundamental assumptions and by indicating problems which arise from those assumptions. Given an interest in the public face of these theories, the presentation will be relatively broad and sketchy. Nevertheless, I believe that even at a first level of investigation, very important considerations can be raised. Although Hegel and Freud have been investigated as philosophers of history by Mazlish (1966), he has not presented us with a direct cross-comparison. Paul Ricoeur's study of Freud (1970) contains an extremely valuable chapter on Freud and Hegel from which I have learned much, but it does not focus on the philosophy of history *per se*. It is my hope, therefore, that by presenting a common outline structure for Freud and Hegel's philosophies of history – and then noting the profound differences within that common outline – we can gain a deeper comprehension of two extraordinarily influential views of human life.

Freud as a philosopher of history

To the best of my knowledge, Freud, who was well read in German philosophy, never read Hegel. In the volumes of *The Complete Psychological Works* (Freud 1964–) there is exactly one reference to Hegel – in which Hegel is cited by a third person. In Ernest Jones' biography (1953–57), there is a single and amusing reference to Hegelian philosophy. At the Weimar Congress of 1911, James Putnam, Freud's American advocate, read a paper entitled 'The Importance of Philosophy to the Further Developments of Psychoanalysis'. Putnam's brand of Hegelian philosophy evoked the following comment from Freud: 'Putnam's philosophy reminds me of a decorative centrepiece; everyone admires it but no one touches it' (*ibid.*, vol II, p.86). On the other hand, Freud was a considerable admirer of Kant and there is a more than superficial rationale for accepting Joseph Fell's suggestion that he was 'a follower of Kant' in his moral views (Fell, 1976). (Hegel's anti-Kantian arguments will, in fact, be lodged against Freud at the conclusion of this analysis.)

The lack of historical filiation makes the overall similarity in their general views about history all the more striking. Both thinkers appear to offer sweeping general theories of history that explain the jumble of the historical record by discovering a less-than-conscious thread of *psyche* or *Geist* which constitutes the inner motive or secret rationale in the manifest content of events. Both see the task of their analysis as bringing this secret spring of history to the light of self-consciousness. The attainment of self-consciousness is seen in turn as the attainment of 'freedom' – and yet both theorists have been sharply accused of a deterministic reduction of historic events to the machinations of an unconscious *id* or a transcendent God. The actual story of history in both theories divides the human record radically between pre-civilised or pre-historical times and civilised. Freud and Hegel claim that a crisis occurs which precipitates a radical change in the nature of human affairs: the shift from primitive to historical or civilised. This crisis haunts the present because the conflict which marks the change is unresolved (if not irresolvable). It is the inner conflict at the heart of civilisation that generates the restlessness, *Unruhigkeit*, which marks the personal and social life of historical mankind. Neurosis, war, revolution and cultural decay stem from the inner contradiction of 'civilisation and its discontents' or 'the unhappy consciousness'.

This characterisation of Freud may seem somewhat surprising to someone interested only in his psychological insights. When the distinguished diplomatic historian William Langer suggested to the American Historical Association that Freud was 'the next assignment' for the historical practitioner, one can be reasonably sure he did not have such a grandiose notion of the task (Langer, 1958). Langer's suggestion was that since psychology has been the historian's stock-in-trade since the days of Herodotus, it would behove the profession to utilise the most advanced work in that field – which he identified with Freudianism. Freud's work commended itself to Langer on two grounds: first, he objected to the casual, armchair nature of most historians' psychologising; second, he found little value in the academic psychology of his day which he believed offered little more than statistical verification for commonplace psychological conjunctions. Langer desired a scientific depth psychology commensurate with the drama of the human past. Freud's attempt to find the hidden springs of extraordinary human behaviour seemed better attuned to the record of revolution, war, trans-cendent faith and black deceit which constitutes much of the cultural record.

Despite the limited scope of Langer's initial assignment, there is a 'natural' progression of Freud's views which press him toward a comprehensive view of civilisation such that his psychology takes on the grand dimensions of a philosophy of history commensurate to Hegel's sweeping scenario of human deeds. If Freudian methods were confined to a scientific explanation of the pathological in history, they could play the same role that standard medical pathologies play in ordinary historical accounts, e.g., the effect of measles on the Amerindian populations as a factor in establishing European domi-nance of the Western hemisphere. Freudian theories cannot be so confined, however, because the realm of the pathological tends to expand to cover the entire historical record. This can be illustrated in three ways – the third of which is crucial.

First, one could regard normal history as systematically pathological. If one accepted literally Karl Popper's condemnation of standard political history as 'nothing but the history of international crime and mass murder', an analyst of the psychotic might well offer the only clue to comprehending such a distressing scene (Popper, 1963, vol. II, p.270). To simple common sense, however, Popper's view may seem highly exaggerated. A second tactic for capturing the historical field for psychoanalysis comes closer to Freud's actual practice: to regard commonplace behaviour as cryptically aberrati-onal. History need not be the record of mass crime; rather ordinary pursuits, like accumulating cash reserves, have a tinge of the compulsive which reveals deeper and more pervasive currents in human affairs than at first supposed. In *The Psychopathology of Everyday Life*, Freud radically extends the scope of his method from manifest neurosis to the minor irrationalities and 'acci-dents' of everyday conduct. An analytic method for our madness is extended to the 'normal' because it turns out that all human behaviour is radically to subtly 'out of place'. From the bizarre displacements of the hysterics to the benign sublimations of the banker, there is something 'off centre,' 'ec-centric' about human action.

The last result is no less unsettling than the earlier claim that history is the record of great crime and madness outright. Not only unsettling, but perhaps unintelligible. Doesn't such a claim fall under the stricture of non-vacuous contrast? If everyone from Nero to the greengrocer is eccentric, we lack a sense for 'sanity' and the Freudian claim turns out to be a disguised definition masquerading as a powerful empirical truth. Freud has frequently been charged with making just such vacuous generalisations, but in this instance I believe he can escape censure – which leads to the third way in which psychoanalysis can lay claim to the realm of general history.

Freud's extension of his interests from the pathological to the everyday was not a result of piecemeal extension of his research, it resulted from a general theory of culture which separates civilised behaviour from pre-civilised behaviour. The needed contrast to the universal psychic aberrations of history is the 'non-aberrational' world of the primitive and precultural. In such works as *Totem and Taboo*, *Moses and Monotheism* and *Civilisation and its Discontents*, Freud developed a general hypothesis about the origins of civilisation from a crisis event within primitive culture. Only *civilised* behaviour involves the universal and systematic displacement of the direct expression of basic desires. Insofar as *history* is the record of civilised peoples it is a story at least akin to madness and the psychoanalyst may prove to be the proper methodologist for the subject. Thus, Bruce Mazlish, a sympathetic Freudian commentator, refers casually to '. . . the group neurosis known as history' (Mazlish, 1966, p.390).

Crisis and history
Philip Rieff introduces a useful distinction between what he calls kairotic and chronological time in his discussion of Freud. *Kairos*, which Rieff interprets in the New Testament sense of 'critical moment', is the sense of time experienced by Freud's neurotic patients and by modern cultures. Freud said that his patients 'suffer from reminiscence'. Time for them is not a simple chronological order of equi-valued moments; time is defined by a crisis which invades and dominates all subsequent experience:

> There has to be a *kairos*, that crucial time in the past which is decisive for what must come after. *Kairos* may be thought of as antinomical to *chronos*, mathematical time in which each unit is qualitatively identical. *Kairotic* time, on the other hand is not qualitatively identical . . . for Freud, memory time is always *kairotic*. (Rieff, 1963, p.26)

For the individual patient, a crisis event (the Oedipal crisis) determines subsequent behaviour. Adult action is constantly coloured, influenced, determined by the unconscious memory of this crisis. A similar crisis on the social level, Freud believes, transformed primitive hordes into civilised societies. In *Totem and Taboo* he speculates that an Oedipal event – murder of the patriarchal father by the sons – created a collective guilt which gives psychic force to civilised social practices. History, the 'neurosis' of history, is separated from an earlier state and precipitated by a profound crisis, 'memory' of which creates the conditions of civilised life and deeply influences the historical course of such societies.

A 'crisis theory of history' which sharply divides human events into pre-civilised and civilised behaviour patterns is also central to Hegel's philosophy of history.

The periods, whether we suppose them to be:

centuries or millenia, which peoples have passed before the writing of history, may have been filled with revolutions, migrations, the wildest transformations. Yet they are without objective history because they lack subjective history, records of history. Such records are lacking, not because they accidentally disappeared through the long ages, but because they could never have existed. (Hegel, 1953, p.76)

Appreciation of the importance of a crisis which divides the *historical* world from the *totality of human events* is central to any understanding of the two theories. For both Freud and Hegel, 'history' is not a record of the comings and goings of mankind in the extent of *chronological* time, but only the analysis of a certain specialised form of human behaviour dominated by kairotic memory. The philosophies of history which they offer in their separate fashions are philosophies of specific, peculiar social *institutions*: the institution of *civilisation*, the institution of the *State* (which Hegel calls 'the definite object of history proper'). A philosophy of history, then, for either man is an examination of a definable set of *values* characteristic of such 'historical' institutions.

The desire to separate pre-history sharply from history proper is expressed in both theories by the notion of a crisis. On the one hand *crisis* may simply mean, as it does in its Greek root, a *separation* of the two periods, but in both cases crisis has the further sense of a moment of conflict and decision. For Freud the crisis which precipitates civilisation is the conflict between a patriarchal tyrant who hoards the erotic goods of the society and a band of brothers who unite to slay him. The ensuing complications – conflict between the brothers and guilt at the murder of the father – produce the psychological constellations and social institutions characteristic of civilisation. For Hegel, the crisis which produces historical modes of thought is the conflict between master and slave outlined in the *Phenomenology of Mind*. Why these particular conflicts are so significant in radically altering human behaviour and how they do or do not create institutions and values associated with *historical* society will constitute the major burden of this essay.

Before turning directly to the nature of these initial crises which determine Freud's and Hegel's views about the nature and meaning of the historical, it is worth emphasising that the actuality of the crisis is of no real significance to the value of the theories. In *Moses and Monotheism*, Freud spends considerable effort trying to substantiate the empirical truth of his claims about the two Moses. No one has been much impressed by this attempt. But historical accuracy is unnecessary. In his clinical practice, Freud had first assumed that the tales of parental sexual assault told him by his patients were shocking revelations of fact. Later he came to believe that fantasy was every bit as potent as fact and that nothing was added by tracing present pain to actual past performance. The Oedipal conflict or the primitive parricide are quite sufficient in mere wish to generate the complexes of neurotic individuals and societies. A similar comment applies to Hegel's story of the master and slave. One need not look for that moment in some dim primeval forest when the actual conflict occurred. Insofar as these conflict stories express factors actually observable in contemporary behaviour, they receive adequate verification. These 'myths of origin' are like any number of ideal constructions used as explanatory concepts in the natural and social sciences, e.g., the frictionless plane, the free market, the social contract.

Patriarchs and Masters

In turning to Freud's crisis of civilisation, it is important to emphasise again the surface similarity of his account and Hegel's. For both theories, history – civilisation arises from a profound and deadly conflict. This conflict is finally resolved peacefully, but at a high price in lingering guilt, pain and unhappiness. Deep inner contradictions are buried in the peaceful resolutions that produce chronic malfunctioning and which become primary explanations for the individual and social changes and aberrations which characterise post-crisis society. Whether and how the basic contradictions generated in the move toward historical institutions can be resolved turns out to be a central difference between Freud and Hegel.

Freud accepted Darwin's supposition that 'the primitive form of society was that of a horde ruled over despotically by a powerful male' (Freud, 1959). In Freud's myth of origin, the sons, chafing at the patriarch's dominance of the erotic goods in the society revolt, kill and then eat the patriarch. An erotic paradise ensues, but the new 'fatherless society' soon breaks down into a Hobbesian war of all against all. Out of a combination of prudence and guilt, the brothers renounce the erotic paradise and formulate a new social arrangement in which the actual father is replaced by the Father God who upholds the restraints of civilisation:

> In Freud's origins myth all history is divided, by the act of parricide, into two stages. With this act, the political stage – submission characterised by guilt – was laid over the primal one. The primal murder signaled not merely the beginning of political society but of all ritual. Politics and religion, understood by Freud as originally ways of reuniting the many under a single authority, came into existence together, as the profoundest expression of the ambivalence of human will. (Rieff, 1959, p.194)

Holding a similarly dour view of primitive human conditions, Hobbes concluded that there was no *summum bonum*, no proper felicity for civilised society; there was only the avoidance of the *summum malum*, the war of all against all. The Hobbesian Leviathan, like Freudian civilisation, runs counter to what men would most like: unbridled self-aggrandisement. Thus, it is the burden of *Civilisation and its Discontents* (Freud, 1961a) that the

resolution of the primitive crisis in the new instruments of civilisation is far
from satisfactory.

As we see, what decides the purpose of life is simply the programme
of the pleasure principle. This principle dominates the operations of
the mental apparatus from the start. There can be no doubt about its
efficacy and yet its programme is at loggerheads with the whole world,
with the macrocosm as much as with the microcosm. There is no
possibility at all of it being carried through; all regulations of the
universe run counter to it. One feels inclined to say that the intention
that man should be 'happy' is not included in the plan of 'creation'.
(Freud, 1961a, p.23)

While the all-powerful pleasure principle will obviously be thwarted by
the decay of the body and the merciless forces of the external world, could
we not hope for happiness from our own creation, civilisation? Not so. 'Our
civilisation is largely responsible for our misery . . .' (Freud, 1961a, p.33).
The renunciation of instinctual pleasure is required by civilisation and is the
deepest source of our discontent.

If we compare this conflict story with Hegel's account of master and slave
we can see a similar problem for post-crisis society. The struggle of master
and slave is resolved when the slave accepts the dominance of the master
rather than death. It is a calculation basically similar to the prudential
calculation of the brothers who prefer established authority to the risk of
death which the post-parricidal anarchy produces. But, just as the resolution of conflict in the Freudian scenario is profoundly unsatisfactory, so
is the solution in Hegel's story. The slave makes the prudential calculation to
save his life, but he does not fundamentally renounce his essential freedom.
The social institution of master and slave is unstable and merely papers over
a basic conflict which remains unresolved. Social institutions which stem
from the core structure of mastery and slavery will all yield 'the unhappy
consciousness' which appears to lie at the heart of historical societies. The
buried crisis of unhappy consciousness is the root cause of the rise and fall
of great states and peoples which so impressed Hegel in the historical
record. One could indeed borrow Freudian medical terminology for Hegel
and suggest that there is a profound spiritual sickness at work in history. In
both theories, then, a severely compromised freedom lurks as a potential
threat to a stable society.

My account of the two conflict stories has been purposely too general;
it has not developed the radical and peculiar turn which marks off post-
civilised from the primitive society either in the Freudian or Hegelian myth.
As an indication that there may be something more to the inner character of
these two myths than has appeared so far, one need only note how Freud and
Hegel differ on the prognosis for a cure to the spiritual illness which constitutes human histoy. Freud adopted a view of historical stages from Comte. In
the beginning there was the pre-civilised animalistic phase of human society;
this is superseded by the religious (neurotic) phase of civilisation precipi-

tated by the parricidal crisis. Freud speculates that this phase will eventually be superseded by the scientific phase in which the 'individual has reached maturity, has renounced the pleasure principle, adjusted himself to reality and turned to the external world as the object of his desires'. Freud is cautiously hopeful that such a scientific stage will occur. As he says in *The Future of an Illusion* (which is the future of our religious/neurotic society):

> The voice of the intellect is a soft one, but it does not rest until it has gained a hearing. Ultimately, after endlessly repeated rebuffs, it succeeds. This is one of the few points in which one can be optimistic about the future of mankind . . . The primacy of the intellect lies in the far, far, but still probably not infinite distance. (Freud, 1961b, p.53)

Despite this expression of qualified hope, Freud is as frequently sceptical about the future and merely stoical about the present. Contrast Freud's caution with the supreme confidence which Hegel places in Reason as the governor and goal of human history:

> The sole thought which philosophy brings to the treatment of history is the simple concept of Reason: that Reason governs the world and that in history things have come about rationally. (Hegel, 1953, p.11)

As we examine the inner workings of the crisis story we will discover the source of divergence.

It is not difficult to suppose that a chronology of human behaviour from the Stone Age to the present day would be an accounting of conflict, murder, domination and revolt. As Hegel indicates explicitly, there may well have been millennia in which the wildest transformations occurred in human affairs and yet none of that will count as *history* in his view. Similarly, it is hard to believe that pre-civilised society in Freud's view was not marked by frequent surly rebellion against the primitive lord. What is it in the focal crisis which generates something so unique in the human story as to constitute a definitive marker for history? What emerges in both stories is a novel *value*, and it is in and around this remarkable new value that civilisation and history are constructed. Briefly stated, that value is what we express in such concepts as the individual, the person, the ego or the self.

The importance of this concept and its radical nature can be illustrated by returning to the comparison made above between Freud and Hobbes on the origin of civilised society. Hobbes' account of primitive anarchy followed by prudential contract omits an essential element of Freud's story. The civilisation which emerges after the primitive parricide for Freud is not only a society of prudence but a society of *guilt*. Hobbes' account is basically an economic or utilitarian account of society and it has all the virtues of such analyses: it appears to give a rationale for the least worst bargain which society offers. A basic issue for both Freud and Hegel is whether such strictly 'economic' analyses of the origin of society will suffice. For Hegel this amounts to the question: will a utilitarian theory of value support the special notion of historical institutions? His answer is clearly that it will not. For

Freud the answer is uncertain. There are times when he appears to think that society can be understood simply through the 'economics' of the libido and yet it is not clear that *civilisation* as it emerges from this myth of parricide can be reduced to the economics of desire.

One could suppose that 'economic' quarrels about distribution of erotic goods had broken out repeatedly in primitive human hordes. Many patriarchs had been slain, many erotic anarchies entered into and then abandoned because of the unacceptable risks. If that were all there were to the story, civilisation as Freud describes it could never have been constructed. There may have been 'revolutions, migrations, the wildest transformations' but until the notion of guilt is generated, the new form of civilised organisation cannot occur. We can see the importance of this new concept by considering Freud's analytic account of the resolution of the Oedipus conflict – the individual crisis which parallels the cultural crisis of the past. What occurs is the replacement of *object* libido by *ego* libido. Specifically, the son gives over his desire for the sexual object (the mother) and seeks satisfaction in *identification* with the person and characteristics of the father. Not *having* the mother, he will *be* the father. How this curious transfer occurs is not my concern; what is important is that without the emergence of the novel notion of ego libido and ego identification, the notion of guilt cannot obtain a conceptual grounding. If the human story can be told solely in terms of the economics of desire, the story of object libido, then guilt remains an empty notion. If the patriarch is hoarding the objects of desire and is disposed of, the survivors may discover that the new arrangements are no better, if not worse, than the former. This turn of events may generate a sense of miscalculation but scarcely a feeling of remorse; the sons may feel stupid, but there is no ground for guilt.

In a model confined to object libido, the actors can only be evaluated in a calculus of object goods. If the patriarch blocks attainment of certain object desires, then he is so evaluated; if the new arrangements prevent attainment of these desires, they are so evaluated. What happens, however, in the crisis of civilisation is that a new, *non-economically* valued object enters into the psychic calculus. In the story of civilisation, the old patriarch who had been murdered out of economic calculation is somehow replaced by a Holy Father who is valued beyond all such calculations. Truly, he is good in himself and cannot be ordered under any rational calculus of human desires (object libido) to be achieved. The Holy Father and his earthy surrogates are thus unique 'objects' for the psyche. They cannot be placed into a rational assessment as means to satisfying object libido. An attack, real or fantasised, on the Holy Father generates incommensurable pain, fear and loathing – it generates, in short, guilt. The new, non-economically valued item is something valued in itself. Thus, the transfer in the resolution of the Oedipus conflict is from object libido to ego libido, to 'satisfaction' not from *having* certain object goods but from identifying with the status of the other who is regarded as good-in-himself.

An analysis which firmly establishes something (the Holy Father) not subject to the calculations of object libido is necessary if the post-parricidal civilisation is to mark anything significantly different from the sorry ups and downs of the whole human record. Freud surely believes a radical re-evaluation has occurred, but he is ambigious about its 'value'. His animadversions against religion, which is the prime social institution of the post-animistic, pre-scientific civilisation would indicate that something improperly commensurate has entered into the calculations of the psyche. As he notes in the very opening sentence of *Civilization and its Discontents*, 'It is impossible to escape the impression that people frequently use false standards of measurement . . . and that they underestimate the true value of life' (Freud, 1961a, p.11). But at this juncture, Freud is unclear about whether the move to civilisation with its attendant guilt and oppressive religious ritual and rigmarole is an advance or a retreat. '[I]t is very far from my intention to, express an opinion about the value of human civilisation' (Freud, 1961a p.91).

One can easily understand the popular interpretation of Freud which would remove the false pieties and attendant guilts of religion in the name of sanity and health, and thus re-establish the rational (economic) world of the object libido. Yet that clearly does not seem to be Freud's aim. What could one make of his central claim for analysis – 'Where id is there ego shall be' – if cure consisted in a return to the calculus of object libido? It is this uncertainty which has led such diverse thinkers as Paul Ricoeur and Ronald de Sousa to argue that Freud's metapsychology and his therapy fail to cohere. When Freud's metapsychological theorising attempts to derive ego libido as a function of object libido, then it becomes impossible to give any definition to the crucial terms which specify the successful outcome of therapy: identification, ego dominance, sublimation and rationality. As de Sousa concludes: 'By drawing attention to the complexity and obscurity of the fundamental notion of satisfaction, the theory undermines its own implicit utilitarianism' (De Sousa, 1974, p.220–21).

One can further illuminate Freud's problems here as well as offer critique by turning to Hegel's account of the crisis situation which generates the new social understanding which we call 'history'. Again we find a need to discover a non-economic account of human conflict. As long as the human story is told as the conflict of simple object desires, it is of no great interest to the historian though it may have been full of 'the wildest transformations'. What is needed is a conflict which introduces a non-economic factor and this occurs in the conflict of master and slave. Not every story of master and slave, however, will serve Hegel's purpose. If the master regards the slave as an instrument to fulfil his object desires, then the relation is conceptually the same as the master's relation to his chattel beasts. If the slave regards the master as merely an overwhelming coercive force, then the relation is essentially no different from the 'slavery' of man to superior natural forces. In such constructions of master and slave, the individual actors are valued in terms of object desires, as means to object desires. They are not valued as actors, in themselves – not in terms of what they *are* but in terms of what they can do or produce. One can well imagine millennia of such dominance relations with their concomitant transformations. None of these cultures will produce 'history'.

The special master–slave conflict which Hegel depicts introduces a non-economic value. The master does not desire the other, but he desires the other's desire. It is the difference between prostitution (an economic relation) and love. Or, putting it more simply, the master wishes not merely the service of the other, he wishes recognition by the other. He wants recognition of the other for *what* he is, i.e., a master. This recognition is not simply a recognition of *fact*, the assertion of superior force and dominance, it is a recognition of *value*: the acknowledgment by the slave that the master's dominance is 'right'. But this kind of recognition is a radically new relation between actors in the human story. The relation of recognition involved (in Freud's terms) a transfer from valuing the actors as means to some object desire (service or security) to valuing of the actor's *status* as an object of inherent value. There is no longer the economic, utilitarian, prudential calculation which evaluates the other as a means to fulfilling my desire, there is recognition of the other as an end, a value in himself. For this reason, Hegel will say that the confrontation 'infinitises' the participants, i.e., it removes the participants from the finite calculation of object goods. The participants in the master–slave relation are 'beyond calculation' or of 'infinite' value from the standpoint of that necessarily finite calculus. This change in human relations is obviously a close parallel to the creation of the Holy Father in the Freudian story of parricide and guilt.

Both the Hegelian and the Freudian crises of culture require what Ricoeur calls 'the reduplication of the self'. Instead of the primitive state of man in which the voracious and solipsistic 'self' goes about seeking whom it may devour – subject to whatever economic considerations may be forced upon it – in the civilised state there are at least two selves: the guilty son and the holy father, the slave and the master. The notion of guilt is grounded on the emergence of ego libido. The Oepidal crisis is solved when the son identifies with the person of the father who is now regarded as beyond the calculus of object libido. Such a process of identification obviously requires the emergence of not *one* new non-calculable item, the (holy) father; it requires *two* since the son must regard himself as ego in order to identify with ego. The Oedipal conflict, then, not only creates a new understanding of father–patriarch but a new idea of son–subordinate.

A variety of astute commentators have traced the reduplication of self in Hegel's account of master and slave (Kojève, 1969; Hyppolite, 1974; Taylor, 1975). In seeking *recognition*, the master makes certain tacit appraisals of the slave and the slave accepts those about himself if the act is not mere show. The master does not wish the obedience of a trained beast, he wishes recognition by the slave that he, the master, transcends the world of mere economic desiring. The master is the one who is willing to forego life itself, the basis of any and all calculations of the object libido, and it is through this willingness to forego life that the master asserts his superiority to all the values of the object libido. The master has a self-concept in which he values himself beyond all economic calculation. He wishes the slave to recognise this special value which he holds as his self-concept. But this requires that the slave accept such an economically transcendent value as genuine value. If the slave is merely cowed by superior force, the master is not recognised for the true superiority he wishes to assert. If the slave, in his heart, believes the master is mad to think that honour is better than death, then the master's search for recognition fails. The slave, then, must accept the truth of the master's world view: that there is a value which goes beyond the economics of desire. But to accept the truth of that view is also to revalue himself: the slave now knows that there is a value beyond the maintenance of life but he is unwilling to act on that value and so 'sinks back into life'.

The various intricacies of this relation are not my concern beyond pointing out that, in both the Freudian and Hegelian stories, the important change that occurs in human affairs in civilisation and history is the emergence of ego-libido or 'self' in a situation of mutuality. In addition, the mutuality which is located as the point of origin is paradoxical since it originates in a profound subordination: the guilty son to father (God), the slave to the master. Having traced the emergence of ego and the 'reduplication' of self which this emergence implies, let us turn directly to the problems of philosophy of history which emerge from the two theories.

The prospects for history
The emergence under either theory of ego (in the special sense of a non-economically appraised value) gives plausibility to the notion that human affairs before and after this emergence should be understood on two radically different models. For Freud, the model is the world of religion and civilisation; for Hegel it is 'history'. The pre-ego and ego periods of human interchange are literally incommensurate since the *measure* of value in the earlier period (object libido: object desire) cannot be applied to the measure of value in the later period (ego libido: the inherent value of 'self'). If such change does occur in human valuation, then the new period requires radical revaluation in comparison to more primitive times. It is this sharp change of value which leads Freud and Hegel to posit a 'crisis' as the origin of the new civilised historical world.

Eventually I wish to ask which of the two theories conforms more closely to certain general notions of history as it is actually constructed by historians. However, before addressing that issue, it is necessary to outline the nature of the story of human affairs which follows from the initial crises outlined in the two theories. The crises determine the nature of post-crisis development and it is that post-crisis story that either will or will not appear to be interesting or useful to a practising historian. Obviously, William Langer thought that

F

Freud's story might recommend itself to the historian in his study, yet many historians have felt that Freud's tale of human behaviour, whatever its worth, was not a story for historians. In fact, if Freud's story is *the* human story, it has been charged that history as it has been conventionally written vanishes from our ken as mere illusion. Hegel's story has had small success with practitioners also, but in comparison to Freud's views it may prove more attractive.

Whether the emergence of ego marks the emergence of *history* in some specialised yet recognisable sense will be put aside, and our immediate interest will be in the new kind of human relationship established by these two crisis stories. The story of humankind will recount the characteristic behaviour of human beings under the new set of understandings. The general human story in the post-crisis period for both Freud and Hegel would be one of instability under social conditions of dominance and subordination. As a most general empirical description of much of historical life such an account is accurate enough. The story of humanity has hardly been a story of stability, tranquillity and equality. It is important to re-emphasise, however, that Freud and Hegel are interested only in a special kind of dominance and instability relations within the whole turbulent chronicle of human affairs.

For Freud, the dominance and instability of civilisation appear to be explicable through unresolved tensions within the initial crisis. Later events are referred back to the earlier crisis for their explanation in what Ricoeur properly calls Freud's 'archaeological' approach to human affairs. The unresolved tension in the initial crisis (for individuals and civilisation) can be broadly characterised as the conflict of nature and civilisation or, precisely, the conflict between the pleasure principle (nature) and the ego (the invention of civilisation). (I interpret Freud's 'super-ego' as a special aspect of the more general world of self or ego which emerges in the Oedipal event.) The story of civilised mankind is the story of the thin and precarious covering of rationality maintained over against the powerful striving of the object libido. The cataclysms of history and the madness of individuals can be attributed to the eruption of these natural forces into human society.

The significance of Freud's general characterisation of the story of civilisation and its discontents can be brought out by noting the difference between his view and Hegel's. In both theories dominance and conflict are inherent factors, but for Hegel the conflict is in a sense *within* civilisation (or history) and not between civilisation and some undigested natural determinant. The Hegelian conflict is not a direct conflict between ego and desire, it is a conflict between egos: the conflict of the ego of the master and that of the slave. (Desire plays a significant role in Hegel's story also, but only *through* the slave. This will be discussed below.) Civilisation is not the best bargain human beings can make with an all powerful nature; it is the 'bargain' that egos make with one another. In addition, the bargain which the egos make with one another is not a prudential bargain alone – to avoid the risks of anarchic pleasure seeking – it is a bargain struck for the purpose of asserting the *value of the ego*: the master's demand to be recognised.

The diverse understanding of the original crisis has profound consequences for the stories which Freud and Hegel project for humankind. For instance, it remains fundamentally uncertain in Freud whether the conflict at the heart of civilisation can be resolved. Freud's stoicism and scepticism are functions of his version of the initial crisis. If the story to be told is a story of a conflict in which nature plays a persistent and destructive part, then the prospects for mankind are likely to be: 'more of the same'. The ground for uncertainty about Freud's views is the unclear relation between Freud as therapist and Freud as metapsychologist. As therapist, Freud gives reason and science a role in human affairs. He can even believe, as therapist, that the still small voice of reason will finally be heard and that a scientific age may succeed our age of religion and irrationality. The problem is that Freud does not appear to have the metapsychology for his therapy. If the initial crisis event is as central and pervasive in men and civilisation as the metapsychology suggests, where is the principle *in that event* for the authority of reason and therapy? Freud posits a powerful object libido countered by the emergent ego with its attendants: guilt, super ego, identification and so forth. It is the conflict between this emergent ego and the clamoring of desire which constitutes our troubled state. However, Freud cannot really bring himself to give full independent standing to the ego. All psychic energy comes from the object libido, from the pleasure principle, '. . . the principle dominates the psychic apparatus from the start'. But if so, what authority can the ego have against this libidinal energy? Ricoeur sums up the point:

> For my part I doubt that Freud succeeded in reducing the fundamental gap between the externality of authority, to which he is condemned by his refusal of an ethical foundation inherent in the positing of the ego, and the solipsism of desire, which stems from his initial economic hypothesis that every formation of an ideal is ultimately a differentiation of the id. (Ricoeur, 1970, p.489)

Let me state this difficulty in terms of a philosophy of history: the ego emerges as the device of the religious phase of history. This seems to be a necessary condition because it is the 'holiness' of the Father God which introduces a non-economic concept of 'ego' into the calculations of human beings. Does this mean, however, that the ego is part of the illusory apparatus of religious valuations? If so, then assigning value to the 'holy' ego is precisely that illusion. And if the ego is not to be good 'in itself', how else should it be valued? The obvious alternative would seem to be by object libido – which would return us directly to the pre-civilised world. Yet Freud clearly never advocated such an atavistic outcome. Freud hopes for a scientific age where ego is expressed in rationality, and reality-testing through science will have authority. But how can an *authoritative* rational ego ever emerge from the causes which Freud displays in his story of origins?

Freud's theory of history, as I have sketched it, has immediate connections through Comte to the Enlightenment views of history which are, like his own, essentially *therapeutic* views of the relation of reason and history. To the Enlightenment, as to Freud, the religious age is a form of 'insanity' from which Reason could now rescue us. But Reason comes *ab extra*, from a theory of human nature discovered above and beyond the history being diagnosed. Psychoanalysis is just such a scientific theory which manages to escape the universal distortions of its own civilised (religious, neurotic) society and so can be used as a therapy from above. It is not at all surprising that later theorists considering this range of claims have argued that Freud's therapy could not escape the power of his own metapsychological myth, that is, psychoanalysis is itself the partial product of an historical situation, not a universal, rational view of human nature.

In contrast to Freud's view of reason (science) *outside* of history acting in some not wholly intelligible fashion as a therapy on historical irrationality, Hegel clearly thinks of reason *in* history. The age of religion for Hegel, in contrast to both Freud and his Enlightenment ancestors, is not mere folly and illusion but contains reason within its structures though in highly imperfect and distorted forms. Hegel would have no trouble affirming what Freud finds it difficult to attest, that the emergence of the ego in the world of spirit and religion is a distinct break from 'animism' *and* a necessary step on the way to 'the scientific age'. The ground of Hegel's strikingly different views is that for him the story of history is not the story of reason versus nature (or reason above nature), it is the conflict of reason with itself. It is the conflict not of the ego with natural desire, but the conflict of egos which emerges from the initial conflict of recognition. One can restate the difference in this general fashion: for Freud, the human conflict appears to be between moral value (as it emerges in the sacred value of the ego in civilisation) and a recalcitrant, amoral nature; for Hegel, the conflict of history is all on the level of value: the *moral* role of master and slave.

We have already detailed the sense in which the initial crisis for history in Hegel is a conflict of egos, the battle for recognition which leads to the para-doxical result of both mutual recognition and subordination of the slave to the master. The paradox in the situation is that *both* master and slave must mutually recognise their inherent dignity and freedom from mere economic evaluation. The slave must know in his heart that the life which transcends desire (shown in the master's willingness to die rather than surrender) is truly valuable or else the recognition relation fails. If then, the Hegelian story of history is the story of mutually recognised freedom – the move from the oriental state where one is free, to the Classical world where some are free, to the modern world where all are free – what has made this task so wayward and full of conflict? One can easily see why Freud is sceptical about progress since he seems to construct civilisation as an irreconcilable conflict between aggrandising libido and civilised restraint. But, since the master–slave relation is based on an implicit recognition of mutual freedom, why has it taken so long to draw that recognition fully into institutional practice? Is the conflict and crisis parallel between Freud and Hegel of my analysis over-drawn?

Any full answer to that question would go beyond the confines of this essay, but one can illuminate Hegel's views here by contrasting him to Freud on the role of desire in the story of civilisation. For Freud, history is the conflict between natural desire and civilised restraint. For Hegel, desire is no less vital to the understanding of historical change but in quite a dif-ferent manner. There is in Hegel what Ricoeur calls 'the unsurpassable character of life and desire' (Ricoeur, 1970, p.469). In the master and slave conflict, what emerges is a value which goes beyond the economics of object desire. The failure of the master–slave relation, however, is that the new value asserted in the life of the master proves to be empty. The moral act of the master is consumed in his willingness to lay down his life to achieve recognition of his lordship. Hegel criticises the master's mode of life by identifying it with the feudal skirmishing of petty lords. The function of the knight is the repeated assertion of the fact that there is a value above life itself – an assertion continually sought in duels of honour. The gesture of lordship becomes a sterile assertion of the new transcendent value, yet it seems the mode of action to which mastership is condemned. It is for this reason that the slave turns out to be the actual mover and shaper of history. The slave refuses the action which asserts transcendent value, he cannot abandon life and desire. However, the slave does not merely sink back into the world of desire since he accepts the superior value of the master. The dilemma of *both* master and slave is: How can a moral life be *lived*? The master chooses *death* in order to assert his superiority to mere desire; the slave chooses *life* but knows that the master's moral choice is better.

The story of Hegelian history, then, revolves about that question: How can the moral life be lived? That may sound like a peculiar question but to Hegel it seemed a problem posed directly by Kant's theory of morality. As W. H. Walsh points out, 'Hegel was continuously preoccupied with the views of Kant; the question what Kant got right in moral philosophy and just where he went wrong is one to which he returns again and again' (Walsh, 1969, p.6). Walsh finally is puzzled by Hegel's ethical views since he is forced to conclude that Hegel lacked Kant's transcendent critical evaluation of actual behaviour. The best (or worst) Hegel might say by way of moral critique would be that some set of customs are 'historically incongruous' (*ibid.*, p.11). Walsh has located a central issue, but I believe there is a more favourable interpretation.

At various points in his ethical works, Kant attempts to locate the pure principle of morality by describing test cases where duty and desire are in conflict. He hopes to show that the *moral* choice lies always on the side of pure duty alone. Heeding the promptings of desire changes the autonomous will into the mere heteronomous will of utilitarian and prudential calculation. What appears to emerge, then, in Kant is yet another conflict scenario for the human psyche: the conflict between duty (pure practical reason) and, desire. While I would not argue that this is Kant's final word on the subject I am prepared to say that his initial word on the subject seems to locate morality as a choice *in opposition to* the promptings of desire. From Hegel's point of view that reduces the moral life to the sterility of mastership. Hegel's question is: can a Kantian moral life be *lived*, i.e., actually carried forth by a creature acting in the centre of manifold desires? As Kant indicates, 'Man is acted on by so many inclinations that, though capable of the idea of pure practical reason, he is not easily able to make it effective *in concreto* in his life' (Kant, 1909, p.4).

Hegel is quite prepared to accept the Kantian view of a moral ego which is an end-in-itself, not to be reduced to a calculus of desires: that is the significance of the story of the master. But Hegel wants to discover the efficacy of such a moral evaluation of the ego in the actual life of human beings. On this issue, Kant and Freud seem to share a certain common predicament. Both suggest that the basic conflict for humanity is the conflict between a manifold of desire and 'morality' (civilisation). Both see the conflict as more or less insoluble. Freud suggests stoicism as an immediate practical outcome; Kant 'solves' the dualism of reason and desire through a postulated hope for immortality. By creating reason *outside* or *above* the actuality of historical life and desire, both Kant and Freud reveal their roots in Enlightenment views of therapeutic reason which Hegel wishes to reject.

Hegel accepts the notion that the moral will is revealed with particular clarity in the rejection of life and desire as the sole determinant of value, but he does not think that the role of reason is *defined* in opposition to desire. Without trying to prove Hegel's point or to explore the intricacies of his discussion, I only wish to point out what a significant difference such a view has on the story line for history. The problem for Hegelian history is, as stated: How can the moral life be lived? If we were to adapt Kantian terms for Hegel, we would say that the conflict of history is a conflict not of reason and desire but of two reasons: pure practical reason expressed in the ego of the master versus the 'impure' practical reason of the slave. The slave chooses both life and (reflected) moral value; therefore, he is not reduced to the sterile moralism of the master: the life of pure assertion of honour and duty. The slave has to discover the means to express moral value *in* life and desire. (As various commentators point out: Hegel's moral views have a linguistic affinity to Aristotle's ethical search for rational desire or desiderative reason.) What the slave does, then, is 'spiritualise' life itself by creating the cultural artifacts which go beyond mere natural desire. It is the story of the slave spiritualising the material conditions of life which constitutes the basic plot line of history. This is a 'sublimation' supported by Hegel's basic theory so that he does not, like Freud, fall back into the economics of desire. Freud's inability to establish a clear, separate value for the ego beyond the economics of desire, means that he is finally unsure how to value the cultural sublimations of civilisation. Are they mere neurotic projections reducible to the basic desire, or do they constitute something quite new and valued on a different standard as the products of the ego? For Hegel the ego has its own story and it is told in genuine sublimations of mere desire.

It is obvious that with theories as rich and suggestive as those of Freud and Hegel, the best that can be hoped for in a short essay is an unsatisfactory sketch of their positions. I believe that the juxtaposition of the two theories, however, is mutually illuminating for the problems raised and also for our general understanding of the significance of historical thinking. Freud (and Freud as a Kantian moralist) will have particular problems trying to discover any story in history. Civilisation and its discontents tends to be a repetitive re-enactment of the unresolved (and irresolvable) crisis which generated this new phase in human society. To be sure, there is a hope from outside and above that reason and science through the therapy of analysis may effect real change, but that will be yet another inexplicable 'crisis' in the chronicle of human action. Philip Rieff is correct about the story of history one would draw from Freud's metapsychology (if not his therapy): '[C]hange becomes constancy, history nature, development repetition' (Rieff, 1959, p.215).

For Freudian *psyche*, historical narrations can only be *examples* of value judgments derived from outside of history: through reason, science and psycho-analysis. For Hegelian *Geist*, historical narrations reveal values which can only be developed in and through history. It is this historicism which troubles Walsh, yet his approval of Kant on this score would appear to leave him with the dilemma of choosing either a transcendent moral theory and a merely exemplary history *or* an immanent moral principle and a genuinely instructive historical narration. One would hope that such a distinguished philosopher of history might find a way to affirm the irreplaceable power of historical thought.

William Langer's assignment of Freudian psychology to the historical profession has hardly met with universal acceptance. Although there have been many 'psycho-histories' written in the recent past, there have been almost as many complaints about the limitations of the genre. My sympathies are with the critics. For all the insight which Freud may give us into the complexities of the human soul, the one thing that I believe he will have great trouble illuminating is *history*. Thus I share Hegel's conviction that historical thinking and historical action mark a unique conceptual understanding of human behaviour in which the *irreducible* value of ego or self is the central issue. In addition, I would agree that this value for the self is not merely a transcendent value *over* actual human life as Kant suggests. Rather, the value of self is expressed *in concreto* in the civilisations of humankind as they are set forth in historical actuality. The story of the self (history) is not a field awaiting transcendent moral evaluation (Kant) or scientific psychoanalysis (Freud), it is a creative story which uniquely reveals the possibilities and the realities of our moral worth. Although few practising historians are likely to espouse the elaborated dialectics of *Die Vernunft in der Geschichte*, I believe that it would be difficult for them to reject Hegel's central insight about the irreplaceable value of historical achievement without abandoning the very task of historical writing. If that central insight can be appreciated, then Hegel's concrete account of the historical pageant could also be recovered.

REFERENCES

Bonaparte,M., Freud,A. and Kris,E., eds. (1954) *The Origins of Psychoanalysis.* New York, Basic Books.

DeSousa,R. (1974) in Wollheim R. (ed.) *Freud: A Collection of Critical Essays.* Garden City, N.Y., Anchor Books.

Fell,J. (1976) in *Der Idealismus und Seine Gegenwart,* von Ute Guzzoni, Bernhard Kary und Ludwig Siep. Hamburg, Felix Meiner.

Freud,S. (1959) *Group Psychology and the Analysis of the Ego,* trans. and ed. James Strachey. New York, W.W.Norton.

Freud,S. (1961a) *Civilization and Its Discontents,* trans. and ed. James Strachey. New York, W.W.Norton.

Freud,S. (1961b) *The Future of an Illusion,* trans. and ed. James Strachey. New York, W.W.Norton.

Freud,S. (1964–) *The Complete Psychological Works,* ed. James Strachey. New York, Macmillan.

Hegel,G.W.F. (1953) *Reason in History,* trans. R.Hartman. Indianapolis, Bobbs-Merrill.

Hyppolite,J. (1974) *Genesis and Structure of Hegel's Phenomenology of Spirit,* trans. Samuel Cherniak and John Heckman. Evanston, Northwestern University Press.

Jones,E. (1953–7) *Sigmund Freud: Life and Work.* New York, Basic Books.

Kant,I. (1909) *Critique of Practical Reason and Other Works on the Theory of Ethics,* trans. T.K.Abbott. London, Longman.

Kojève,A. (1969) *Introduction to the Reading of Hegel,* trans. J.H. Nichols, Jr. New York, Basic Books.

Langer,W. (1958) The Next Assignment, *American Historical Review,* 63.

Mazlish,B. (1966) *The Riddle of History: The Great Speculators from Vico to Freud.* New York and London, Harper & Row.

Popper,K. (1963) *The Open Society and its Enemies.* Princeton, N.J., Princeton University Press.

Ricoeur,P. (1970) *Freud & Philosophy: An Essay on Interpretation.* New Haven, Yale University Press.

Rieff,P. (1959) *Freud: The Mind of the Moralist.* Chicago, University of Chicago Press.

Rieff,P. (1963) in Mazlish,B. ed. *Psycholoanalysis and History.* Engelwood Cliffs, N.J., Prentice Hall.

Taylor,C. (1975) *Hegel.* Cambridge, Cambridge University Press.

Walsh,W.H. (1969) *Hegelian Ethics.* New York, St Martin's Press.

6. Convertibility and Alienation

NATHAN ROTENSTREICH

I

The subject of the following analysis will be the impact of Vico's basic concept of *verum factum*, which is called the principle of convertibility (Otto, 1977a; Pompa, 1975, pp.15ff.) or congruence, upon the dialectics of the notion of alienation – *Entfremdung* – in Marx's version of that notion. In spite of the well-known reference to Vico in the note to the first volume of *Das Kapital* (Marx, 1972b, p.393 note), it is not our point to argue that Marx was directly influenced by Vico's idea. Our point, and this has to be analysed in some detail, is that systematic philosophic thinking has a certain structure which in turn leads to affinities between individual systems, disregarding whether or not there is a conscious indebtedness and hence a conscious sequence, of one system to the other.

The notion of convertibility in Vico's sense is understood here in accordance with the interpretation of the congruence between *verare* qua 'thinking' and *facere* qua 'doing' or 'creating'. That notion is reinforced by the well-known statement of Vico's that all things are contained in our inner self, and that things persist as long as we apply our mind (*nostra mens*) to them. The historical world, in Vico's famous dictum, is certainly created by man, and, therefore, its essence is bound to be rediscovered (*ritrovare*) in the modifications of our own mind.

II

The notion of alienation, as philosophers have employed it, seems at first glance to contradict the principle of convertibility and its concomitant continuity from creation to rediscovery of the origins of human products in human acts, which may broadly be termed identification or re-identification. For alienation, again broadly speaking, connotes the transfer or the shift to the object which becomes external to the person and his nature. But it has to be observed here that there is a basic difference between Hegel's presentation of the concept of alienation and that of Marx. If we take the *Phänomenologie des Geistes* as representative of Hegel's view, alienation is the motion of the spirit to become something alien or different from itself, that is to say, an object for itself. Here the German term *Gegenstand* (object) invites, as it were, the projective interpretation of the concept, that is to say, an object is posed as something external *vis à vis* the spirit but still facing the spirit; thus the notion of the alienated *Gegenstand* is only transitory. The posing of the *Gegenstand* appears also to have only an instrumental validity, that is to say, it is there in order to be 'sublated' (*um dieses Anderssein aufzuheben*). Thus we have to distinguish here between the activity of spirit, which is manifest implicitly in the notion of alienation, and its product qua object; because of the lack of self-awareness or self-consciousness of the individual mind, the latter does not know that it is involved in the dialectic process of projection and sublation. The two steps, though successive, are inherently correlated. This process takes place for the sake of spirit's self-evolvement and self-manifestation (Hegel, 1921, p.37). Thus *en route* we may not know that rhythm of the spirit, but from the point of view of a – or the – comprehensive philosophical position that rhythm becomes discernible. Thus *verare* and *facere*, or to put it differently again the convertibility, is preserved, but not immediately so – if we again use here a Hegelian term. What is significant for our attempt to understand the line from Vico to Marx is that convertibility takes place in Hegel's understanding on the level of philosophy as a synoptic understanding of *mens*; it does not take place on the level of history, as Vico assumed. On the contrary, it can be assumed that history is *an sich* (in itself) grounded in convertibility, but is not so *für sich* (for itself). The merger between *an sich* and *für sich* occurs on the level of philosophy.

III

Turning now to our analysis of Marx's concept of alienation, it has to be observed from the beginning that for Marx alienation is not a creation of objects for the sake of their sublation, that is to say, for the sake of the spirit's finding itself – in Vico's sense. It is a transfer, a transfer of ownership, and thus essentially, a derangement of the human position in history, and in a more amplified form – it is eventually an undermining of the ontological status of man. It is because of that trend that we find in Marx the basic notion that alienation is the devaluation (*Entwertung*) of the human position and *pari passu* a transfer to the world of things which becomes imbued with values (*Verwertung der Sachenwelt*). We shall look into some selected statements of Marx in order to throw light on the issue before us and eventually to see Marx's problematic position through the conceptual framework of Vico's principle of convertibility.

When Marx discusses alienation, he immediately speaks about the indifference (*Gleichgültigkeit*) characteristic of the relation between the labourer, who is the bearer (*Träger*) of the living work, and the labour conditions which are of an economic, that is to say, rational and thrifty, character (Marx 1972b, p.36).

It is therefore no chance that Marx speaks not only about the indifference characteristic of the created world, but also about its ossification (*Verknöcherung*), in the sense that the inner relationship between the producer and the product is ultimately reversed and covered up. Marx uses the term *subsume* in the sense that workers are subsumed under the capital. We are aware of the fact, of course, that subsumption is used in the basically logical sense, e.g., when a particular case is subsumed under a rule, or species or genus. This very connotation of subordination is indeed already a reversal, an act of making the thing into a person and making the person into a thing (*Verkehrung, Personifizierung der Sache, und Versachlichung der Person*). (Marx, 1972–73, vol.26, pp.366–7, vol.28, pp.255,519). It is because of that reversal that the harmonistic trend characteristic of Hegel's concept of alienation, or let us call it the teleological interpretation of alienation, cannot in Marx's view hold water. We may interpret Marx's position in the following way: one could assume a distance between a present form of exhibition or manifestation of the spirit and its ultimate form. But a perversion of the basic form in the present form cannot be understood as serving the *telos* of the rediscovery of the mind or spirit according to the principle of convertibility.

To be sure, there is an additional aspect to alienation as it appears in the economic sphere: the economists of the capitalist world take the specific historic form of the social world, as it becomes manifest in the capitalistic production, as a universal and eternal form. They take the specifically historical – and thus a particular – form as a truth of nature (*Naturwahrheit*). Therefore they interpret the particular conditions of production as absolutely necessary, that is to say, as non-historical and, therefore, as conditions which are, according to nature and, by the same token, rational (*naturgemäss und vernünftig*). (Marx, 1972–3, vol.28, p.255). But because the phenomenon of alienation is by definition identified and recognised in the economic sphere, it has, despite its pseudo-ontological interpretation, a basically economic meaning, namely, that in the capitalistic system the worker is a non-owner (*Nicht-Eigentümer*) of the conditions of production, neither of the land he is working nor of the tools he uses for his work. Hence the capitalistic system, historically and humanly speaking, defies the principle of convertibility. It defies it on the level of productivity qua activity and defies it on the level of interpretation, since a particular historical stage qua capitalism is taken as an absolute form. This aspect of Marx's analysis of estrangement as not conforming to convertibility is enhanced by the notion of interest. Hence we have to turn to an analysis of that notion.

IV

Summing up the first point related to the notion of alienation it can be said that, according to Marx, not only history is to be conceived from the perspective of the principle of convertibility, but the very position of man *vis à vis* his surroundings has to be regarded in the same light. Yet, history brings about a derailment of the human situation and thus undermines not only its own principle but also the very status of man. It can be said, therefore, that underlying the line from Vico to Marx is the ontological rendering of the principle of convertibility along with the critical evaluation that human history is not faithful to its own *raison d'être*. There is a clash between the fundamental, i.e., ontological status of man and the historical reality or, to put it differently, convertibility in history does not imply a guarantee that the basic human position will be – and is – maintained in history.

Parallel to the historical lack of congruence between the ontological position and that in real time in terms of the actual or concrete human situation, is the understanding of the notion of interest. Here, first a comparison between Kant and Marx is apposite. Marx takes the concept of interest, as he does *vis à vis* alienation, to be historically grounded, while in Kant there is no historical interpretation of the notion of interest and its position. This has to be observed – though in Kant one can identify a kind of implication or even anticipation of the notion of estrangement. The latter notion is implied in Kant's well known description or definition of enlightenment as man's release from his self-incurred tutelage. Tutelage, as explained by Kant, is man's inability to make use of his understanding without direction from another (Kant, 1963, p.3; Rotenstreich, 1979a). One could suggest that tutelage and its concomitant direction toward another is a form of self-alienation, though in Kant that alienation is confined to the lack of courage to use one's own reason. To put it differently, this mode of alienation is confined to the rational faculties of man and to the absence of their proper activisation. Therefore the overcoming of tutelage or of self-alienation in this sense is the establishment, i.e., re-establishment, of man's rational sovereignty or spontaneity. That process occurs in history, though history is not understood here as a comprehensive realm. It is confined to the relationship between human rationality and the historical circumstances which have to be overcome, whereby rationality is the norm meant to be prevailing in the circumstances to come.

When we now look into Kant's analysis of the concept of interest, it has to be observed that Kant makes a distinction between pathological interest and practical interest. As regards the pathological interest, we encounter a dependence on principles of reason placed at the service of inclination, that is to say, reason merely supplies a practical rule for meeting the needs of inclination. Whereas in the direction of practical reason we encounter only a dependence of the will on the principles of reason for itself. In the pathological interest our interest lies in the object of the action while in the practical interest proper our interest lies in the action itself. Therefore, there is a difference between taking an interest in something, which is the practical interest in the strict sense of the term, and acting from interest, which signifies our urges or our pathological interest (Kant, 1964, pp.81 note, 117–8 note). We can sum up, therefore, this description or juxtaposition of interest and interests as connoting a concept the centre of which is whether or not our will is dependent on reason as the incentive or on our inclinations as our driving factor. For Kant the distinction between the two levels of motivation is clearly one of a non-historical character, since it stems from the basic equipment of human nature, composed of sensuality along with rationality or reason. It is in this context that Kant speaks about the renunciation of all interest, obviously in the sense of the pathological interest and not in the sense of practical interest proper. To be sure, Kant makes some concession when he refers to the mere fact of deserving happiness, which can by itself interest us, even without the motive of sharing this happiness. This is so, although Kant himself observes that only a rational being can take an interest in something: non-rational creatures merely feel sensuous impulses. This again is a concession in the sense that even sensuality as such is not of an instantaneous character and is accompanied by, or absorbed in, a sort of guidance by reason. Even so, namely, while the rigid distinctions are somehow blurred, there is no attempt to set the motivation by interest into historical, i.e., changing, circumstances.

When Hegel speaks about interest, he refers to interest 'for me' as having a subjective worth 'for me'. Again, in a way, similar to Kant's juxtaposition, Hegel mentions immediately in the context of the subjective worth of interest the distinction between end and means: 'In contrast with this *end* – the content of the intention – the direct character of the action in its further content is reduced to a *means*' (Hegel, 1924, para.122, p.104; Hegel, 1942, para.122, p.82). It is because of this consideration that Hegel speaks in terms of interest about the singularity (*Einzelnheit*) which has to be satisfied in the execution of the most objective ends. I myself, as this particular individual, do not and should not want to perish in the execution of the end. This, as Hegel puts it, is my interest, and as such should not be mistaken for selfishness (Hegel, 1927, p.377). Again we notice in Hegel the distinction between the particular position of the individual and the objective end, though the sharp contradistinction, as put forward by Kant, is, to say the least, attenuated. This is so because the preservation of the status of the individual is considered to be eventually and essentially congruous with the objective end. It is from this point of view that we have to look at Marx's understanding of interest as having a historical connotation and thus, as such, as related to the process and dialectics of alienation. We now turn to that part of our exploration.

V

The history of the term and concept 'interest' is a long and varied one. Let us only emphasise a kind of constant hard core pertaining to that concept, because that emphasis will throw some light on Marx's interpretation of the concept irrespective of the question whether or not he was aware of the shifts which he introduced in this context and, indeed, this is of secondary significance. We emphasise in the concept the aspects of *utilita* or *bonté*, while the two aspects merge in that of *advantage*. Now, within the boundaries of that permanent core, one of the major distinctions which have been brought forward is that between private advantage and common weal. For Kant, as we have seen, the very coincidence between sensuality and pathological interest already implies the basic relationship of interest to the individual, or, in traditional terms, to *utilita propria*. Hegel, too, emphasised the personal or private aspect of the notion of interest, but in a sense different from that present in Kant. Hegel, because of his criticism of dichotomies, gave legitimisation – a limited one indeed – to that personal or private aspect.

Looking now into Marx's exploration, or perhaps pronouncements, we encounter immediately Marx's saying that the personal interests, despite the persons themselves (*den Personen zum Trotz*), develop always into class interests. As such, they are common interests (*gemeinschaftliche Interessen*), and they become independent *vis à vis* the individual persons. They take the independent shape of *common* interests and as such are in opposition to the real individuals. Once that basic contrast emerges, the next step is to give to these common interests the position of projected ideal interests qua religious ones, holy ones, etc. It is clear that Marx, by using the notion of turning interests into independent ones (*Verselbständigung*) applies to the notion of interest qua advantage or utility the apparatus of alienation and concurrently the same terminology which he applied to that term and notion. Indeed, he says, the personal behaviour of the individual is bound to turn into a thing (*versachlichen*) and to become alienated. That projective character of the interest is maintained, but it is viewed as a product of life and not as a product of thinking – and Marx probably hints here at Feuerbach. This shift from the personal to the common sphere is present in what Marx called theoretical communists who are concerned with history as discerned in the whole of history. In order to pinpoint that issue, it can be said that the shift is of a generic character, but in each period it has to be identified in terms of the specific shape it takes. The whole contradiction between the personal and private is in practice continuously both annulled and created (Marx, 1952, pp.236ff.).

It has to be observed at this point that though Marx presents the shift towards the general or the common interest as a shift from personal interests to class interests, that shift occurs against the background of history or against the primary involvement or belonging of individuals to the species qua *Gattungswesen*. Hence we cannot define the shift from the personal to the collective as alienation and all that goes along with that concept or deviation. We can only make the distinction between the primary collective existence and the subjugation which occurs in history whereby the sovereign person ceases to be what he ontologically is and meant to be and becomes estranged from himself. It is evident that the concept of estrangement and the concept of interest are two corollary concepts in Marx's theory.

An attempt to get out of the straightjacket of estrangement or interest by addressing ourselves to the idea in the Kantian sense to the moral obligation – for instance – or to the interest in the practical sense against the pathological one, cannot hold good since the idea as such is both powerless and is only a projection of real life. Marx observes that the 'idea' always exposed itself to shame (*blamierte sich immer*) in so far as it differed from 'interest'. On the other hand, it is easily understood that every 'interest' which appeals to the masses and penetrates history, when first appearing on the stage of the world, exceeds by far its real boundaries as delineated in the term 'idea' or in the 'representation', and usurps the place of *human* interest as such. This projection is called by Marx an illusion though it determines the 'tone' of each historical era. The French revolution is a case in point; it gave rise to pathos and enthusiasm, although the masses were not emancipated by the revolution; on the contrary, they remained essentially static in terms of their living conditions. The revolution substantively affected a limited mass and did not embrace the totality (*nicht die Gesamtheit umfassende, eine beschränkte Masse war*) (Marx, 1972a, pp.85–6). To sum up this analysis, we could say that the idea, as used by Marx in the context, refers to what has since become the common term 'ideology'.

Leaving aside the terminological questions, the following can now be said: interests are not primarily given, and thus are not basically prescribed or determining factors of human nature. They are of a social and historical character. As such they move the individual from his own sphere to the pseudosocietal sphere, because they move him to entities qua classes, and not to the entity qua humanity. The trend and the norm of human emancipation is to liberate human beings both from estrangement and from the predominance of interests, in order to maintain the continuity, i.e., convertibility, between the producer and his product or between the creator of history and the historical *status quo* which is a *status quo* of the class-structure, in spite of the changes which occur in history. The principle of convertibility, being the principle explaining history in its occurence and status, becomes therefore the principle guiding it or pointing to its focus or *telos*. That principle becomes both an analytical tool and a criterion of evaluation of the human condition which empirically defies its own principle, since the changes occurring in history are so fundamental as to bring about the convertibility proper. The principle of convertibility is maintained but its manifestations do not coincide with its essence. Thus history is a process and a situation not only dominated by interests and estrangement but also by the lack of congruence between what is going on in it and what is the wellspring of history and at the same time its objective. Precisely since Marx does not adhere to the Kantian dichotomy between sensuality and practice proper, he turns Vico's principle into a moral idea, maintaining at the same time its explanatory position or relevance. We can say that, whereas Hegel placed the moral idea on the level of speculative reflection where the identity of the subject and object, i.e., convertibility, will be achieved by way of a dialectical articulation, Marx attempts to place the achievement and realisation of the moral idea on the level of history and thus not relegate it to the level of speculation. This again explains the impetus towards the coalescence between the ontological and the ethical aspects of convertibility.

VI

The principle of convertibility, as inherited from Vico, has mainly an onto-logical and epistemological connotation: *verum ipsum factum* is meant to bring into relief the fact that history is created by man and is thus accessible to his understanding. This idea is obviously present also in Marx. But Marx gave it a broader and even a totalistic interpretation: if history is created by man and open to his understanding, there has to be and ought to be a continual interaction from man to history and from history to man (man connoting here: men). This is the meaning of Marx's notion that emancipation is not just man's liberation through the assertion of certain rights, like for instance a right in the legal and political sphere or the right to free worship. Emancipation for Marx is the restoration of the very basis of human existence which in this totalistic interpretation of convertibility is man himself. Thus Vico's principle is understood as pointing in the direction of the meeting between the *telos* of history and its very beginning or basic factor. As long as there is a gap between interests which involve man in partial and partisan situations and ideas which point to the overriding *telos* of history, the principle of convertibility is not realised in practice. Along with the totalisation of convertibility goes its moralisation. The addition of that ethical component seems to be Marx's main contribution to and amendment of the notion of convertibility – as will be shown presently.

Let us look into one or two of the major expressions of that ethical inter-pretation of convertibility, which is the other side of the coin of the analysis of estrangement and of interest. When Marx speaks of the accumulation of capital, he points, as is well known, to the corresponding accumulation of poverty and misery describing the latter as '*Akkumulation von Elend*', hard-ship in work, '*Arbeitsqual*', slavery, ignorance, brutalisation and moral degradation. These opposites, as Marx describes them, are the compensating lot of the class which produces its own product qua capital. It has to be observed that it is evident that the description of the various features which are comprised under the general heading of *Elend* are mainly of a human character. That character accompanies poverty in its limited economic or financial sense. At this point Marx refers to an analysis by 'a Venetian monk, Ortes', who uses the expression of equilibrium in the sense that in a nation the economic good and the economic evil are always in a state of equilibrium, implying that the abundance of goods for some people always causes their scarcity for others. It has to be observed that indeed the Italian text as quoted by Marx uses in this context the two terms '*bene*' and '*male*'. This is open to what seems to be a warranted interpretation, namely, that whereas the economic *good* is an ambiguous term in the first place, because it carries the connotations both of goodness and of commodity, the term '*Böse*' or '*male*' is less ambiguous because it does not point only to a privation but also to an evil in the moral sense (Marx, 1972b, p.615).

Since a moral interpretation is implied here, and the notion of the equilibrium points to a static situation and therefore also to interests and to estrangement, it is appropriate to say that the static equilibrium has to be replaced by a dynamic convertibility which will maintain the continuity between the producer and his product. Therefore, *pari passu*, the immoral situation in which, according to Ortes's description, great riches owned by some people are always causing many others to be deprived of the basic necessities, will be overcome. Since the quantitative aspect of the majority is here alluded to, it can be said, in line with the spirit of the quotation and Marx's adherence to it, that the interest of the majority is coterminous with the convertibility between the interest and the idea. Hence we are again led to our conclusion that because the historical situation as it stands defies, in terms of the concrete mainfestation, man's moral position, the adherence to *verum ipsum factum* is meant not only to open history to human understanding and to present it as a sphere in which the human mind is sovereign. It is also a point of departure for the realisation through historical forces of the moral idea of the sovereign man. Here, convertibility pertains not only to mind and history but also to historical reality and the moral ideal, which is both a historical ideal and a moral interpretation of man's ontological status in and *vis à vis* history.

That moral interpretation has an additional expression and at this point in terms of the relationship between man's value and the direction of his activities. As long as man is viewed as endowed with specialised capacities, he may be regarded as essentially turning in the direction of a partial expression of his activities, and thus as having partial and partisan interests. These interests, in turn, inhibit any possible identification by and of him with the totality of history and its ideal *telos*. As long as we remain on the level of philosophy in general in the *Hegelian sense*, or of philosophy of history in *Vico's sense*, we may assume that history is open to human knowledge because it is created by human beings. Yet this relationship does not necessarily connote the possibility of an identity between every concrete human being and the process of history. We can understand history as a human product without implying that human beings are responsible for that product. It seems plausible to assume that Marx's ethical interpretation of convertibility prevented him from granting that duality which is embodied in the reflection on history as being different from the subject-matter of the reflection. Marx moves in the direction of his version of the *uomo universale* who, as a being endowed with comprehensive capacities, will be able to become identical with the comprehensive historical realm. It is probably for this reason that Marx says that man will be hunting in the morning, fishing in the afternoon, etc,. without ever becoming a hunter, a fisherman (Marx, 1947, p. 22, interpreted in Rotenstreich, 1973), or any kind of specialist since specialisation makes it impossible for man continuously to identify himself with his social and historical activity. The totalistic interpretation of convertibility, that is to say, the combination of the ontological, epistemo-

G

logical and ethical elements, is supplemented by the universalistic utopia of man who, as a non-specialised being, will be able not only to survey history but eventually to identify himself with it. Man is identical with it at the beginning of history; that identity will be redeemed as an outcome of the process which will overcome estrangement and interests. This is meant by the previous saying about the totalistic interpretation of convertibility which eventually results in the conception that moral activity is not intervening in history but emerging out of it and coalescing with it.

VII

At this point – and we turn to critical comments – Marx imposed on history too much and, in a kind of symmetry, devalued the moral intervention of the human beings in the process, an intervention which indeed can occur only in a piecemeal way. There is no convertibility between history and morality.

One may wonder whether convertibility is applicable even on the level of knowledge. History as a course of events created by human actions becomes a reality, and, therefore, it imposes on historical cognition the need or the task to decipher it. We can be aware of the broad ontological status of history, namely, that it has been and is continuously created by human actions and still be bewildered by the motivations of these actions – which in many cases are multi-faceted and even multi-dimensional – no less than by the results of these actions. The latter leave us in an ongoing situation of facing the enigmatic character of history since in many cases we lack a standard (even in terms of time) for when to look for the results and where to look for them. To adduce an obvious example: the Communist revolution did not take place in the Western world within the context of the industrial proletariat, but in the rural societies of Tzarist Russia and of China. In addition: human actions, once they occur, become to some extent detached from the agents; the *ipsum factum* which is indeed an adequate description from the point of view of the ontological status of history and of the causative relations present in it, does not provide the clue to the detailed understanding of the historical events once we do not consider the origin but the facts.

If this is so in terms of our cognitive approach to history, it is *a fortiori* so in terms of the moral intervention in history. Suppose that we could say that human actions, giving rise to historical events and to their momentum, are manifestations of freedom. That manifestation would still not guarantee the realisation of freedom in the historical realm in terms of detached freedom, i.e., freedom of thought, expression and enjoyment of the public services and the goods – commodities – of civilisation. The first does not guarantee the second, because the second amounts to piecemeal interventions in historical circumstances. In many cases we are puzzled by those circumstances – not less than in the cognitive sphere, when attempting to understand the events *sine ira et studio*. Morality can be understood in the Kantian sense as an imperative toward the universality of mankind. But how to realise in practice here and now that imperative is an open question and,

as such, minute acts of intervention within the context of the historical reality are called for and only minute acts are possible. History may be viewed as a sphere but historical acts are of a piecemeal character only (Rotenstreich, 1979b).
Hence it is not enough to trace reality as it exists to the course of events and to the underlying human creativity. There can occur clashes between one mode of human creativity and another as, for instance, between an aesthetic and a moral evaluation of a work of art. This is even more so in terms of the overriding human creativity exhibited in history and detailed acts of human creativity exhibited in moral acts aiming at shaping of history. Hence there is no convertibility between history and morality, because (a) morality intervenes in history here and now and (b) there is no end or stop to these acts of such an intervention. Moreover, every act elicits a response which is an act just the same, imbued with the essence of acts as piecemeal interventions in the sphere of history.

REFERENCES

Grassi, E. (1976) Marxism, Humanism and Imagination in Vico's Works. In Tagliacozzo, G. and Verene D.Ph. (eds.) *Giambattista Vico's Science of Humanity*. Baltimore, Johns Hopkins Press.

Hegel, G.W.F. (1921) *Phänomenologie des Geistes*, ed. G. Lasson, 2nd ed. Leipzig, Meiner.

Hegel, G.W.F. (1927) *Encyklopädie, Sämtliche Werke*. Stuttgart, Fr. Frommanns Verlag–Günther Holzboog.

Hegel G.W.F. (1924) *Gründlinien der Philosophie des Rechts* ed. Lasson. Leipzig, Meiner.

Hegel, G.W.F. (1942) *Philosophy of Right*, trans. with notes by T.M. Knox. Oxford, Clarendon Press.

Kant, I. (1963) What is Enlightenment? trans. by Lewis White-Beck, included in *Kant on History*. Indianapolis/New York, Bobbs-Merrill.

Kant, I. (1964) *Groundwork of Metaphysic of Morals*, trans. and analysed by H.J. Paton. New York, Harper & Row.

Marx, K. (1947) *The German Ideology*, ed. (with an introduction) R. Pascal. International Publishers, New York (Parts I and III).

Marx, K. (1952) Die Deutsche Ideologie, *Der historische Materialismus, Die Frühschriften*, ed. S. Landshut and J.P. Mayer, 2nd vol. Leipzig, Alfred Kroner.

Marx, K. (1972a) Die heilige Familie, Marx, K. and Engels, F., *Werke*, vol. 2. Berlin, Dietz Verlag.

Marx, K. (1972b) *Das Kapital*. In *Werke*, vol. 23. Berlin, Dietz Verlag.

Marx, K. (1972–3) *Theorien über den Mehrwert*, 3 vols. In *Werke*, vols. 26, 27, 28. Berlin, Dietz Verlag.

Otto, S. (1977a) Faktizität und Transzendentalität der Geschichte. Die Aktualität der Geschichtsphilosophie G.B. Vicos im Blick auf Kant und Hegel, *Zeitschrift für Philosophische Forschung*, 31, (1), 197–214.

Otto, S. (1977b) Die transzendental-philosophische Relevanz des Axioms 'verum et factum convertuntur.' Überlegungen zu

Giambattista Vicos Liber Metaphysicus, *Philosophisches Jahrbuch*, 84, 32–54.

Pompa, L. (1975) *Vico: A Study of the 'New Science'*. Cambridge, Cambridge University Press.

Rotenstreich, N. (1973) Human Emancipation and Revolution, *Interpretation*, 3/2, 3, 205–20.

Rotenstreich, N. (1979a) Enlightenment: Between Mendelssohn and Kant. In Stein, S. and Loewe, R. (eds.) *Studies in Jewish Religion and Intellectual History*. Presented to Alexander Altmann on the occasion of His Seventieth Birthday. Alabama University Press, pp.263–79.

Rotenstreich, N. (1979b) *Practice and Realization: Studies in Kant's Moral Philosophy*. The Hague/Boston/London, Martinus Nijhoff.

7. Collingwood's Doctrine of Absolute Presuppositions and the Possibility of Historical Knowledge

REX MARTIN

I

Collingwood believed that every system of inquiry has its basic presuppositions, which are logically ultimate and independent of one another, and that these presuppositions are, from the standpoint of any given piece of inquiry or explanation, *a priori*. He called them 'absolute presuppositions'. More particularly, Collingwood thought there was an *a priori* element in historical explanations (see especially, Collingwood, 1946, pp.245–6; 1940, pp.196–7). Similarly, W.H.Walsh remarks that the 'notions' typically employed in the explanations given by historians 'appear to contain an element which is not due to experience, but may be called *a priori* or subjective according to taste' (Walsh, 1967, p.69). In one of his more recent writings, Walsh identifies this *a priori* element with 'the form of practical thinking' or what he also calls 'the general schema of the practical syllogism' (Walsh, 1976, pp.282–3, 285; see also pp.286, 288).

Supposing Walsh's later insight to be substantially sound, can we find evidence that Collingwood subscribed to some such 'general schema'? Consider, for instance, his claim that the 'historian of politics or warfare, presented with an account of certain actions done by Julius Caesar, tries to understand these actions. . . . This implies envisaging for himself the situation in which Caesar stood, and thinking for himself what Caesar thought about the situation and the possible ways of dealing with it' (Collingwood, 1946, p.215). It *implies* this because, for Collingwood, actions occur in a context of states of affairs and are responsive to some degree to the situation the agent envisaged.

Indeed, Collingwood laid this precise point down as a general principle when he said that the cause of an action is 'made up of two elements, a *causa quod* or efficient cause and a *causa ut* or final cause. The *causa quod* is a situation or state of things existing; the *causa ut* is a purpose or state of things to be brought about. Neither of these could be a cause if the other were absent' (Collingwood, 1940, p.292; see also p.293). Thus, in the example of Caesar just cited, the historian would try to understand the action performed – say, Caesar's crossing the Rubicon – not only by 'envisaging the situation in which Caesar stood' but also by thinking through the intention or purpose Caesar had formed as a way of resolving that situation.

The historian does this in his investigation of a particular action of

Caesar's because, more generally, he thinks that we provide an explanation of anyone's action when we can show that (1) the agent did perceive himself to be in a certain situation, (2) where he might be moved to do some deed – described as *A* – and (3) has a purpose or end in view relevant to dealing with his situation and (4) could be taken as seeing or believing that *A* would accomplish, or help accomplish, this end. In Collingwood's language (1) gives the *causa quod*, the efficient cause or motivation of the action, and (3) states the *causa ut*, the relevant purpose or intention with which the agent acted. And (2) says that the action performed would be regarded as plausibly motivated in that situation, (4) that that same action could be regarded as a means to the end identified. These four points are connected in a complex way and constitute a coherent view of what is involved in an action and, correspondingly, in an explanation of an action. They give us the general form of an action-explanation: we can explain 'the agent did *A* because (1) and (2) and (3) and (4)'. Of course this general form is susceptible to expansion and further explication (see Martin, 1977, esp. pp.71–9; also Donagan, 1962, pp.182–92; Donagan, 1966, pp.150–1; Donagan, 1969, pp.77–81) but it will suffice to indicate the sort of general schema Collingwood was committed to in his theory of explanation by re-enactment. Let us say then, that this schema is, or points to, an absolute presupposition of scientific history.

II

Collingwood's account of absolute presuppositions, as we have it principally in Part I of his *Essay on Metaphysics* and also in his *Autobiography*, is very complex; so, in indicating an affinity between the general schema for action-explanations and what he called absolute presuppositions, I do not mean to suggest that the schema conforms in every detail to that account. We can presume conformity, however, on the main points. Thus we will treat the general schema as an instance of what Collingwood says about all absolute presuppositions; then we will consider whether its character as an absolute presupposition poses any special problems for the schema as a presupposition of historical knowledge in particular.

Perhaps Collingwood's central claim is that absolute presuppositions are not propositions at all. But his reason for saying this was rather eccentric and open to doubt: he claimed that a proposition is always asserted in a certain context and that it 'arises' and takes its meaning, so to speak, out of the specific matrix that it presupposes. (See in particular his discussion of the logic of question and answer; Collingwood, 1939, pp.31–9.) Since it stands to reason that not every matrix can itself depend on a logically prior one, he concluded that there must be some that are simply ultimate: these, by definition, would not be propositions; they would be absolute presuppositions. What he meant, though, when he said absolute presuppositions are not propositions is clear enough; he meant they can be neither true nor false (see Collingwood, 1939, pp.66–7; 1940, esp. pp.32–3 and also pp.53–4).

It should be noted that the claim that an absolute presupposition can be neither true nor false is qualified by Collingwood in a significant way. For he did identify a certain sense in which an absolute presupposition can be true/false. We might take him here, rather roughly, as distinguishing between our conception of some general feature of the world and our description or formulation of this conception (see Collingwood, 1940, pp.33, 55, 60).

Now a descriptive formulation can be true or false, for it is an attempt to identify, more or less accurately, what particular conception of things does organise a given universe of discourse. For instance, a person might assert (truly) that most politically active people in Europe and North America in the twentieth century, as evidenced by the kind of political life they lead and the things they say when they argue politics, do not hold to the notion of a divine right of kings. Since such statements are characteristically made by historians, Collingwood said that these statements, even when made about absolute presuppositions, are actually 'historical' in nature (Collingwood, 1940, pp.49,77,81,163). Polemics aside though, what he was saying here is that so-called metaphysical statements are attempts to convey accurately what was in fact absolutely presupposed in a given science or universe of discourse; and metaphysical statements, taken in this way, can therefore be true or false (Collingwood, 1940, pp.40,47,54,81,101,168).

So, on this reading of Collingwood, the general schema for action-explanations can be formulated and can, when written down, be regarded as true or false; for it is simply an attempt to state accurately how we conceive actions to happen and how, accordingly, they are to be explained. The general schema is here merely a conceptual representation. But what of the conception it represents, can *that* be true or false?

It was in answer to this question that Collingwood made his claim that absolute presuppositions are altogether incapable of having truth-values. There is, his argument goes, no clear way in which any such conception could be regarded as true or false. For it is difficult to see what they could be referred to in order to determine their truth-value: as absolute they presuppose nothing, nothing is logically prior to them; whereas all of our network of knowledge claims, by which we do determine truth or falsity, for example, by going to the facts of the world, already presuppose them (Collingwood, 1940, pp.30,32,46,147). So, clearly, the way in which we could determine an absolute presupposition to be true or false would have to be vastly different from the way in which a statement *within* the universe of discourse organised by such a conception would be determined true or false (see Collingwood, 1940, pp.147–53 in particular). Once this is said, there seems to be no other way – at least no obvious or accredited way – to assign them truth-value at all. Indeed it becomes difficult to identify even a sense in which they could be true or false.

In sum, the description of an absolute presupposition can be, as to accuracy, true or false; but the content itself of the basic conception can be neither true nor false. Absolute presuppositions are not propounded; they are just supposed (Collingwood, 1940, pp.28,48,92,163); and their 'logical efficacy' comes, not from their being true, but simply from their being supposed (Collingwood, 1940, pp.27,32,39,42,52,101).

Now that we have clarified, somewhat, Collingwood's contention that absolute presuppositions are not propositions, it might be useful to consider briefly the connection that some have seen as holding between Collingwood's *Essay on Metaphysics* and A. J. Ayer's *Language, Truth and Logic* (1936). Both Knox and Donagan believe that 'between 1936 and 1938 Collingwood radically changed his mind about the relation of philosophy to history' (Donagan, 1962, p.12; see also Knox, 1946, pp.x–xi). Donagan contends, further, that this break stemmed from Collingwood's having read Ayer's book (first published in 1936), with the result that 'he had come to endorse Ayer's view that the propositions of traditional metaphysics are unverifiable . . .' (Donagan, 1962, p.15; see also p.14).

I think Donagan's insight is very shrewd here. There is clear textual evidence that Collingwood had read Ayer attentively; indeed he devoted an entire chapter of his book to Ayer's critique of metaphysics (Collingwood, 1940, pp.162–71; see also pp.5 and 19). I do not think we should take Collingwood as *endorsing* Ayer's view, however; rather, we could better regard the *Essay on Metaphysics* as a clever and well-devised attempt to get around Ayer's principal strictures. For the essence of the *Metaphysics* is to deny the exhaustive dichotomising of all meaningful statements into two exclusive classes, the analytic and the factual-empirical, by arguing that a third class of such statements, the philosophical, exists. At the same time, Collingwood accepts Ayer's thrust that the statements of traditional metaphysics have no truth-value. Ayer's point here, though, was that the traditional formulations are incapable of taking truth-values because, in his jargon, they are 'unverifiable' and therefore nonsensical; Collingwood's was the very different point that absolute presuppositions can have no truth-value because, though meaningful when stated, they are not basically propositions at all. In Collingwood's account, the presuppositions are not conceived as *pseudo*-propositions, hence nonsensical, but rather as *non*-propositions to which the application of the term 'nonsensical' would be wholly inappropriate.

One other important point in common between Ayer and Collingwood, and one that I have never seen cited, is that both men took the archetype of true statements to be those of the *natural* sciences, especially physics. (See Collingwood, 1940, pp.62,66,68,84,169; but note also p.85, where Collingwood broadened the notion of science to include the social sciences and history as well – and by extension metaphysics itself.) If there is any significant change between the 'earlier' and the 'later' philosophy of Collingwood, it is his increasing respect for natural science and his willingness to take physics as a paradigm of human knowledge. Although he was never wholly successful in throwing off the tendency to historicise all knowledge, Collingwood's maturing 'later' philosophy could fruitfully be regarded as a series of attempts, in part against his own inclinations, to establish the autonomy of the natural sciences alongside the autonomy of the historical ones. And we can view the *Essay on Metaphysics* as a placing of the logically ultimate and logically independent absolute presuppositions of physics and the other natural sciences on a par with those of history and the other sciences of mind (see also Martin, 1977, chapter 2).

These latter presuppositions, those of the sciences of mind, like the former set, constitute the nature of our understanding within a particular universe of discourse and they govern the explanations we give there in individual cases. But if our explanatory practices should prove inadequate, in any of a variety of ways, then we change what we do; and it is through such changes that change can occur in the organising conceptions themselves. For these basic conceptions are not in our collective unconscious, as shadowy, incipient propositions available for dredging up by psychologists (see Collingwood, 1940, pp.102–3), or out there somewhere in Plato's heaven; rather, they are *in* the explanatory practices and knowledge claims themselves. The basic conceptions are objective features, though implicit ones, of any ongoing science. They are a part of the institutional setting, the procedures, of science in a given society (see Collingwood, 1940, pp.194, 196–7).

The main point here can be illustrated by going to linguistics. When speakers of a language make judgments as to whether utterances are grammatical, they do so in terms of standards or rules which are part of the operative reality of the language. The rules which the linguist works up and writes down are rule-statements: more or less accurate formulations of the objective rules. In the same way, what might be termed the 'real rules' or basic conceptions of a system of knowledge are objective standards and conventions to which people conform when they frame and evaluate knowledge claims or hypotheses, when they offer or criticise explanations, when they 'automatically' follow a narrative or a proof, and so on. What might be called the rule-statements here are more or less accurate formulations, made by the philosopher, of these basic conceptions; they are a way of talking about certain regularities of behaviour.

But the basic conceptions themselves are, simply, ways of behaving. They are not statements but, rather, proto-statements. If we were ever to formulate them explicitly, the formulations would be meaningful but they would not have, except descriptively, any truth value at all.

Collingwood's notion that an absolute presupposition cannot be separated from the statements that presuppose it (contrary to Louis Mink's idea that an absolute presupposition can be treated as an *a priori* concept – see Mink, 1969, esp. pp.144–51) leads to the idea that absolute presuppositions are simply a part of scientific practice itself. They are ingredient there as foundation or ground. The function of basic conceptions – or absolute presuppositions, as Collingwood called them – is not to be propounded but to be supposed (see Collingwood, 1940, pp.32–3, 163). Basic conceptions govern the explanations we give and the inquiries we undertake. We exhibit these conceptions simply in 'doing' science in the way that we do (see also Martin, 1977, p.210.)

A striking doctrine (very like Wittgenstein's notion of a language game; see Martin, 1976b, especially section 4; and Martin, 1977, pp.203–10) lies at the heart of Collingwood's distinction between basic conceptions and their formulation. Absolute presuppositions, the basic conceptions themselves, are not propositions; they are objective patterns and structures in our way of knowing. They are neither right nor wrong, true nor false; they just are. We can, of course, put these structures into words, try to formulate and thereby describe them. Indeed, this is the only way we could come to know that they are there at all, or what they are. And such statements can be, as I have been at pains to emphasise, true or false.

These formulations, however, are not simply reportorial in nature; rather, they are logical or dialectical conclusions to complex arguments. The metaphysician does not perceive absolute presuppositions, for they do not pre-exist as something that can be perceived, or introspected for that matter. One can become conscious of an absolute presupposition only by formulating it. They must be argued to: one reasons from the explanatory practices and from the knowledge claims in a given science to the presuppositions that must be involved.

Accordingly, I would be reluctant to regard Collingwoodian metaphysical statements as essentially *descriptive* in nature as Walsh, for example, has done (Walsh, 1972, esp. p.149). They are more accurately viewed, I believe, as, analytic constructs, as rational reconstructions (see Collingwood, 1940, p.101).

Collingwood himself often called these formulations 'historical', but this is perhaps somewhat misleading. They are 'historical' insofar as they do strive for accuracy in the rendition of a particular or individual case; but the method of their formulation is logical or dialectical, rather than historical, in character. And, to put the matter polemically but rather bluntly, there is no thought to which the metaphysical formulation stands as its *re*thinking. There is no fact, other than the soundness of the argument involved, that could determine a metaphysical statement to be true or false. In the case of such statements there is no distinction between their truth and their adequate formulation. Absolute presuppositions can be known, but only by reason.

In addition to Collingwood's central contentions, that absolute presuppositions are not propositions and that they can only be rendered (propounded) historically, he suggested a number of other important – but secondary – ways in which absolute presuppositions could be characterised. He claimed that absolute presuppositions are probably culturally delimited (Collingwood, 1940, pp.60,72), even though the persons who live in a given culture are largely unconscious of them (see Collingwood, 1940, pp.48, 101–2); that these presuppositions are conjoined in a rather loose amalgam, or 'constellation' as he called it (Collingwood, 1940, pp.66–7); that this amalgam is held together under a kind of pressure or strain so that it tends to change over time (Collingwood, 1940, pp.75–7), with the result that the absolute presuppositions themselves are subject to change and always changing (Collingwood, 1940, p.48n). But absolute presuppositions cannot be changed directly, for they are held unconsciously. For this same reason they cannot be adopted or discarded directly either. They are not like fashions or fancies that one can capriciously put on or take off (Collingwood, 1940, p.48n). Rather, absolute presuppositions 'come with the territory', with the 'doing' of any science. Absolute presuppositions are properly seen as commitments that we have, or are driven to. They are at a far remove from being gratuitous, let alone perfectly gratuitous as Shalom (1955, p.710) has claimed.

Much of this is clearly intended to contrast with the Kantian account of the principles of human understanding, with its categories and its forms of intuition and its synthetic *a priori* propositions (see Collingwood, 1940, pp. 179–80). Moreover, these secondary contentions of Collingwood are all quite interesting – and quite consistent with other things that he said, for example, with his criticism of the idea of a science of human nature (see Martin, 1977, chapters 1 and 2) – but it is worth noting that none of them are *entailed* by his central contentions about absolute presuppositions. It is, nonetheless, possible to hold all these contentions, the main ones and the secondary ones, as a single, self-consistent view of the nature of science. And it is quite evident that Collingwood, basing his claims on work he had done as a historian of scientific ideas (in particular Collingwood, 1945;1946, parts I–IV), did hold precisely this view.

Presumably, then, the view he held about absolute presuppositions and science generally would control his view in the particular case: that of the science of history and of the absolute presupposition(s) implicated in the historical way of knowing. And this would include the absolute presupposition which governs explanatory re-enactment, the mode of explanation which Collingwood believed to be characteristic of contemporary, scientific history. This presupposition is the one pointed to by what was earlier summed up under the name 'general schema of the practical syllogism'. Accordingly, we should expect *this* absolute presupposition to exhibit the important characteristics of *all* absolute presuppositions: it will be non-propositional and susceptible to having, other than descriptively, no truth value at all; it will be, though widespread, culturally delimited; people in that culture will by and large be unaware that it even exists; it will be the result of earlier – indirect – changes, will be subject to further change, and so on.

III

The question we want to consider now is whether these characteristic features of absolute presuppositions pose any special problem for this one absolute presupposition in particular and for the science that it founds.

We might do well at the outset to note an asymmetry which, according to

Collingwood, holds between the study of nature and that of mind. 'In the case of nature, [the] distinction between the outside and the inside of an event does not arise. The events of nature are mere events, not the acts of agents whose thought the scientist endeavours to trace' (Collingwood, 1946, p.214). The sciences of nature are concerned with a subject matter that has no thought-side; it is mere event. Natural science may have its absolute presuppositions but what it studies does not. The sciences of mind, however, not only have absolute presuppositions themselves but study something which also has them. And, if we can credit Collingwood's account of absolute presuppositions, we can expect the presuppositions of the people under study sometimes to differ significantly from those of the ones who do the studying.

It is not clear, though, that the differences I have cited, between natural science and the sciences of mind and, within the latter, between the absolute presuppositions of, say, historians or anthropologists and the absolute presuppositions of those they study, are of any great moment. But it should also be noted that Collingwood devoted very little analysis to this specific problem. His attention was deflected, no doubt, by his one-sided preoccupation in the *Essay on Metaphysics* with the issue of the absolute presuppositions of natural science, in particular, physics. Here the fact that different scientific ages had different absolute presuppositions did not matter, if one was prepared to accept the validity of alternative, non-competing explanations (as Collingwood was, see 1940, esp. p.304) and if one was committed to a broadly progressive view of the development of science, in which older absolute presuppositions could be superseded by newer and better ones (see Collingwood, 1946, pp.321–34, esp. p.332; for the logic behind his view see Collingwood, 1933, and Martin, 1974, esp. p.249.) The matter may stand quite differently with a science of mind, however – a point Collingwood failed adequately to consider in the *Metaphysics*.

Let us suppose that the ancient Chinese (or the Incas or some prehistoric tribe) had certain absolute presuppositions that governed their scientific explanations of human behaviour. Some of these would concern *agency*; they would, when formulated, serve to characterise that society's conception of individual human actions: how they happened and, correspondingly, how they were to be explained.

That basic conception of action would be shared throughout the society in question, not just by its historians but also by the everyday agents in the society (see Collingwood, 1940, p.60, on the assumption of social sharing; note that he treats the assumption as merely a 'probable' one). This basic conception – if put into words, presumably accurately – would yield a formula that characterised action and its explanation in the eyes of that society in a way exactly analogous to what the 'general schema of the practical syllogism' does in our present-day society. But such a basic conception would be there and have its effect whether formulated (or formulated accurately) or not.

Now, let us consider the possibility that the people of this past society explained action and presumably acted on the basis of a paradigm for actions (or behaviour, if you will) which was significantly different from the one we are familiar with, that is, in the general schema. The character of the difference we are contemplating can perhaps be brought out more fully by considering an example.

A historian might say that Brutus' intention (to save the republican constitution of Rome) explains his action (joining Cassius' conspiracy against Caesar). To say that this intention explains that action is to have proper grounds for that particular statement. Among these would be evidence that Brutus did this thing and that Brutus had this intention; we would need a motivational setting for all this too, in Brutus' perception of Caesar's threat to the existing Roman constitution. But we would also need the practice, the basic conception, of giving such explanations; here we would turn to the idea, familiar from the general schema, that intentions (under certain conditions) give rise to actions.

We can readily imagine an alternative explanation for Brutus' deed in which the operative intention cited was, for example, Brutus' desire to rid himself of an envied political rival. But this alternative explanation still has crucial features in common with the original explanation: in both cases the intention as described could be a plausible reason for Brutus' action and, more important, in both cases the same basic conception of action-explanation is being presupposed: the action is explained by referring it to an intention, with respect to which the action is a means or a way of accomplishing that end envisioned.

We could, next, imagine an explanation in which the intention as described and the deed did *not* cohere as intelligibly connected. Often the explanations offered by psychoanalysts, at least preliminarily, have this character. Still, it is possible to treat such explanations as conforming to the general schema whereby actions are explained as means to, or ways of accomplishing, some specific end (see Martin, 1976a, pp.325-8). Of course we do not regard psychoanalytic explanations, in which odd or unfamiliar patterns of connecting particular intentions with particular deeds are relied on, as coming from another culture. But differences of culture might well give us such unfamiliar or strange patterns, and in abundance.

An even more profound difference is possible, for we can conceive the situation in which the basic conception of action pointed to by the general schema was not presupposed or employed at all in the understanding of human behaviour. Deterministic historical-materialist explanations, in which talk of individual motivations and intentions was suppressed or immediately discounted by translation into terms of class struggle, the categories of Marxist political economy, and stages of historical development,would provide an example. Again, the difference here is arguably not a difference between cultures or periods, but we could readily imagine a culture different from our own in which human behaviour simply was not understood or explained in conformity with the absolute presupposition that we are familiar with in the general schema.

In that society human behaviour would not be understood as motivated through the agent's conception of his situation; it would not be understood as involving, further, an intention or end-in-view which, if achieved, would resolve whatever was problematic in that situation, as the agent conceived it; and behaviour would not be understood as a way, or as part of achieving, such an end. The categories of situational motivation, intention, means/end behaviour simply would not be employed in that society; they would have no purchase there. Human behaviour and its explanation would run along an altogether different track.

This is, specifically, the sort of difference I am concerned with. Such a difference can be counted on where there is a marked temporal or cultural distance between agents and investigators. Thus, historians and anthropologists, in particular, would typically be faced with situations of just this sort (see the argument of Collingwood, 1946, part v; also Martin, 1977, esp. chapters 2 and 11). The question is whether such a difference would pose a problem for these investigators.

Presumably, when people today explain actions done in the present they do so in accordance with the 'general schema of the practical syllogism' and do so, in part, because they believe that actions actually do happen in this way. Now, were such people to turn to the past (or to another culture) they would still conform to this same explanatory paradigm. It may prove necessary for them to vary the factual filler considerably or even to adapt themselves to different standards of appropriate behaviour within the framework provided by the general schema; but, so long as they are concerned with human behaviour, the same paradigm, the same basic conception of actions, is invariably employed. The historian (or the anthropologist) literally cannot do otherwise so long as he is concerned with actions, in particular to explain them scientifically. For him to do otherwise, to neglect or reject the paradigm, would be to fail to understand past actions as actions. If past actions are to be intelligible, in the only way that actions are intelligible, to him and his audience the behaviour under study must be conceived as conforming to that paradigm. That behaviour must, accordingly, be filtered through the relevant paradigm, the absolute presupposition for action-explanations common to the historian and his society.

But if we allow a difference, of the sort I have already described, between the action paradigm of the people under study and the action paradigm of those who do the study, then we guarantee not just that the self-understanding but even that the very conception of being an agent, of acting at all, which is implicit in past actions, will not carry over to the study of them by the present. What counts as behaviour (the way it is conceived), what counts as intelligibility in behaviour, the very framework for explaining behaviour is itself different between the people, in the past, under study and the people, in the present, who do the study. Thus, the basic conception of action held in the past would not as such, without translation or some sort of reworking, yield intelligibility to the present. And what the present necessarily employs, its own paradigm, would create the same discordance, were the situations reversed, with the people of the past studying (*per impossibile*) those of the present.

It would appear that the present, under the condition of profound difference that we have delineated, could not understand the past on its own terms at all. This seems sufficient at least to question the possibility of historical knowledge.

One response to the problem I have cited is to say that what is pointed to by the so-called general schema of the practical syllogism is, like the regularities of nature, actually culturally invariant. Science may change but not nature. Ways of doing history may change but not the very framework of human action. Just as the fire burns in Athens as it does in Persia so we can expect Athenians and Persians to be moved to act by their conceptions of their situation, to form relevant intentions, to engage in means/end behaviour. In any case, there just is not *in fact* the kind or degree of difference between agents in different cultures or in different times that the argument of this section has relied on.

Perhaps not. But we could readily imagine the possibility of such significant differences. Some versions of Marxism, as I have already indicated, if they ever really got built into a society and penetrated popular consciousness accordingly, would establish a framework for explaining behaviour and presumably would engender action on a basis significantly unlike that of the general schema for intentional action. Or a religion devoted – fanatically, we would say – to the will of God and inculcating a kind of wholesale submissiveness to divine determinism could have, in time, a similar effect. Or a radically Skinnerian society or one in which behaviour was understood wholly cybernetically. More to the point, a person who was true to the teaching of *An Essay on Metaphysics* would have to accept such a possibility. A Collingwoodian, in the face of evident cultural diversity and changes wrought in the course of history, would have to presume a significant, perhaps even a total, difference between the absolute presuppositions of one time or place and those of another.

Another response to the problem would be to say that science is one thing and mere opinion another. We do not credit the views of another age or culture or social group, either about the heavens or about themselves. This is what science is all about; it is the antithesis of superstition and ignorance, the very stuff of any 'climate of opinion'. And after all, when we think about it, Skinnerians and psychoanalysts are not deterred by the fact that their subjects of study have a self-understanding and a conception of action radically different from the science of behaviour each of these groups of scientists respectively espouses.

Quite so, but this is because each group of practitioners regards its science as true and the opinions of others, where they conflict with that science, as false. It is not open to a Collingwoodian, however, to think this. The doctrine of absolute presuppositions forbids him to think that his paradigm of action-explanations, other than as regards descriptive accuracy (which applies only to his own society, in any case) is true; action-explanation paradigms that directly conflict with his, so long as they are actually supposed and efficacious in their social operation, are not thought false by reason of this conflict.

So, neither of the responses I have canvassed are open to the Collingwoodian. Indeed, the person who accepted Collingwood's account of absolute presuppositions, with its emphasis on the cultural determinateness of absolute presuppositions and on their tendency to change radically over time, must be prepared to accept the localisation and nonpersistence of any one of them, including the general schema to which Collingwood's theory of explanatory re-enactment is itself committed. The problem, then, is whether the Collingwoodian can give an account of historical knowledge on the assumption that absolute presuppositions themselves may differ, probably will differ sharply, from culture to culture or age to age.

And the prospects for Collingwood's own preferred account of history are not promising. His concept of re-enactment seems to demand an internal understanding of past agents, for it sets the presumed thought of the agent as a standard and requires, as a necessary aim or goal, that this thought can be accurately recreated by the investigator (see Martin, 1977, pp. 59–62). But the investigator would, if the doctrine of absolute presuppositions is correct, have to include, in making explicit the thought of past agents, elements which rendered that thought unintelligible to him. So, in merely recreating the thought of the past faithfully, he necessarily would fail to understand it. And if he employed the standard of intelligibility available to him (for the present-day historian it would be that represented by the general schema) then the historian could understand the thought and action of a past agent only by going well beyond a mere reproduction of them.

It may well be that Collingwood intended by re-enactment more than a faithful recreation of the action-involved thought of past agents; I think that he did. Even so, a problem remains where the very bridges by which the historian would cross the gap of cultural or of temporal difference – the various rules of intelligible material connection or, more crucially, the basic schema of action-explanation itself – are not transcultural. For then the present-day historian can at best project his forms of understanding onto other cultures or onto the distant past; but this is not the same thing as really understanding, as understanding from within, that other culture or other period. So if the proper understanding of another culture or period is conceived as an internal one, as it is in Collingwood's re-enactment theory, then it follows that proper or real understanding is impossible.

The demands of re-enactment and the implications of the doctrine of absolute presuppositions are evidently at cross purposes. Even if we could make Collingwood's doctrine consistent with *some* versions of historical inquiry, it would not appear possible to make it consistent with his own favoured version, the theory of re-enactment. The doctrine of absolute presuppositions seems to rule out, as impossible, historical knowledge – where such knowledge is taken to include those very features Collingwood characteristically emphasised. The problem I have been developing would bear down acutely, then, on the complete Collingwoodian; for it does not seem possible to subscribe both to Collingwood's doctrine of absolute presuppositions and to his theory of explanatory re-enactment in history. There appears to be a tension, amounting perhaps to an inconsistency, here within Collingwood's own philosophy.

IV

To conclude that this tension – this apparent inconsistency – is insurmountable would, however, be premature. Let me show in the concluding section of this essay how the two elements in his overall philosophy can in fact be seen as 'consupponible' (the term is Collingwood's; see Collingwood, 1940, pp.66,331).

It has been said that two different cultures have differing absolute presuppositions regarding the happening of human behaviour and its proper explanation. But how can one say this? Why do we not say instead that one culture has a conception of human behaviour and the other one does not? The main reason one might be inclined to treat human behaviour as a factor common to both cultures is that there is a stock of instances appropriate to the one absolute presupposition and a stock appropriate to the other; and there is a significant overlap between these two stocks.

If there were not stocks of covered instances in each case, then we could not regard the basic conceptions as ones that were actually supposed, as ones that governed the understanding of behaviour – as to how it happened and so on – in their respective cultures. And if the instances of behaviour picked out by the absolute presupposition(s) of the culture doing the study were not roughly the same as the ones that would be picked out, as instances of behaviour, by the absolute presupposition(s) of the culture under study, then there would be no problem of the sort we are here concerned with. Unless there was an overlap of instances, the differing absolute presuppositions would establish alternative modes of inquiry but not competing explanations. Though there would be differing absolute presuppositions and, accordingly, different ways of explaining, there would not be different ways of explaining *the same thing*.

Only when we reach the point of contrasted ways of conceiving or explaining the same thing do we reach grounds for the sort of metaphysically based scepticism about historical knowledge that surfaced in section III. It was the putting together of differences between agent's understanding and investigator's understanding of *the same piece of behaviour*, with the requirement of internal understanding implicit in Collingwood's notion of re-enactment,

H

that created the problem of genuine historical, or anthropological, knowledge in the first place.

In sum, then, each of the differing absolute presuppositions arises in its own particular cultural milieu and has thereby its own peculiar battery of descriptions and covered instances which normally attend it. But each absolute presupposition must, nonetheless, be conceived here as a member of the *same* family of presuppositions, that is, the family concerned with the happening and ultimately the explanation of human behaviour. And, more important, there must be, under each of the differing absolute presuppositions, a set of instances which are the same, no matter how differently described they are in each of the cases.

What makes for the overlapping character of these absolute presuppositions is the fact that the stock of normally covered instances can be extended, in the case of one absolute presupposition, to include instances that were originally part of the preferred stock of the *other* one. And, presumably, this extending of instances could run in the other direction as well: so that the original stock of instances under the other culture's absolute presupposition can be extended to include new and different instances. So, differing absolute presuppositions with different original extensions get locked together through the (partial) overlap of their covered instances, through the interpenetration of what were originally wholly different stocks of covered instances.

Just as this idea of interpenetration or overlap is necessary for the problem I have been discussing to arise, so it also provides a necessary basis for resolving that problem. For what can stand between, and bridge, two cultures is the *practice* of assimilating mutually alien absolute presuppositions by extending their 'stock' of covered instances so as to interpenetrate, thereby bringing together the presuppositions themselves.

A particular basic conception such as the general schema of the practical syllogism ought not, on this showing, to be regarded as a way of translating the detail of another culture into our categories: for the way we talk and think constitutes but one of the styles that can be accommodated within a given family of basic conceptions. And just as this family is culturally neutral with respect to what detailed kinds of instances can ultimately be accommodated under it so it is logically neutral with respect to the cultures and 'forms of life' themselves. It is the property of no one society or period.

Accordingly, rather than say that we project our cultural perspective, via the use of the general schema, onto another culture or period, we might do better to say that the schema itself is projectible in two different directions, to cover *our* thought and conduct and that of the society under investigation. Hence, the oft-repeated claim that we understand other periods or other cultures by 'analogy' with our own is somewhat misleading. It is not the 'likeness' of things, or the similarity of alien things to the things we are familiar with, that governs our bringing them together. Rather, the crucial fact is that they can all be brought together under the same basic conception, which happens to have these disparate things among its extension, as part of its stock of covered instances.

Now the basic conception has this character, not because these alien things were part of its original extension, but because explanatory practice can assimilate instances from other stocks and thereby assimilate basic conceptions, from other periods/other cultures and from our own, to one another. It is in this way, by assimilating instances and thence absolute presuppositions to one another, that transhistorical, or cross-cultural, understanding becomes possible.

But is this really an *internal* understanding? There are many ways, it should be clear, in which it is not. I am not suggesting that the investigator can experience in himself the inner side – the fugitive thoughts, the conviction of beliefs, the naturalness of behaviour – the feeling of living as a participant in the other culture. For the investigator is not attempting to duplicate or to acquire the interior dimension of life in the other culture. He is not going to share their beliefs, or their social horizons, or their view of the world.

Nor does the notion of internal understanding which I am developing require that the investigator's rules (of intelligibility) in some way reproduce the rules which persons in other cultures have formulated, or which they could articulate upon request. Indeed, sometimes there is no rule, at least none that the participants have been able to put into words. (And this is the usual case with absolute presuppositions; for they have effect, Collingwood believed, even though the people who live in a given culture are largely unconscious of them.) But in this regard the investigator stands no differently to other periods/other cultures than he stands to his own – and, hence, than any indigenous investigator would stand to *his* native period or culture. So, if no one native to a particular period or culture could readily formulate the rule (though the participants there did seem to be following one – at least to the extent that they, or anyone, could say whether or not something was being done correctly), then all anyone could offer would be a construction (in the form of a rule-statement) which more or less accurately formulates certain objective features in that society. And where a variety of such formulations are workable, then each would be acceptable (Hanson, 1975, p.65; Hanson and Martin, 1973, sect. 4, esp. pp.203-4).

In no event is the historian or anthropologist engaged in the spurious task of attempting to recapitulate in his own mind the deeply buried subconscious cognition of participants. Rather, this whole business of duplicating or sharing or recapitulating – whether the duplication is said to be of native feelings or beliefs or rules (either articulated or seemingly unexpressible) – is beside the point. What I have called internal understanding is not conceived as the duplication of anything in the native mind or culture at all. On the contrary, the model of internal understanding I am advocating involves the assimilation of native rules (or rule constructions, as the case may be) and not their duplication.

By assimilating instances from other stocks we are able to draw rules and basic conceptions together, from other periods and other cultures and from our own, and thereby assimilate them to one another. The understanding so achieved is internal because it allows us to use their basic rule *as a rule of intelligibility*; for, as assimilated to the basic rule (of intelligibility) from our society, it is conceived as a different way of formulating that rule – hence as a redescription of it (the reverse, of course, is true as well). And the understanding achieved is internal because it allows us to bring their actions, intentions, beliefs and so on – when assimilated to our stock of instances – into line with a basic rule of intelligibility which, in principle, both investigator and participant can use. Or it might be better to say that the understanding is internal inasmuch as it is possible to bring their actions, intentions, beliefs, etc., and our own under the same family of rules and of basic conceptions.

Assimilation so conceived is not a matter of duplication. For it requires not only that the one set of rules remain distinct from the other but also that the difference in their formulation be retained as well.

We do not, of course, have to accept their rule of intelligibility (nor they ours); it is required merely that we be able to follow it (and they ours). Nor must one share the belief or engage in the action that has been assimilated to his stock of instances. For what is at issue is not the advisability of behaving or believing in a certain way but, instead, the intelligibility of it. And this is something that is to be determined by assimilating instances to instances, rules to rules, and, if need be, absolute presupposition to absolute presupposition.

This practice of assimilating allows us to follow, in the sense of make intelligible, the material connections between particular actions, intentions, beliefs, etc., of agents in another culture or in another period. Indeed the practice of so assimilating *is* the following of those connections and, hence, is to count as internal understanding.

There need not be, and probably is not, an ideal rule which, if formulated, would bring together and make explicit what these rules – or what these absolute presuppositions – have in common. Bluntly put, the investigator does not in fact understand alien behaviour by bringing it under some very general rule that covers both his behaviour and that in the other culture; rather, he associates his rule with their rule through the overlap of (previously) 'covered' instances in the case of each. But we have no single overarching rule, nor do we require one. What we do have is a practice of assimilating disparate rules to one another.

One might say that the practice of assimilation is *like* bringing disparate phenomena under a single rule (that is its regulative idea) – like it, I say, except that there is not (necessarily) any such rule there. In the absence of such a rule (which is the usual case presumed in history) we make do with what I have called a family of rules. It bespeaks a messier situation, but the logic is similar to that of the ideal-rule case.

Thus, if my account of assimilation is sound and can be applied to absolute presuppositions themselves, as I have attempted to do in this paper, then it gives us the sketch of a solution to the problem we are concerned with. The theory of assimilation, in which no ultimate 'ideal' rule is required for completion, allows absolute presuppositions to retain their distinctness and their logical ultimacy. (Any theory that did otherwise would probably deny, in effect, their character as absolute presuppositions.) And the theory allows us to retain, indeed to emphasise, the point that practices of scientific inquiry and explanation are culturally determinate – localised and delimited – and the point that the basic conceptions behind these practices, if accurately formulated in words, would describe something that differed from culture to culture, from period to period, either as the result of sheer cultural distance or as the result of inevitable and ever deepening long-term changes within a given culture.

Thus it is possible for a Collingwoodian to believe that the absolute presupposition of contemporary, scientific history is not a constant; to believe that 'the general schema of the practical syllogism' (which formulates this presupposition) has a history, has very likely changed during that history, and is subject, inevitably, to further changes; to believe that this presupposition, whether changing or not, is not universal; and to believe that it has no special exempted truth value (for, as an absolute presupposition, it can have no truth value at all). And it is possible to believe, as Collingwood himself apparently did (Collingwood, 1946, pp.11–17), that some societies have no practice of history at all and that our own society has a practice which itself has changed over time and hence is not only internally different, at the various points in its career, but also different from the practice of history in other societies. It is possible to believe these things and yet to regard as still eligible, as not deformed or deflected, the claim that the understanding characteristic of contemporary historians or anthropologists can have cross-cultural range, transhistorical scope, and can count, despite radical differences between past and present or between one culture and another, as an internal understanding of the culture or period under study.

It is possible, in short, to apply the general analysis of absolute presuppositions to the special case of the absolute presupposition of history and at the same time to allow for a historical understanding of the past which is tolerably like that which Collingwood described under the heading of re-enactment. Insofar as our study is concerned, then, with the internal consistency of Collingwood's own position, we can resolve the matter by saying that Collingwood's doctrine of absolute presuppositions does not rule out the possibility of historical knowledge as he conceived it.

REFERENCES
Ayer, A. J. (1936) *Language, Truth and Logic*. London, Gollancz; New York, Oxford University Press.
Collingwood, R. G. (1933) *An Essay on Philosophical Method*. Oxford, Clarendon Press.

Collingwood, R. G. (1939) *An Autobiography*. Oxford, Clarendon Press.
Collingwood, R. G. (1940) *An Essay on Metaphysics*. Oxford, Clarendon Press.
Collingwood, R. G. (1945) *The Idea of Nature*, Edited by T. M. Knox. Oxford, Clarendon Press.
Collingwood, R. G. (1946) *The Idea of History*, Edited with an introduction by T. M. Knox. Oxford, Clarendon Press. (Page citations are to the printing of 1956; New York, Oxford University Press.)
Donagan, A. H. (1962) *The Later Philosophy of R. G. Collingwood*. Oxford, Clarendon Press.
Donagan, A. H. (1966) The Popper–Hempel Theory Reconsidered. In Dray, W. H. (ed.) *Philosophical Analysis and History*, pp.127–59. New York, NY, Harper & Row. (Essay originally published in *History and Theory* 4 (1964), 3–26.)
Donagan, A. H. (1969) Alternative Historical Explanations and Their Verification, *Monist* 53, 58–89.
Hanson, F. A. (1975) *Meaning in Culture*. London, Routledge & Kegan Paul.
Hanson, F. A. and Martin, R. (1973) The Problem of Other Cultures, *Philosophy of the Social Sciences* 3, 191–208. (The present paper draws, sometimes verbatim, on this article.)
Knox, T. M. (1946) Editor's Preface. In Collingwood (1946), pp.v–xxiv.
Krausz, M. (ed.). (1972) *Critical Essays on the Philosophy of R. G. Collingwood*. Oxford, the Clarendon Press. (Besides the essay by Walsh listed below, there are relevant essays in this volume by Nathan Rotenstreich, Stephen Toulmin, and Michael Krausz. There is a comprehensive bibliography of works by and on Collingwood, pp.327–48.)
Martin, R. (1974) Collingwood's *Essay on Philosophical Method*, *Idealistic Studies* 4, 24–50.
Martin, R. (1976a) Explanation and Understanding in History. In Manninen, J. and Tuomela, R. (eds.) *Essays on Explanation and Understanding*, pp.305–34. Dordrecht, Holland, D. Reidel.
Martin, R. (1976b) The Problem of the 'Tie' in von Wright's Schema of Practical Inference: A Wittgensteinian Solution, *Acta Philosophica Fennica* 28, 326–63.
Martin, R. (1977) *Historical Explanation: Re-enactment and Practical Inference*. Ithaca, NY, Cornell University Press. (In the writing of the present paper I have drawn, sometimes verbatim, on this book. In particular this is true of section IV of the paper; see Martin, 1977, pp.230–6 esp.; also pp.236–40 and 249–52.)
Mink, L. O. (1969) *Mind, History and Dialectic: The Philosophy of R. G. Collingwood*. Bloomington, Indiana, Indiana University Press.
Shalom, A. (1955) R. G. Collingwood et la métaphysique, *Les Etudes philosophiques* 10, 693–711.
Walsh, W. H. (1967) *An Introduction to Philosophy of History*, 3rd ed. London, Hutchinson.
Walsh, W. H. (1972) Collingwood and Metaphysical Neutralism. In Krausz (1972), pp.134–53.
Walsh, W. H. (1976) The Constancy of Human Nature. In Lewis, H. D. (ed.) *Contemporary British Philosophy* 4th series, pp.274–91. London, Allen & Unwin.

8. Is Speculative Philosophy of History Possible?

LOUIS O. MINK

It may seem strange to ask whether speculative philosophy of history is 'possible'. Whatever is actual is possible, and there on our shelves are speculative philosophies of history from Augustine on. There is a story of the Indiana farmer who was asked whether he believed in baptism by immersion. 'Believe in it?' he said; 'Hell, I've *seen* them do it'. And so we have, indeed, seen them do speculative philosophy of history. The question is whether there is any legitimate defence of it as a truth-claiming form of inquiry – or whether, like astrology, it is a subject which, no matter how it may flourish in popular culture, fails to meet any reasonable set of criteria for claims to advance knowledge.

Even so there is something strange about the question. Speculative philosophy of history has no contemporary practitioners. There are plenty of Hegel scholars, but Hegel-interpretation, even when accompanied by reasons for agreement or disagreement, is not the same thing as the practice of speculative philosophy of history. Historical materialism is very much alive, although diffused among a proliferating variety of Marxisms, but it has become less a philosophy of history or even a discipline in which questions of philosophy of history are explored than a guide to which areas and problems of ordinary historical research are more interesting than others. Eric Voegelin, the one living scholar who might be called a philosopher of history in the tradition of Spengler, Sorokin and Toynbee, has explicitly abandoned, in the fourth of his projected five-volume *Order in History* (published seventeen years after the third volume) his original enterprise of demonstrating a single line of meaningful development in Western history from the ancient Near East to the present. The facts, he found, and candidly admitted, have been too intractable for any power of unitary interpretation. Whether or not there is an inverse relation between the steady accumulation of concrete historical data and the ability to discern large-scale patterns in them, it does seem that the cumulative expansion of monographic history has been accompanied by a steady disappearance of philosophies of history in the classic pattern. So one might guess that speculative philosophy of history thrived on historical ignorance and could not survive the unassimilable achievements of specialist history. Not a very good guess, though: the decline of philosophy of history did not in fact accelerate through the nineteenth century, and Spengler and Toynbee flourished long after Ranke introduced modern professional history.

It is also true that philosophy of history in the classic manner is ill suited to the culture of modern universities with their emphasis on sustained professional criticism. Systems of any sort, and the single-minded concentration and prolonged gestation which they require, are hardly possible in this environment, and their products, like Voegelin's, are apt to be ignored as irrelevant to swiftly changing conceptual and rhetorical fashions. Even the American historian of a few decades ago who introduced himself to Jacques Barzun by saying 'I am the Age of Jackson' has been succeeded by younger social historians who would not want to claim expertise extending beyond the household economics of the working class in Boston between 1890 and 1920. But even this can hardly account for the total demise of speculative philosophy of history as a subject and as an activity.

So if one looks around to see what is happening in speculative philosophy of history today, it appears that it in some ways resembles space biology. It is a discipline wholly without subject-matter. There are in fact space biologists, but (as yet) not a single piece of evidence for the existence of life originating outside the earth's atmosphere; space biologists therefore are limited to designing instruments for the detection of extraterrestrial organisms if indeed any such exist. There are critics of speculative philosophy of history (including presumably all of the contributors to this volume as well as the philosopher of history whose career occasions it) but there are, today, no speculative philosophers of history to criticise. But we still elaborate arguments which may achieve applicability if a speculative philosophy of history should announce itself.

The difference between speculative philosophy of history and space biology, of course, is that there *have been* speculative philosophies of history. Thus there is a subject-matter, though it has become intellectual history. But no one professes speculative philosophy of history or presents a reasoned defence of propositions resembling those of the great speculators from Augustine to Toynbee and Spengler. As an activity or profession, philosophy of history today means analytical or critical philosophy of history, not the theory of the historical process – of *res gestae* – but the theory of historical inquiry – of *historia rerum gestarum*.

It was C. D. Broad who originally gave currency to the distinction between 'critical' and 'speculative' disciplines, but he had in mind particularly the difference between philosophy of science and philosophy of nature. The difference between critical philosophy of *history* and speculative philosophy of *history* has long seemed standard, but it was in fact introduced for the first time by Professor W. H. Walsh (1951) in his *An Introduction to Philosophy of History*. I intend to argue that the distinction is pernicious – or rather that it has been understood in a pernicious way – but Walsh's innovation was in itself benign and guileless in intent. Addressing an English-speaking philosophical audience which had not yet learned to call Collingwood a philosopher of history, he had to convince them first of all that a 'philosophy of history' was not necessarily Hegelian or Spenglerian moonshine. And his distinction was for this purpose immediately and unqualifiedly successful. It connected the accepted problems of theory of knowledge with 'critical philosophy of history' and relegated the unpopular claims of metaphysics to 'speculative philosophy of history'. Walsh himself had greater sympathy with such claims that he could expect from his professional audience. Even so, there is a tentativeness about his discussion of 'speculative philosophy of history' which is quite different from anything in his discussion of 'critical philosophy of history'. Partly this is due to the fact that Spengler and Toynbee, the contemporary examples of speculative philosophers of history, were not philosophers at all, and Walsh's strategy was to ask what philosophy *as such* can contribute in principle to the understanding of either the historical process or the activity of historical inquiry. It was hard enough to convince anyone of the latter, given the 'bias against philosophy of history which has been a permanent feature of British philosophy' (Walsh, 1967, p.14). Nevertheless, Walsh did boldly devote three chapters (a third of his book) to speculative philosophy of history, and discussed Herder, Kant, Hegel, Comte, Marx and Toynbee. His verdict on the type is, as he says, 'mixed': speculative philosophy of history, he concludes, is in one way 'utterly wrongheaded'; in attempting to 'comprehend history from the outside, [it] cannot have any appeal for working historians' (Walsh, 1967, pp.149–50). The merit of speculative philosophy of history is that it *did* have salutary effects on historical studies, for example by provoking dissatisfaction with 'loose chronicles and empty moralising' passing for history. But the only reason Walsh gave why speculative philosophy of history should continue to survive at all is that some people still demand a 'moral justification of the course history has taken'; and speculative philosophies of history will presumably continue to appear 'so long as evil is looked on as constituting a metaphysical problem' (Walsh, p.150).

This is of course not even a weak defence of speculative philosophy of history as a project; it is not a defence at all. Elsewhere in the same book Walsh argues that historians cannot avoid historical interpretations based on their deeply ingrained moral and metaphysical beliefs, for example about human nature (Walsh, 1967, pp.105,108). But evidently these do not necessarily include moral and metaphysical beliefs about the historical process itself; such beliefs, Walsh evidently holds, are at best optional extras, and philosophy must therefore prudently defer to the consensus of 'working historians' that they be thoroughly eschewed.

It emerges from all this that for Walsh speculative philosophy of history has two main defining features: it deals with the historical process *as a whole* (and it therefore must include the entire human future in the historical process, although Walsh does not make a point of emphasising this); and it seeks to discern in this process a *meaning and purpose* (Walsh, 1967, p.20). Claims about the 'main moving factors' in history (as in the Marxist theory of history) are not philosophical at all, in Walsh's view, but for better or for worse have the form of empirical hypotheses. It follows that there are theories of history, for example some forms of historical materialism, which are not speculative philosophy of history at all. Still, they go beyond the description and explanation of a single series of events, so they are not just ordinary history, either. Since they are in some sense philosophies of history but not *speculative* philosophies of history, one can conclude that the distinction between critical and speculative philosophy of history is not exhaustive. This is my inference, not Walsh's conclusion. But Walsh does not suggest that there is any appropriate philosophical interest in theories of history which are neither speculative philosophies of history (by his definition) nor ordinary history (in the regard of what he calls 'working historians').

So a reader of *An Introduction* could be forgiven for carrying away the impression that critical philosophy of history and speculative philosophy of history divide between them exclusively and exhaustively the whole field of philosophy of history. And for nearly twenty years the distinction itself went unchallenged. Of course this has not been just on Walsh's authority. There are deeper reasons why the distinction between critical and speculative philosophy of history has seemed so fundamental and unproblematic. I do not of course mean by 'reasons' such things as that the distinction satisfied the desire of most philosophers and historians to lump Hegel, Spengler, Toynbee and – as a dividend – Marx, together and dispose of them all together as a *type* without having to engage them critically one by one. By 'deeper reasons' I mean rather that the distinction nested neatly into dominant conceptual schemes and thereby acquired their entrenched authority. And these reasons can be found in Walsh's own discussion; they serve, I think, as the justification he would give for the distinction, even though he presents it as if it needed no justification, just clarification of its terms.

One reason is that it simply carries over the difference – or whatever one accepts as the difference – between epistemology and metaphysics. A second reason, also alluded to by Walsh, is that it corresponds to the well-known ambiguity of the term 'history' in English and some other languages. In one sense 'history' refers to the actual nexus of happenings in time, in another sense to the report, analysis and explanation of those events, or, as Collingwood would say, to the activity of asking and answering questions about them. This is of course the difference between *res gestae* and *historia rerum gestarum*, and it was noted at least as early as Hegel (1953, p.75), who proposed to reunite the two meanings. A third reason is that philosophy is, as Collingwood (1946, p.1) said, thought 'of the second degree', that is, thinking about the activity of thinking about any object. (It is revealing that late in *The Idea of History* Collingwood (1946, p.307) gives exactly the same definition of *history* – 'thinking about the act of thinking' – which at the beginning he gives of *philosophy*; but this is of course consistent with his expansion of the term 'history' far beyond the limits of anything that 'working historians' do merely as such.) Thinking about historical events themselves, which is what historians do, would of course be thought of the first degree. There is a specious clarity about this reason: first and second degree are made to seem as distinct as the ordinal numbers themselves. But as soon as one reflects that 'historical events' are at least in some small part *constituted* by thought itself – surely no one believes that the investiture controversy or the Renaissance is a *datum* – it is no longer clear that thought of the first degree is completely distinguishable from thought of the second degree, except for a narrow range of possible objects – i.e., events which are in a one-to-one relation to data. Beyond this, the contrast between thought of the first and second degrees is reducible to the two meanings of history: history-as-past-actuality and history-as-present-knowledge. And this reason in turn reduces to the difference between epistemology and metaphysics. There are not three reasons but three expressions of the same reason. And whether critical philosophy of history and speculative philosophy of history as types are mutually exclusive and jointly exhaustive depends on whether epistemology and metaphysics are so. There are of course those who think that they are, but only because they regard metaphysical statements as meaningless or pseudo-statements. This is not Walsh's own view, of course. Any decent regard for the history of Western philosophy must reveal at least that from Plato to Wittgenstein the question has been not whether epistemology and metaphysics are related but how they are.

I think myself that epistemology and metaphysics presuppose each other: that is, that any adequate theory of knowledge will have acknowledged or unacknowledged metaphysical presuppositions about what there is and is not to be known; and any metaphysics must be able to explain at least how, if it were true, we could come to know it. (Even a revealed theology must have an epistemology of revelation.) But I do not propose to argue this thesis in general, only in its particular application to history.

Every philosophy rests on certain beliefs or intuitions; they can also be called 'insights', at least phenomenologically, because they tend to occur at certain moments of intellectual confusion as transposing the meaning and force of a whole set of beliefs. Everyone knows, for example, that the past is inaccessible to any direct inspection, and that this is true not just for practical reasons, like the inaccessibility of very distant objects or very small particles, but *in principle*. The inaccessibility of the past is not epistemological (though it is that, too) but ontological. But people *believe* this in more or less deeply entrenched ways. It is an occupational habit of historians to believe it but simultaneously to believe that it is not logically or conceptually connected with any other beliefs. The historian's response is typically 'Of course, but so what?' On the other hand, the realisation that the past is literally *nowhere* comes for some people – including myself, and I suspect Walsh, though he might express it less dramatically – like a bolt of lightning which illuminates the entire landscape. And in the darkness following the lightning, and until it strikes again, we try to reconstruct bit by bit the complex picture which was illuminated briefly but powerfully. 'My God!'

we say, 'It's *really* true, the past isn't there at all. There's no *there* for it to be. Whatever a history signifies, it's not anything that we can even conceive being placed side-by-side with the history to observe the degree of resemblance.' Meanwhile the historian gets on with his work, humming Ranke under his breath. My point is not that the historian's response is wrong. He has or hopes for his lightning-bolts of illumination too; it is just that they are not ontological, but something more like configurations of data. Still, the logic of the situation is independent of how deeply embedded one's belief is. The significant part of the historian's response is not the 'So what?' but the 'Of course!' This acknowledgment is a metaphysical assertion – by someone who happens not to be very interested in metaphysical assertions, but that does not change its character.

So the ontological inaccessibility of the past is one example of the conceptual inseparability of epistemology and metaphysics. Characteristically, Walsh's acknowledgment is made by the way in his discussion of the correspondence and coherence theories of truth – apparently a topic belonging wholly to the 'critical philosophy of history', and one which he does not connect with 'realism' and 'idealism' or constructionism. Concerned with other problems, such as whether there are primary facts from which every element of interpretation is absent or eliminable, it is only in passing that he observes that 'we cannot carry out the full programme of the Correspondence theory *because we cannot examine the past*' (Walsh, 1967, p.89, italics added); at the same time he undertakes to justify (with careful qualifications) the Correspondence view that 'there is an attempt in history, as in perception, to characterise an independent reality' (*ibid*). It should not be a surprise to find the Correspondence and Coherence theories making metaphysical claims: they always have. But it does imply that if epistemological and metaphysical beliefs are in some cases inseparable, and if critical and speculative philosophy of history are distinguished as respectively epistemological and metaphysical, *then* critical and speculative philosophy of history are in some cases inseparable. Walsh does not draw this conclusion simply because he has in effect renamed as 'critical' all metaphysical problems of history *except* the question whether the *whole historical process* has a single meaning or pattern, with moral significance.

To put it differently, only theodicies, actual or secularised, count as speculative philosophies of history for Walsh. Meanwhile, metaphysical problems tend to be referred to the commonsense ontologies of 'working historians'. But then it becomes inexplicable how, as Walsh himself in fairness is anxious to acknowledge, the Great Speculators could have had 'insights which later historians were to turn to good account' (Walsh, 1967, p.149). Such insights could not have derived merely from the mistaken claim to have disclosed the moral meaning behind the historical process as a whole.

The distinction between critical and speculative philosophy of history, tendentious as it turns out to be, could not remain forever unchallenged. And in fact the last decade has produced at least three books, two by historians and one by a philosopher, which take dead aim at the distinction, or rather at the received opinion that the legitimacy of critical philosophy of history and the illegitimacy of speculative philosophy of history are opposite sides of the same coin. Haskell Fain's (1970) *Between Philosophy and History* even bears the subtitle 'The Resurrection of Speculative Philosophy of History within the Analytic Tradition'. Peter Munz's (1977, p.7) *The Shapes of Time* describes itself as 'written to bridge the gap between analytic and speculative philosophy of history'. And Hayden White's (1973, p.xi) *Metahistory*, while mainly a study of the origin in linguistic tropes of the forms of narrative emplotment, has as one of its sub-themes the rejection of any fundamental distinction between 'proper history' and philosophy of history: both, in White's view, are expressions of common metahistorical engagements and differ only as relatively implicit and relatively explicit statements of metahistory. Yet these three books are quite dissimilar in most respects. They converge only as legitimations of the enterprise of speculative philosophy of history, and even in that respect their arguments are very different.

For Peter Munz (1977), the difference between 'ordinary' history and speculative philosophy of history is a difference of degree, not a difference of kind. What historians ordinarily do is to assemble sub-events into events, and events into large events. So the characteristic historiographical act is a construction, and it is brought about by introducing generalisations. Munz actually undertakes to defend the covering-law model of explanation, and sometimes calls the linkages of events 'general laws', but it is clear that he intends to include generalisations of every sort, even trivial generalisations of the 'Nobody likes to be shot at' sort. Sometimes he calls them 'universal', which I think means only that they apply to more than one case, hence go beyond the 'individuality' or 'uniqueness' which historians are so fond of claiming as the special characteristic of their subject-matter. Sometimes the historian uses generalisations familiar to the people he's talking about; his way of linking events, that is, would be intelligible to them. Munz calls such cases 'explanations', and contrasts them with 'interpretations', in which the historian uses generalisations unknown to and even unintelligible to the people he is talking about.

Now there is no reason why events cannot be assembled into larger events, and those into still larger events, and so on indefinitely, so long as plausible generalisations can be found to connect them. So for Munz, speculative philosophies of history differ from ordinary historical narratives only in scale – and, one might add, in boldness. Because they deal with very large-scale events (not perceptible as single wholes to the people living through them), they depend more on interpretation than on explanation. Also because they deal with very large-scale events, (their generalisations may be misperceived (but only misperceived) as developmental laws. Developmental laws (if there are any) would entail the inevitability of processes subject to them; and they could also be used to predict the future, conditionally or unconditionally. Munz rejects both the imputation of inevitability and the possibility of prediction. He even imposes on all history what he calls the 'Postulate of Absolute Praeterity', an absolute prohibition of all future-referring statements to any kind of history, from ordinary to speculative. For philosophy of history, he says, it is not the laws but the *events* that are big. The ordinary historian connects the monarchy of Henry VIII with the reign of Henry VII; the philosopher of history connects it with the decline of feudalism (Munz, 1977, p.288). Most historians, I presume, would say that both of these are manifestly forms of 'ordinary' history; but the objection oddly supports Munz's point. There *are* differences of scale in the construction of historical narratives, and no upper limit can be established *a priori*. Historians do think of events as made up out of smaller events and as parts of larger events (as in battle – campaign – war) and are as incapable of stating criteria for a largest event as they are for a smallest one. After these considerations it should not be surprising to find that Munz regards Toynbee's work as 'the most powerfully suggestive philosophy of history ever thought out' (Munz, 1977, p.299). Munz obviously reads Toynbee very differently from the way Walsh does; each emphasises in Toynbee features which the other leaves out entirely. Walsh emphasises the last four volumes of *A Study of History* and convicts Toynbee of prophecy – of predicting the future of Western Civilisation, especially the coming synthesis of the 'four higher religions'. This violates Munz's injunctions against prediction, but Munz ignores Toynbee's prophecies and concentrates instead only on his patterns of civilisations which have run their course.

Even of this earlier Toynbee, Walsh judges that he was 'not an historian' at all, since 'his interest was not in particular events but in repeated patterns', and to enquire into historical law 'is not identical with doing history in the ordinary sense' (Walsh, 1967, p.163). Evidently for Walsh history in the ordinary sense is limited to particular events even though it orders them into a 'significant narrative'. This is dramatically opposed to Munz's claim that any description of an event necessarily presupposes a generalisation not directly derived from whatever evidence makes the description of the event referential.

If the transition from ordinary history to speculative philosophy of history is as seamless and continuous as Munz claims, then why have historians and philosophers alike been nearly unanimous in seeing them as categorically different? Munz's answer is that ordinary history is commonly but wrongly regarded as a transcript of 'what really happened', a more or less successful attempt to provide a copy of historical reality. Historical realism, that is, is comfortable with particular facts, uncomfortable with 'laws' or theories; the former are reality-referring, the latter not. If, however, even ordinary history is recognised as inescapably a construction rather than a transcript, then the gulf between ordinary history and speculative philosophy of history disappears, or rather is transposed into continuously variable degrees of scale.

If Munz is unique among historians in not only adopting the covering-law model but even claiming that it bridges the gap between ordinary history and speculative philosophy of history, Haskell Fain is unique among philosophers in doing analytical philosophy of history without even mentioning covering laws. This is not quite true; he adds to his book an Epilogue discussing covering-law explanation, but, as he ruefully admits, his nerve failed at the last moment. Still, it is only an Epilogue not only formally but logically – that is, nothing he has to say about the covering-law model is required for his argument proper.

Fain's purpose is explicit: it is to 'shatter the powerful stereotype' which distinguishes the 'brackish swamp called speculative philosophy of history' from the 'clear lake of analytical philosophy of history' (Fain, 1970, p.13). In the end, the only difference between these which he acknowledges is that speculative philosophers of history deal with the kinds of philosophical problems that cluster around the narrative aspect of history whereas analytical philosophers of history are primarily interested in how historical facts are established and explained (Fain, 1970, p.216). As sympathetic as I am to Fain's enterprise, I do not think that this difference supports the language. The difference is really just a difference between two areas of analytical philosophy of history. Fain's subtitle, 'The Resurrection of Speculative Philosophy of History Within the Analytic Tradition', seems to confirm this. By Fain's definition, *he*, not Hegel, Marx, Spengler or Toynbee, is the speculative philosopher of history, and the questions of speculative philosophy of history are such obviously critical questions as 'What are the criteria for deciding whether the account of a given incident belongs to a given narrative structure?' and 'Does narrative intelligibility presuppose theoretical explanation (or require it for its completion), or does it supplant theoretical explanation and make it superfluous?' These are clearly conceptual questions belonging to critical philosophy. At the same time they broaden the scope of critical philosophy of history beyond the narrow scope imposed by exclusive attention to the 'establishment and explanation' of facts. In fact – and I think this is the point – they broaden it enough to invite attention to the likes of Hegel and Marx. Walsh intentionally or inadvertently forged an exclusive alliance between the critical philosopher of history and the 'working historian'. The latter's province is the 'establishment and explanation' of historical facts; the former's is the analysis and clarification of the principles of such establishment and explanation. The two are complementary. The 'speculative philosopher of history', muddled as he is, is not (for Walsh) an historian at all, and as philosopher he can only attempt the hopeless task of deducing the empirical content of historical knowledge from wholly *a priori* premises.

Fain, however, like Munz claims significant continuity between 'ordinary history' and 'philosophical history'. The difference between them is primarily one of rhetorical form. Histories are narratives, and every historian necessarily provides (through his choice of descriptions) narrative units ('episodes'), narrative organisation, and the narrative unity of a story with beginning, middle and end. Ordinary history does this, so to speak, unreflectively; philosophical historians are more self-conscious, and take pains to justify their narrative units and narrative organisation (Fain, 1970, pp.209, 233). This, and apparently only this, accounts for the 'rhetorical' difference between ordinary history and philosophical history. The latter simply makes explicit and undertakes to justify what in the former is present but implicit. Received opinion and shared commonsense are great labour-savers, and of course no one should be surprised if 'working historians' simply adopt them and push on, since they have lots of other labour-intensive work, while philosophers tirelessly play cat-and-mouse with them, because they do not. In any case, the speculative philosopher of history – that is, Fain himself for one – shares a subject with the philosophical historian, even though the former approaches it from the side of criterial analysis and the other from the side of problems of narrative coherence; and that subject is the coherence between a story-line and the material which it purports to organise – between plot and action, so to speak. Fain is actually more sympathetic to Hegel than is Walsh. According to Walsh, Hegel attempted to deduce the plot of history, though not its details, from purely philosophical premises, that is, from the categories of his logic (Walsh, 1967, p.149). Of course such an attempt cannot but pain yet once more Walsh's faithful 'working historian', but it pains Walsh too. Fain, however, perhaps at the cost of ignoring Hegel's distinction between understanding and reason, sees even claims about the march of the world-historical spirit as not 'deductive' at all but rather as an attempt to provide a narrative unity among widely-separated historical deeds by redescribing them in such a way that they appear as episodes in the same story. As with Munz, this effort does not reveal a rational history behind empirical history, but a larger story beyond the collection of smaller stories. Fain does not say so, but one could guess that the criticism of such a philosophical history would be of the legitimacy (with respect to supporting evidence) of proposed redescriptions; since if they fail so does the narrative unity which depends on them. (This is in fact the kind of criticism that Pieter Geyl and others made of Toynbee: not that Toynbee selected facts to fit his theories but that he selected descriptions to fit his plot-forms; so that a sequence of events might be called 'challenge and response' or 'rout and rally' if it came at the prescribed stage, while another sequence of events not relevantly different but occurring at a different stage would not be so described.) As Fain understands Hegel, his history of freedom might be wrong throughout, but not because of the *kind* of history it is. To show that it is wrong would require two kinds of argument, one more historical and the other more philosophical. On the one hand, essential descriptions could be faulted as arbitrary or inadequate; on the other, the essential descriptions could be shown to be insufficient to support the degree of narrative unity claimed. But even if philosophical history on such a scale should prove to exceed human capacity, this would be a practical difficulty and not an impossibility in principle.

Hayden White's (1973) *Metahistory* is in the first instance intellectual history of nineteenth-century historiography, but it is to ordinary intellectual history as philosophical history is to ordinary history. Although he discusses four historians – Michelet, Tocqueville, Burckhardt and Ranke – and four philosophers of history – Hegel, Marx, Nietzsche and Croce – the whole argument maintains the continuity of historiography and philosophy of history rather than their differences. Note that Marx appears as philosopher of history rather than as historian, despite the fact that a whole chapter is devoted to the *18th Brumaire*. I think too that it would be right to say that even if Spengler and Toynbee had fallen within the chronological limits of the nineteenth century they would still not have been suitable subjects for *Metahistory*, or at least not more than many others, since *Metahistory's* scheme of categories is unrestricted in application. But Spengler and Toynbee are neither characteristically historiographers nor characteristically philosophers of history, as *Metahistory* sees both. Fundamental for *Metahistory* is the notion that different types of historical imagination are figured by the dominance of one or another of four linguistic tropes – metaphor, metonymy, synecdoche and irony. These appear most importantly not in casual rhetoric but in the transformation of the chronicle of events into narrative by choice of a mode of emplotment. The primary modes of emplotment turn out to be the classic literary genres of Romance (metaphor), Comedy (metonymy), Tragedy (synecdoche) and Satire (irony). For our purposes, the important point is that White regards philosophy of history as inescapable in any history, since it is a conception of the historical field and its processes. In the great historiographers, such a conception was not directly avowed but was 'displaced' to a mode of narrative emplotment. Speculative philosophy of history simply makes such conceptual constructs explicit; thus Croce appears in *Metahistory* as a philosopher of history despite the fact that (thinking primarily of Hegel and Marx) he denied the possibility of philosophy of history. The metahistorical level is common to both 'proper history' and philosophy of history; they are distinguished only in emphasis and explicitness (White, 1973, p.427).

White's view is unabashedly relativistic. So in fact are Munz's and Fain's, though neither makes a point of it. But both the latter envision alternative plot-lines without suggesting any way of resolving competing and incompatible claims. *Metahistory*, on the other hand, avows a limited relativism, since it recognises no more than four types of emplotment, though it specifically rejects any possibility of a rational choice among them. Of course something accounts for an historian's choice of one mode of emplotment rather than another, but what that choice expresses is both extra-historical and extra-philosophical; it represents an aesthetic or political preference, as a matter of individual taste or commitment. In practice, moreover, quite different histories can be written in each of the historiographical genres. For the linguistic tropes generate not only modes of emplotment but also metaphysical claims (corresponding to Stephen Pepper's four World Hypothe-

I

ses), explanatory strategies and political commitments; there are four of
each, uniquely associated with the four linguistic tropes as are the modes of
emplotment. But since these constrain historiographical thought without
determining it, no historian can in practice escape at least sometimes adopting an explanatory strategy or a political position appropriate to a different
fundamental trope; and in fact the struggle to deal with the consequences of
such incoherences not understood as such is what primarily evokes origi-
nality in the great historians, though it would inspire only gaps or evasions in
the less gifted. Finally, critical philosophy of history has, as I understand
Metahistory, no prospect of providing criteria which might resolve the
conflicting metahistories. How could it, when the difference among explanatory strategies is generated by and just as irresolvable as the difference
among the tropes themselves? The arguments made by critical philosophers
of history could appear in the scheme of *Metahistory* only as the rationalis-
ation of one explanatory strategy or another.

Now how do all of these stand with respect to Walsh's original distinction?
That they all converge in rejecting it is interesting but perhaps no more than
that; after all, they appear here together only because I selected them for just
that reason. They might represent nothing more than a *folie à trois*. But they
do by contrast throw into high relief a certain arbitrariness in Walsh's
distinction. Speculative philosophy of history is marked out by Walsh as
making claims about the historical process as a whole, and as providing a
moral justification of that process. None of these three views characterises
speculative philosophy of history in either of these ways; none, that is, limits
speculative philosophy of history to theodicy by definition. All of them
argue that there are inescapable continuities between 'ordinary history' and
philosophy of history characterised in some way that by Walsh's definitions
is neither critical nor speculative. What should this middle ground be called?
Fain simply calls it 'speculative philosophy of history' but that is awkward
because as Fain uses the term it excludes precisely those views which Walsh
calls 'speculative', which then would require to be renamed, no doubt to
everyone's confusion. One suspects that terminological ingenuity is not
what is wanted, if the difficulty lies in the distinction which inspires it. And
that difficulty is that since the distinction is not exhaustive it leaves almost
entirely indeterminate the middle ground of continuities between ordinary
history and philosophy of history. This middle ground is not only real but
central; it is occupied by what White calls 'a conception of the historical
field and its processes', what Fain means by 'narrative organisation', and
what Munz regards as the 'generalisations' which link events to larger events.
All of these are two-sided: they appear *in* histories as the structure of represented historical process or development, and they are also subject to
philosophical analysis and criticism as conceptual constructs. So there is a
distinction – roughly between the implicit deployment of concepts (as in
narrative emplotment) and their explicit statement and development. But
this distinction displaces the received distinction between 'critical' and

'speculative' philosophy, which, having served its purpose, may now, like so many similar distinctions, be decently interred in intellectual history.

What is at stake, it might be said, is the possibility of the conceptual impoverishment of history as an ongoing activity. Historians have often risked this by their insistence that history is not 'theoretical' and is concerned only with the particular and the 'unique'. But in fact new concepts inevitably invade historiography, not unadorned but transposed or in White's term 'displaced' into structural forms, that is into story-lines. Thus this is a necessary locus of historiographical innovation, and it is not incompatible with the professionally recognised mode of innovation, which is to put new questions to old archives or old questions to newly identified ones. As historians succeed in domesticating new concepts, even implicitly, philosophers of history will be quite happy to point out to them what they have done.

REFERENCES

Collingwood, R. G. (1946) *The Idea of History*. Oxford, Clarendon Press.

Fain, H. (1970) *Between Philosophy and History*. Princeton, Princeton University Press.

Hegel, G. W. F. (1953) *Lectures on the Philosophy of History*, English trans. by Robert S. Hartman. New York, Liberal Arts Press.

Munz, P. (1977) *The Shapes of Time*. Middletown, Connecticut, Wesleyan University Press.

Walsh, W. H. (1951) *An Introduction to Philosophy of History*. London, Hutchinson.

Walsh, W. H. (1967) Revised and retitled edition, *Philosophy of History: An Introduction*. London, Hutchinson.

White, H. (1973) *Metahistory*. Baltimore and London, The Johns Hopkins University Press.

9. Precision in History

J. L. GORMAN

'The interpretations of one historian are indignantly repudiated by another', says W. H. Walsh in his *An Introduction to Philosophy of History* (1967, p.97), 'and how to reconcile them is not apparent, since the disputes are not merely technical (over the correct interpretation of evidence), but rather depend on ultimate preconceptions which in this case are emphatically not universally shared.'

It is in this way that Walsh provides a preliminary statement of the problem of historical objectivity, a conception of the problem which directs our attention to the repudiation, by a reader, of an historical account. Such repudiation – and its converse, acceptance – are very typically emotive in character, but there remains the philosophical problem of whether repudiation or acceptance can be rationally founded.

It is usual for philosophers to attend directly to the question of the rational nature of an historical account, without any intermediate consideration of the nature of our acceptance or repudiation of it. One particular argument which has been used is that historians necessarily express themselves in vague and imprecise terms, and that, in consequence, history is necessarily a subjective matter. In this essay an argument with such a conclusion will be examined, and criticised in terms of an analysis of the reader's assessment of the statements that appear in historical accounts, in order to understand the place which precision has in what purports to be an expression of historical knowledge. Only then may we consider the dependence of historical disputes on 'ultimate preconceptions', and formulate the question of how the assessment of an historical account can be rationally founded.

I

The argument which we shall examine is taken from an article by Joel J. Kupperman (1975). We shall approach the problem with the following notion: that it is necessary, although not sufficient, for objectivity in history that historical statements be objective, and that it is necessary, although not sufficient, for an historical statement to be objective that it offer a superior description of what it describes to any alternative statement, interpreted within the same theoretical context (Gorman, 1974). The qualification 'interpreted within the same theoretical context' is added at the recommendation of Kupperman; the merit of doing so is examined later.

It is necessary for us to examine our assessment of historical examples, and we will take for this purpose those which Kupperman provides, selecting from his longer passages (1975, p.378):

1. 'Julius Caesar was assassinated by a group of men, some of whom feared the concentration of power that he represented'.
2. 'Julius Caesar was killed by a group of men, some of whom were extremely jealous of his power'.

Kupperman invites us to recognise that the first statement is superior, and that this superiority is due to the greater precision of its language. Our assessment of superiority here, however, could be quite unfounded – whether reason can be had for such an assessment is an essential part of the problem of objectivity – but Kupperman both interprets our assessment of superiority as being an assessment of precision, and also offers two factors which enter into such an assessment. These might be said to give reason for the assessment, but it is not the kind of reason which will allow for a claim to historical objectivity.

Kupperman's first factor is that the use of one word rather than another involves comparison with other matters of which the word is also used. Pointing out these similarities, even with a normally inappropriate word, gives historical enlightenment.

The second factor is that the choice of a word is often a choice of how much to say. The historian may wish to refer to the wider background of the event he is describing by using some words rather than others.

On the basis of these factors Kupperman's historian makes his choice of description; but the enlightenment this provides is short term, for once a description becomes well established, it becomes a cliché, following which any new description – making different comparisons or referring to different background material – will be superior. Historical superiority is therefore a relative matter. Scientific precision, on the other hand, which is in terms of fineness of measurement, does not raise these problems. Kupperman concludes that history is necessarily less objective than science.

The premises of this argument are all problematic. One, however, is particularly implausible. The argument depends upon our accepting that superiority of historical description lies in novelty. Thus, if we are bored with the cliché, with the old and familiar, then we shall embrace the new and unfamiliar, so that, if it is superiority in such stimulation of our interest which is at issue, then objectivity is impossible, for superiority of this kind is a subjectively relative matter. However, Kupperman gives us no reason to believe that it is this kind of superiority that is involved in our assessment of historical statements for comparative objectivity.

A statement has many features. For example, it may be an interruption, ungrammatically expressed, the twenty-fifth made in the course of the morning, ill-founded, or false. But none would suppose that superiority in terms of politeness – perhaps where one statement is an interruption and another is not – is relevant to the superiority of historical description. There are very many grounds for the superiority of one statement over another, but very few are plausibly relevant to our ordinary assessment of the superiority of historical description, quite apart from the question of whether such assessments are rationally supportable. It is extremely implausible that it is the mere *novelty* of outside comparisons and width of background referred to that exercises the reader to indignation, and is an essential feature of historical assessment.

Thus, even if we accept that the superiority, in terms of historical description, of one statement over another lies in Kupperman's two factors, we need not accept that it lies in the novelty of those factors, and we are therefore not driven to the conclusion that history is necessarily less objective than science. It remains open to a sceptic, nevertheless, to suggest other subjective grounds for determining superiority of historical description, and it would be better to avoid a succession of arguments about such possible grounds by analysing more accurately our assessment of the differences between statement 1 and statement 2.

We should note, first, one very plausible candidate for interpreting the notion of superiority of historical description. The truth of a statement is surely required for objective historical description, and may similarly be supposed to be a factor in our assessment of comparative superiority. But throughout this essay it will be assumed that the requirement of truth, itself necessary but not sufficient for historical objectivity, is met. Following Walsh, we shall suppose that, here, truth is merely a technical matter, and properly supported by evidence. Both statements 1 and 2 we then assume to be true, for the purpose of the argument, and therefore, although truth is an essential part of what we look for in our assessment, it cannot explain the superiority we judge statement 1 to have over statement 2. Nevertheless, there will be many other examples of historical description where truth is the crucial factor marking superiority.

Part of the judgment that statement 1 is superior to statement 2 lies in the judgment that the first part of statement 1 is superior to the first part of statement 2, and here we note the presence of the word 'assassinated' rather than 'killed'. 'Assassinated' has a smaller extension than 'killed', and it owes this smaller extension to the additional information about Caesar which it provides. 'X was assassinated' is equivalent to 'X was killed deliberately, in order to remove him from a position of power', and the additional information is that X was in a position of power, that the killing was deliberate, and that the former was the reason for the latter. Note that this additional information is not 'implicit' in saying that Caesar was assassinated; this is rather part of the meaning of 'assassinated', and is in a straightforward way made explicit by using this word. To judge that statement 1 is superior to statement 2 is, in part, to judge that it is better to make explicit this additional information.

Let us now consider statements 1 and 2 in a more normal context, as competitors for a place in a full-length account of the occurrence, nature, and significance of Caesar's death. We may imagine the readers of this account to be wholly ignorant of Caesar's situation. They will need to be told of his position of power. There are many ways in which they might be told this. One particularly mischievous way of doing so would be to leave the information to be provided only by using the word 'assassinated', so that *only through this word* would the ignorant reader learn of Caesar's position. There are, of course, many more reliable ways of successfully communicating this information to the ignorant reader, and these might involve slightly more expansive sentences, such as 'Caesar was in a position of power', or still more effective means, such as yet more lengthy expression, the condensed but memorable phrase, the metaphor (with its negative analogy which is properly to be ignored), and so forth.

Distinguish, therefore, a statement from the sentence which is used to make it. In spite of this distinction, it remains the case that a statement is only specifiable by means of a sentence; there is no commitment here to the existence of statements in any objectionable sense, and no more than a metaphysically superficial contrast is required for the argument. Nevertheless, a number of different sentences may be used to make the same statement, and the same sentence may be used to make different statements. A statement may be made in a number of different ways, and some of these will be more effective than others in communicating information (conceived in the form of statements, the familiar vehicle of knowledge) to readers of a certain level of knowledge and understanding.

We may agree that the additional information provided in the first part of statement 1 by the use of 'assassinated' makes that statement superior, in that part, to statement 2. But, given the distinction now drawn between sentences and statements, it by no means follows that *sentence* 1 is superior to *sentence* 2. Our judgment that statement 1 is superior is only a judgment that the additional information ought to be made explicit somehow, and is not an endorsement of the superiority of a particular sentence. The *sentence* 'Caesar was assassinated . . .' may well not be the best way of making the *statement* that Caesar was assassinated . . .; indeed, we have seen that such a sentence would be a particularly ineffective way of communicating the statement to an ignorant reader.

Our present concern is to analyse the superiority of historical description, conceived as a problem of objectivity. We have seen that superiority lies, at least in part, in the provision of information, in the statements that the historian makes. We have noted that these statements may be made by many different sentences, and it follows that these different sentences, in that they express the same statement, will *all be equivalent in cognitive content*. Given this cognitive equivalence, it follows that there is no cognitive problem, no problem for historical objectivity, in deciding which sentence to use to make the statement at issue. The historian's problem of choice of language, then, involves two decisions: first, about which statements ought to be made; and secondly, about how these statements are most effectively to be communicated to a given readership by means of written sentences. The former is an epistemological problem; the latter is not.

Kupperman, in recognising the superiority of statement 1 over statement 2, has sought to ground objectivity in the precision of its language. There is, certainly, a sense of 'precision' in which 'assassinated' may properly be described as more precise than 'killed', and such precision derives from the smaller extension of 'assassinated', an extension which is limited by the additional information which 'assassinated' involves. But we have now seen that the use of the word 'assassinated' is only one of many ways in which this additional information may be communicated, and it follows that the use of word-precision is only one of many ways, only one of many rhetorical devices, which are available to the historian to make given information explicit. It is not, in itself, a cognitively superior mode of expression, and we have seen that it would be a mistake to rely on precision to impart information.

In a *properly written* full account, therefore, the additional precision which 'assassinated' has over 'killed' is cognitively redundant, since it merely repeats information which is made more effectively explicit elsewhere. From a rhetorical or literary standpoint, 'assassinated' merely serves as a reminder of that information, as a signal that it is about to be given, or something similar. If word-precision is doing any cognitive work in an account, then it is likely that there will be something rhetorically wrong with the account, for it is probable that only great concentration from the reader will enable him to grasp what is being said.

There is, however, another sense of 'precision' which is of greater epistemological importance. We will often describe an account which contains certain additional information as a more precise *account* than another; although it is the presence of the additional information alone which makes it so, and we will be unable to identify any particular *word* or *sentence* as necessarily contributing, through its 'precision' in the first sense, to the precision of the account. Used of individual words, 'precision' has to do only with the economy of expression; as a ground of assessment of historical description, on the other hand, 'precision' has to do with what information is made explicit. How this latter information is made explicit is a literary problem of communication, which may or may not be solved by the precision of language.

'Precision', therefore, in its second, epistemologically important, sense, involves the giving of a greater amount of information about the matter described. On this analysis, we will find that precision is interpreted in a way which permits one account to be more precise than another. We will also find that the notion of 'greatest' precision is not available to us, for it is always possible to find additional information about the matter described.

Thus the superiority of one historical statement over another has been analysed, in part, in terms of the provision of information. Kupperman's two factors may similarly be understood as problems of what information ought to be supplied; they are not, it should now be clear, factors which have anything essentially to do with the precision of words. Subjective grounds were suggested as determining his two factors, and the sceptic may similarly be imagined to suggest subjective grounds as determining all selection of information. But it is not the case that just any true information will do, the provision of which will make a statement superior to statement 2, for example. 'Caesar was killed and grass is green' is not superior to 'Caesar was killed', so far as historical description is concerned. Superiority cannot lie in the mere maximising of information, even information about the matter in hand: we would never allow that the longest historical accounts are the most objective. Greater and greater precision (in the second, epistemologically important, sense) is not required; we recognise well enough what information ought to be included, and clearly it is the maximising of *relevant* information which is at issue here. Our judgment that it is better to make explicit the additional information which 'assassinated' includes involves a judgment that this information is relevant, as well as true, and it presupposes that an assessment of the relevance of the information which is, or might be, supplied is a necessary part of our assessment of an historical account, a part which must have rational support if the account is to be objective.

II

Analysis of the superiority of the first part of statement 1 over the first part of statement 2 is only part of the problem. We shall next examine the last parts of the two statements. 1 has 'some of whom feared the concentration of power that he represented', and 2 has 'some of whom were extremely jealous of his power'.

It is not the case that these are merely different ways of saying the same thing. Each sentence is used to make a different statement. These statements are not incompatible: perhaps some of the group feared Caesar's power, while others were merely jealous; perhaps all of the group both feared his power and were jealous. It would be necessary to make clear exactly what is meant, and assess the alternatives for truth. Where one is false, naturally the other will be superior.

Where both are true, however, the problem becomes more difficult. The juxtaposition of the first and last parts of the statements 1 and 2 is only an appropriate way of expressing the information they contain if we suppose that the fear or jealousy they mention is offered as part of the explanation of the killing of Caesar. The superiority of the one statement over the other, in their latter parts, would then depend on the relevance of what is mentioned to a successful explanation. We are not in a position to judge which, if not both, emotion is more relevantly a part of the explanation; both seem equally credible. On our present understanding of the matter, both might be relevant, and both ought then to be included in a full account, and thus we need not judge either of statements 1 and 2 to be superior to the other in this respect. Nevertheless, if we do decide between them, our assessment will be on the bases that the analysis has already disclosed, those of truth and relevance.

III

Our examples of historical description have now been exhaustively analysed, and it has been argued that the superiority which we judge one to have over the other lies in its expressing a superior selection of relevant and true information. In general, such superiority requires superiority in truth and relevance, and word-precision is not involved. While the imprecision or vagueness of a word may lead to doubt about whether it is truly applicable to some subject-matter, there will always be another way of making a true statement about that subject-matter. Even if all words are vague, this remains the case. Such vagueness, by appropriate re-expression, may easily be relegated to an irrelevant area of discourse. We are merely being intransigent if we insist on an 'objective' answer to the question whether Napoleon was really short or just middle-sized, for example. Stipulative definition and the introduction of technical terms are nevertheless available as a last resort, although it may be noted that historians, by their usual modes of discourse, plainly find ordinary language precise enough.

Consider, however, a problem of choice of description which is not so easily understood in terms of precision, and which may lead, in a more familiar way, to that indignant rejection which Walsh notes: whether to describe an individual as a labourer or as a member of the proletariat. If the problem were merely whether to describe him as a labourer or as an agricultural labourer, then, given that we accept that both descriptions are true, our assessment of the superiority of one over the other will be an assessment of whether the additional information given by the precision of the second description is relevant information to give. However, relevance cannot be the foundation for our choice between the 'labourer' and 'member of the proletariat' descriptions, for the following reasons.

'Relevance' is not a property of statements considered without reference to context, but a *relational* property: statements are relevant or irrelevant to some account. It is necessary, when assessing a statement for relevance, to know what it is supposed to be relevant to. The account in question is often obvious, but even with statements 1 and 2 it was necessary to provide some outline specification. Statements do not carry with them a fixed relevance-value, like a truth-value, regardless of where they appear. A statement will sometimes be relevant, and sometimes not.

'Labourer' and 'member of the proletariat' have different connotations, and thus to use one rather than another is to make explicit one set of information rather than another set, although the sets overlap. We could in principle specify some account, and ask which of the two descriptions is superior in relevance to it. If the account were a Marxist one, then the latter description would probably be more relevant than the former; if it were non-Marxist, then the reverse would be the case. But this easy result obscures the point of our assessment for relative superiority of these two descriptions, for it suggests that we might find one description inferior to the other on the ground that it is only relevant to accounts antecedently regarded as unacceptable. Thus it implies that a rejection of the 'proletariat' description, say, is on the ground that it is relevant only to accounts which are Marxist in character and unacceptable for that reason. Such a rejection requires the latter assessment, that Marxist accounts are rejected; but part of the unacceptability of a Marxist account (given this judgment) lies in the presence of statements expressed in such unacceptable terminology as the 'proletariat' description involves. The same problem of superiority of description would arise again here, while the requirement of relevance would *ex hypothesi* have been met. Thus the suggested interpretation of our assessment is circular and ineffective. The indignant rejection of the 'proletariat' description is not an assessment that it is irrelevant.

Rather, it is clear that judgments as to which description is superior do differ to emotional extremes, and are made without qualification; they are not contingent on any particular account. Since such judgments are not relative to any particular account, they cannot be based on an assessment of relevance, for relevance is relative to a particular account. It follows that no criterion of relevance can decide between the two descriptions.

It is next necessary to consider whether our assessment of the superiority of one of the two descriptions is an assessment of its truth. It is certainly possible that we can assess them for truth, but it is not what is involved here. Thus we simply have no reason to suppose it false that our individual is a member of the proletariat, and, on the contrary, much of the evidence had for supporting the belief that he is a labourer will also support the belief that he is a member of the proletariat. Terms like 'proletariat' are commonly introduced in such a way that they bear relations of necessity or sufficiency to terms like 'labourer'. Thus the inferior description here is not being judged so on the ground of its falsity.

It may be said that the use of certain terminology 'commits' the speaker to a certain theory, and that we may understand the supposed rejection of the 'proletariat' description in terms of the rejection of the theory of a Marxist kind which is thus 'involved' in the use of this term. 'Commitment', to play such an important part in the problem of objectivity, will need to be explicated. It is not a logical commitment; there is no inconsistency in describing a person as a member of the proletariat while holding Marx's theory of history to be false. It might be argued, however, that the commitment can be regarded as a conversational implicature (Grice, 1975), where certain features of what is said in a certain context enable information to be communicated which is not logically or conventionally stated or implied. A familiar example from the literature (Grice, 1961) is of a tutor writing a reference for a student. The tutor writes 'Jones has beautiful handwriting and his English is grammatical', and the reader of this will naturally infer that Jones is appalling at philosophy, although this is neither stated nor logically implied.

Supposing that the notion of a conversational implicature can be sufficiently explicated to enable us to show how the use of 'proletariat' commits the speaker to a specific theory – a most ambitious task, one perhaps too implausible to undertake – it will still remain to be shown what kind of assessment is involved in the rejection of the theory to which we are committed by such a use. Such a theory may be held false; but we recognise in the philosophy of science that falsifications, at most, are only of the current articulation of a theory, and that there will be attempts, which may be well founded, to re-articulate the theory to avoid these falsifications. Such re-articulation may be no more than an unfounded *ad hoc* device; but it could equally be a quite rational development of the theory.

A theory is more than merely a set of statements held true; at least a part of what is additionally involved is a conceptual scheme, a means of classifying the world so that theory can express judgments about it. The rejection of Marxist theory will involve rejecting such a classificatory scheme; it will involve rejecting the idea of providing a pigeonhole labelled 'proletariat' into which some people are placed, so that either true or false statements may be made about them. It follows that 'commitment to an unacceptable theory' involves a prior assessment of the acceptability of a conceptual scheme of classification, a scheme represented in words like 'proletariat'. Thus the suggested interpretation of our assessment is circular and ineffective.

It should be noted that the use of the *word* 'proletariat' is only one of many ways of expressing a particular classification. In accordance with an earlier result of this essay, which word is used has to do with which *sentence* is used to express the statement at issue. A statement may be rejected on the ground of the conceptual scheme involved even though the set of sentences used to make that statement contains no *obviously* 'theory-laden' words like 'proletariat' at all.

In our assessment of the superiority of one historical statement over another, therefore, we look for truth, relevance, and the involvement of an acceptable conceptual scheme of classification. The two decisions which the historian has to make involve, first, the making of statements; here the decision is constrained by whatever rational limits there may be to the claims to truth, relevance to the particular account being written, and the acceptability of a conceptual scheme of classification. Secondly, the historian must choose appropriate sentences to make these statements to a given readership; here the decision is constrained by literary and rhetorical limits on the effectiveness of communication.

IV

This argument began with the assumption that it is necessary for an historical statement to be objective that it offer a superior description of what it describes to any alternative statement, interpreted within the same theoretical context. What is involved in the superiority of historical description has now been analysed, and shown to consist of superiority in terms of truth, relevance, and the conceptual scheme of classification. It is next necessary to examine Kupperman's added qualification, 'interpreted within the same theoretical context', included in the condition for objectivity.

This qualification was introduced in order to avoid a possible objection deriving from the work of P. K. Feyerabend. Feyerabend holds that a scientific theory is an entire world view, such that experience itself, instead of acting as a check on such a theory, is rather understood, conceptualised, and expressed in accordance with it. So understood, a description of experience cannot be regarded as just a copy of experience, a copy of a fact in the world, for different descriptions will be appropriate, depending on the theory that is held.

Added to this philosophy of science is a philosophy of meaning, involving the claim that the meanings of the terms used in descriptions of the world are provided by the theory, so that no vocabulary (apart, possibly, from logical constants) is shared by two different theories. The theories are then incommensurable, that is, neither has any logical relations whatever with the other. Since the world is conceptualised differently for each, the theories share neither sense nor reference, and it is concluded that it is impossible to find a sense in which two speakers from different theoretical backgrounds can be making statements about the same world at all. Such ultimate preconceptions are 'emphatically not universally shared' (Walsh, 1967, p.97).

We are looking for a way of determining which of two statements is superior. But we can only compare them for superiority if they are about the same thing, if they share the same world. They only do this, however, if they share the same theoretical context, and this is the reason for Kupperman's qualification. Note that this is not a reason for holding history to be less objective than science, for the same problem arises for both.

Kupperman has, however, used this argument of Feyerabend's in an inappropriate way. If this argument is correct, then the expression 'interpreted within the same theoretical context' in the condition for objectivity is redundant, for that condition is limited to the superiority of one statement over another in describing *what they do*, and since they can only share the same object of description if they are already within the same theoretical context, the qualification is unnecessary. We may then reduce the condition to just this: that it is necessary for an historical statement to be objective that it offer a superior description of what it describes to any alternative.

Feyerabend's argument then reappears in the difficulty of whether and when we have *alternative* descriptions of the *same* matter. If this argument permits such alternatives, then objectivity requires that one be superior to all the others; but, since all are expressed within the same theoretical context (since they share the same object of description), there is nothing further in Feyerabend's argument to prevent such objectivity. On the other hand, if Feyerabend's argument does not permit alternatives, then the statement assessed is self-evidently the only suitable description of what it describes, and therefore absolutely superior, and we can hardly deny objectivity to it.

Neither horn of this dilemma permits Feyerabend's objection to affect the issue, and this is because the question of the relativity of reality to theory is begged by the expression 'of what it describes' in the condition for objectivity. If Feyerabend is right, then we are not entitled to assess the superiority of description by reference to what is described. Rather, superiority lies with the 'theoretical context' itself, and we will need to determine what a 'theoretical context' in history is. Perhaps each statement is its own theoretical context; or each account; or each 'philosophy of history'.

The most natural interpretation of Feyerabend's position here would require us to hold that each conceptual scheme of classification, of a kind already exemplified – Marxism, say – is itself a 'theoretical context'. But it is in the choice of and clash between such alternative approaches that the issues of objectivity in history become so acute. How to reconcile, or decide between, such differing interpretations may not be apparent, but it is crucial that we be able to ask which of two such theoretical contexts is superior. By including Kupperman's qualification in the condition for objectivity such a question is ruled out *ab initio*. It may be that Feyerabend's position should be taken seriously, but to admit this is not to say that we should give him his conclusion, and define objectivity in terms of it.

For good reason, then, we should hold only that objectivity requires that a statement offer a superior description of what it describes to any alternative. Supporting a claim to objectivity will then require rationally supporting the claim that the statement at issue is superior in terms of (as now shown) truth, relevance, and the conceptual scheme of classification. Feyerabend's problem will then re-appear in the question whether the latter claim can be made good, whether superiority in these three ways can be rationally assessed as such.

V

The claim that objectivity requires that a statement be superior to 'any' alternative is unclear. The requirement may be for superiority over all *possible* alternatives, or only over those alternatives *actually* available. The former requirement would be for certainty, while the latter would be for a rational, although revisable, acceptance. The issue is between a 'justificationist' and a 'fallibilist' approach (Popper, 1969, p.228).

Justificationism in science seems to require something which is logically impossible, the valid deduction of a general statement from a finite number of singular statements. By introducing a fallibilist notion, Popper was able to argue for the rational acceptability of scientific laws, even though deductive certainty was not available. Scientific theories, while they may be well founded, can be at best no more than provisional.

Historical statements are typically singular in form, and not general. There is no logical difficulty in their being the conclusions of valid deductive arguments, the premises of which are a finite number of singular statements. Whatever place there is for science in history, whatever difficulties there may be in the evidential support for historical statements, there is no obvious analogy for the problem of induction. There is no *prima facie* reason to reject justificationism, and thus no need to introduce a fallibilist approach.

It may well be that further work on the nature of the support for historical statements will require the introduction of a fallibilist approach, if problems of appropriate logical difficulty are disclosed. But such problems will not be disclosed at all unless we adopt, initially, a justificationist approach; unless we strive, with Descartes, for certainty. The initial adoption of a fallibilist approach may set us a goal which is too easily reached, and we might never know what more might have been achieved. The value of the argument requires that we accept the strong, justificationist, position: that superiority of description be over any *possible* alternative. The condition for objectivity should be understood in this sense.

VI

Objectivity, therefore, requires that an historical statement offer a superior description of what it describes to any alternative. Analysis of our assessment of such superiority has shown that, in a typical case, we assess truth, relevance, and the conceptual scheme of classification. *All three*, and not just truth (as many analytical philosophers would claim), are essentially involved in an expression of historical knowledge; all three must be rationally supported if a claim to historical knowledge is to be made out. Nothing at this stage of the argument prevents this requirement for objectivity from being met, nor suggests that it can be met.

The argument further shows a solution to the perennial problem of the relationship between history and literature. However the three cognitive elements are supported, there remains the separate problem of how to communicate these matters. Statements must be expressed in sentences, and so history necessarily involves literary or rhetorical elements. There will be many ways of communicating information, and how well it is done is important, for historical knowledge is worthless unless intelligible and communicable. There are literary and aesthetic standards; history is welcome if it can be great literature.

But literary grounds of assessment do not affect the cognitive content of historical accounts. It is a mistake to suppose that criteria for rhetoric prevent *a priori* the possibility of rational standards for truth, relevance, and the conceptual scheme of classification. There is no reason why objectivity and literature should not be easy bedfellows.

REFERENCES

Gorman, J. L. (1974) Objectivity and truth in history, *Inquiry* 17, 373–97.

Grice, H. P. (1961) The causal theory of perception, *Aris. Soc. Supp. Vol.*35, 121–52.

Grice, H. P. (1975) Logic and conversation. In Cole, Peter and Morgan, Jerry L. (eds.) *Syntax and Semantics*, vol.3 *Speech Acts*. New York, San Francisco, London, Academic Press.

Kupperman, J. J. (1975) Precision in history, *Mind* 84, 374–89.

Popper, K. R. (1969) *Conjectures and Refutations: The Growth of Scientific Knowledge*, 3rd ed. (revised). London, Routledge and Kegan Paul.

Walsh, W. H. (1967) *An Introduction to Philosophy of History*, 3rd ed. (revised). London, Hutchinson.

10. Historian Malgré Moi

J.R.LUCAS

'Which I don't believe ever actually happened.' I was in Edinburgh, planning our next series of Gifford Lectures on the Development of Mind. We were talking of the evolution of language, whether man, as a communicating animal – λογιστικόν ξῷου – was basically an ape, garbed in linguistic customs, or had some special angelic aspect to his nature. There had been some reference to the legendary encounter between T. H. Huxley and Samuel Wilberforce, Bishop of Oxford, at the meeting of the British Association in Oxford on Saturday, 30 June 1860, in which Huxley was supposed to have wiped the floor with Wilberforce, and established once for all the supremacy of science over religion. And then I heard myself adding the rider, that, apparently, I did not believe it ever actually happened. The conversation flowed on. But my own *obiter dictum* stuck in my mind, and later I began to wonder about what I had said, whether it was true, why I had come to hold a belief about it. When the Giffords were out of the way, I tried to resolve the matter by looking up contemporary records and seeing exactly what Wilberforce and Huxley had said. But there were no full contemporary records, only partial or much later accounts. The most authoritative of modern writers, Owen Chadwick, gave guarded support to my feeling that the received account was unreliable, but many sorties to the Bodleian between tutorials failed to reveal what actually happened. The problem caught hold of me. The more I went into it, the more I realised that whatever had happened, it was not as was generally believed. In the end I wrote up the results of my inquiries, read it to a society in Oxford, and, after much rewriting, published it in the *Historical Journal*, seven years after the original conversation.

I learnt many lessons from my foray into history, and it is worth dwelling on them, partly because, being an issue in the history of ideas it raises questions of intellectual rather than practical or moral values, and makes it that much easier for the philosopher to see the interplay between values and historiography, and partly because philosophers thinking about the nature of history tend to think of it as consumers rather than producers (Dray, 1980, p.4). And the fact that I was not a professional historian made me more aware of the special perspectives of the producers' point of view. The producer has an axe – many axes – to grind. Only if he is very anxious to achieve something will he go to the labour of reading original sources, ferretting out the facts, drafting and redrafting his text, checking references and correcting

K

proofs, and as he hones down each paragraph, he will become increasingly aware of the different, and often conflicting, ends he has in view. I wanted to tell a story, the story of what happened in the University Museum one summer Saturday, 120 years ago. But I did not just want to tell a story: I wanted to set the record straight. I came to the conclusion that Wilberforce had been unfairly treated by the popular account, and I wanted to vindicate him. But simply to show that Wilberforce had not said exactly the words attributed to him and had not been trounced by Huxley would have been an incomplete exercise. To understand the words used by each, it was necessary both to set them in context and to evaluate them with the benefit of hindsight: Huxley's attack on Wilberforce appeared in a very different light when it emerged that he had been making a number of polemical interventions throughout the meeting of the British Association in 1860, and that in the previous April he had published in the *Westminster Review* a very similar attack on Darwin's critics generally; more important was to try and see the real issues in the debate – what exactly were Wilberforce's criticisms of Darwin? How did Huxley seek to counter them? – And to decide how cogent the points on either side were. This was an exercise not of history but of biology, and one on which there has been much work in our own time. In order to reach a fair judgment on the arguments adduced in 1860, it was necessary to consider the subsequent development of Darwinism. Only in the 1940s had the science of genetics been worked out fully enough to yield a theory of gene drift; only in the 1940s could Wilberforce's criticisms of Darwin's theory be adequately countered. The standpoint from which his arguments should be viewed is not a simple historical one. And, finally, even if I could arrive at a fair assessment of the debate, I should still have a further problem of explaining why the false one had taken root and flourished: the received account of what had happened on 30 June 1860 was, in point of historical fact, false: but that it was the received account was in itself an indubitable historical fact, and one which needed understanding and which in turn revealed something important about the way men thought.

Part of my concern was to discover what actually was said. It was an aim that is, untypically in history, completely attainable. There might have been a short-hand writer making a full transcript – as it happened there were two journalists present – or, more modernly, there could be an undoctored tape-recording. In this, speech differs from action generally. We cannot in principle have a complete picture of, say, the battle of Leipzig, because there are indefinitely many points of view, and even if we imagine a television camera at every position and pointing in every direction, we should, in selecting from the infinite quantity of video-tape, be leaving something out. A conversation or debate, by contrast, has only one focus. The sequence of words actually uttered is definite and central. And although on occasion we might seek for further, non-verbal, information – was Wilberforce smiling insolently when he turned to put his question to Huxley? – we could, with only a few supplementary pictures, obtain all the additional information we require. In principle we could have a complete account of the debate, as complete as that given by Hansard or the portrayal on television of the enthronement of the Archbishop of Canterbury. It may not in practice be possible to achieve an absolute accuracy and absolutely complete account, because of the inadequacy of the records, but it is something to be aimed at. I could intelligibly hope to produce, as an end result of my labours, a three-hour television programme, showing exactly what happened, no more and no less.

Debates and conversations are untypical, because they are almost entirely constituted by words, and words are already interpreted into definite discrete units. Since the facts to which our account must correspond are themselves already interpreted, one standard objection to the correspondence theory of truth is obviated (Walsh, 1951, p.76). Others however remain, both epistemological and hermeneutic. Although in the case of verbal activities our knowledge is not necessarily inadequate, in practice it often is, and the reconstruction of what actually was said is open to the same doubts and difficulties as cloud the discovery of other things men do. The evidence of witnesses is partial. Neither of the two journalists present recorded the interchange between Wilberforce and Huxley at all – itself a significant fact (*Jackson's Oxford Journal* 1860; *The Athenaeum*, 1860). One of the chief witnesses – Hooker – changed his story, and at the end of the century gave all the credit to Huxley whereas he had said, writing to Darwin the day after the debate, that Huxley had been ineffective and it fell to him, Hooker, to stand up for Darwin's theory (Huxley, 1918, pp.525–7). One source of great importance was the review Wilberforce had written of *The Origin of Species* a few weeks earlier (Wilberforce, S., 1860 pp. 225-64). It clearly formed the basis of his speech, and one contemporary said there was nothing in the speech that was not in the review (Tuckwell, 1900, p.51; Huxley, 1918, p.526), but even so there must have been some compression and there may have been a significant change of emphasis. These are real problems, but not insuperable ones, nor ones peculiar to history. A court of law can decide whether, beyond reasonable doubt, the accused committed a crime. A geologist can conclude that the Isle of Wight once joined on the Isle of Purbeck, or that South America, Antartica and Australia were once part of the same continent. In each case the conclusion is not open to direct inspection or any other form of independent verification, and in each case the inference is not deductively necessary. There is room for philosophical doubt. But although sceptical arguments can be brought forward, they can also be countered, and history is in no worse case than other disciplines. What is important for the writer of history is the balance between argument and conclusion. I could not simply tell the story of what happened: I had all the time to be arguing for my version rather than the received account or other, *prima facie* plausible, ones. In a court of law the forensic purpose is dominant. There is only one question at issue – 'Did the accused undoubtedly commit the crime?' But history is seldom concerned with just one fact. I needed not only to argue for my version but also to relate it, and was constantly finding the one enterprise obstructing the execution of the other. Writing history, I found, was much more difficult than writing philosophy, where argument and exposition seem more readily to blend. The available facts were too gritty, too unevenly spaced to be harmonised with the flow of the narrative while at the same time bearing their share of evidential support. Geologists, I have noticed, have, with a few, shining exceptions, similar difficulty in combining clear exposition with effective argumentation. More praise to those historians who succeed in being clear and cogent at the same time.

A verdict is not a simple finding of fact; it is a finding of fact relevant to some system of law or rules. We are interested in establishing whether the accused actually did what he is said to have done, because if he did, he broke the law and is liable to punishment. What happened in the University Museum on 30 June 1860 was important not simply as a chunk of the past, but because it was construed as a decisive confrontation between science and religion. Darwin's theory of evolution had attracted a lot of attention, but had not yet won the support of the scientific community at large. The meeting of the British Association provided an occasion for scientists, professional and amateur alike, to debate the merits of the new theory, and for some, notably Hooker and Lubbock, to avow their adherence; but the majority remained unconvinced. As a debate within science, it was significant but not decisive. It revealed the main lines of dispute, and the arguments on either side, but it settled nothing. Victory went to the Darwinians only gradually over the next twenty years as more and more geological evidence came to light, and showed that, whatever difficulties there remained in explaining exactly how genetic differences arose and were disseminated, species had, in point of fact, evolved in the course of geological time.

In his review of *The Origin of Species*, Wilberforce was at pains to allow that Darwin's theory could be true, and that, if sufficient evidence for it were forthcoming, man would have to pocket his pride and acknowledge his kinship with the mushrooms. But sufficient evidence had not been produced as yet, and there were a number of considerations that counted against. Over the whole course of human history species had been immutable, in spite of intense selective breeding of domestic animals; and even where, as with pigeons and horses, different breeds within the species had been developed, they still were members of the same species, and rapidly reverted to type when allowed to run wild. Again, members of different species could not produce fertile offspring, from which it followed that identity of species was a hereditary property, and it was logically impossible for non-human ancestors to have human descendants. None of these were negligible arguments. Even the last, which gave Huxley the occasion for his sally at the British Association meeting, was put to me with great vigour by J. H. Woodger, on the way back from church at a Logic conference in Manchester in 1960, and, under a different guise, has been the subject of many articles in recent years (e.g., Dummett, 1975; Wright, 1975). Darwin acknowledged the force of Wilberforce's criticisms, and as soon as his health allowed, set to work on dogs, in order to meet them.

To give a true verdict on the scientific merits of Wilberforce's criticisms, it was necessary to delve into the intricacies of Darwinian theory, and to raise fundamental issues in the philosophy of science. It was of crucial importance that Darwinian theory was not a simple static theory, which was either true or false, and, as it turned out, true, but a complex interweaving of observation, hypothesis and explanations at different levels, which was itself evolving to accommodate fresh evidence and meet fresh criticisms. In one aspect evolution was a putative fact, inadequately established in 1860, on account, as Darwin reasonably pointed out, of the extreme imperfection of the geological record, but later established beyond reasonable doubt. In another aspect – the one that appealed to Hooker – evolution was an organising idea, a paradigm, enabling biologists to impose a coherent pattern on their subject matter. The most original aspect was Darwin's scheme of explanation, 'the survival of the fittest'. It had intuitive explanatory appeal, and accounted for many of the phenomena Darwin had observed; but it did not explain in detail the transmission of inherited *traits* from parent to offspring, it did not account for the origin of variation, and appeared to be incompatible with the observed stability of species. Modern Darwinians can give explanations in terms of genetic theory which allow for the origin of mutations, account for the survival of genes that, in the gene complex prevailing in the population, are favourable and explain the sterility of hybrids and reversion to type. But these are twentieth-century refinements. In 1860 Mendel's theory of genes lay far beyond the horizon. The criticisms of Wilberforce, Owen and the majority of professional biologists were both cogent, and at the time unanswerable. Wilberforce's criticisms of Evolution should be likened to those made of quantum theory seventy years later by Einstein. Although Einstein could not bring himself to believe that God plays dice, most physicists now can and do believe just this. Although the conceptual difficulties in quantum mechanics exposed by the Einstein – Podolski – Rosen argument have not been satisfactorily resolved, most physicists are convinced by the success of quantum mechanics in explaining and predicting observations that it is substantially true, and take it on trust from their mathematical colleagues that there is no possibility of embedding it, by means of hidden variables, in a deterministic framework. It is still largely a matter of trust, as it was for biologists between 1880 and 1940. There is enough going for either theory to enable it to surmount formidable difficulties. Although they could not explain why favourable changes were not diluted out of existence, or why species were genetically stable, biologists at the end of the nineteenth and the beginning of the twentieth centuries were sure that explanations would one day be found, much as physicists today believe that a satisfactory conceptual framework for quantum mechanics will one day be developed in which the difficulties raised by Einstein,

Podolski and Rosen will be satisfactorily resolved or effectively dissolved. In the mean time they are prepared to wear the difficulties on account of the other great merits of the theory.

Wilberforce and Huxley were both confused about the philosophy of science. So are we. Like them we have a moderately good idea of the empirical tests a good theory should be able to pass, but an inadequate grasp of the conceptual requirements it should satisfy. Darwin's theory was explanatory at one level, not at another. Quantum theory explains many phenomena, but cannot as yet give a coherent account of the objective properties corresponding to non-commuting operators. What the different conceptual requirements are, and how much weight should be given them, is still unclear. Darwin's account of the origin of species could be regarded as a simple empirical hypothesis, and as such was in due course established as a fact; but its chief appeal was as an organising idea, which was open, like the indeterminism of quantum mechanics, to deep theoretical objections. It could also be considered at a number of intermediate levels, each with its own advantages and difficulties. The records show that these points were touched on at the meeting of the British Association but not, so far as we can see, that they were dealt with adequately. But then an adequate treatment of the philosophy of biological science has yet to be given.

The verdicts on the performances of Wilberforce and Huxley were in each case Not Bad. The arguments they put forward were relevant and weighty. They sometimes were arguing at cross-purposes, but most of what they said was to the point. Huxley was too polemical and failed to hold his audience, Wilberforce failed to appreciate the different conceptual aspects of the theory of evolution, and put too much weight on the *Sorites* argument. But in the intellectual situation of their time, they both performed well, each contributing usefully to the informed discussion of Darwin's theory. Modern historians have failed to appreciate this because they have insufficiently understood the theory of evolution. They have unwittingly assumed that because Wilberforce criticised Darwin and we are all Darwinians now, therefore Wilberforce was Wrong. They have not seen that the evolutionary theory we now believe to be true has evolved a long way from the evolutionary theory Wilberforce criticised, or that the criticisms he put forward have been influential in the subsequent refinement of Darwinian thought. In judging what was done in 1860 they have unconsciously assumed a post-1880 standpoint, and a somewhat *simpliste* one at that. Many philosophers of history condemn the 'Whig Interpretation of History', and say that we should not judge one age from the standpoint of our own. The example of Wilberforce shows both the strength and the limitations of this critique. The Whig Interpretation of History sees the history of ideas, like that of political institutions, as a steady progression leading up to the present, and judges them according to the contribution they appear to have made to our present position. Against this, it is entirely right to insist that in judging what was done in 1860 we must remember that it was done in 1860. In 1860 the geological evidence for evolution was thin. More evidence might emerge and might prove conclusive, as Wilberforce acknowledged, but it was quite reasonable to be sceptical then, whereas it became increasingly unreasonable later on. In 1860 Dalton's atomic theory carried with it the doctrine of the immutability of elements: the immutability of biological species was not only supported by strong empirical evidence but was in tune with the background assumptions of physical science. A decade later Mendeléef discovered family resemblances between different elements and produced his periodic table, but the doctrine of immutability remained; I remember in the chemistry textbooks of my youth the transmutation of elements being held up as one of the absurd ideas of the mediaeval alchemists. Wilberforce in 1860 was being quite reasonable, whereas the same points made at the end of the century would indeed be obscurantist. To this extent the Whig Interpretation of History is, indeed, wrong. But the conclusions drawn by its critics have often been either that historians should eschew value judgments altogether or that each age should be judged entirely by its own lights. Both are wrong. A value-free account of the meeting of the British Association would have been incomplete. It might show that Wilberforce and Huxley had not uttered the words attributed to them, but even to decide whether Wilberforce was being flippant or Huxley rude would involve some judgment of value, and to decide whether Wilberforce was putting forward good arguments or bad is an essentially evaluative exercise. Value-free history is defective, because history is about the actions of agents, who, in deciding what to do, are judging what had best be done in their situation as they see it. Wilberforce was criticising Darwin's theory, and putting forward what he took to be cogent objections to it. No account which avoids the concept of cogency can be adequate. And equally in the wider field of non-intellectual activities, value-free accounts are inherently inadequate.

The alternative conclusion – that each age should be judged entirely by its own lights – is more tempting. But I found I could not understand the 1860 debate solely in 1860 terms. Although the Whig judgment was too *simpliste*, I found I needed to master modern thinking on evolution in order to evaluate, to understand, even to notice, the points being made by either side. Arguments were being canvassed, and in order to judge arguments it is necessary to decide whether they are cogent or not, and cogency is a timeless property. Only by considering the fully worked out theory could I assess the cogency of various arguments for and against. Wilberforce's contention that the available geological evidence was insufficient to ground a Baconian induction was cogent, but was reasonably countered by Darwin's point that a great deal of the geological evidence had perished anyway. Wilberforce's argument that no known species had changed during the course of recorded history was cogent, but was reasonably countered by the immense time scale posited by Darwin. Wilberforce's point about regression to type was cogent, and exposed a major weakness in early Darwinism, whose significance can only be appreciated in the light of the theory subsequently developed to meet it. It might seem as though I was being also a Whig, only judging from the standpoint of the 1940s instead of the 1880s, but what I was really doing was to judge the cogency of the arguments from the timeless standpoint of the fully developed theory, which, as it happened, was only available in the 1940s. If, as I believe, the main lines of the theory of evolution are now fully worked out, there will be no significant alteration in the assessment of Wilberforce's scientific arguments. On more general issues of the philosophy of science we have not yet reached a state of final clarity, and are correspondingly less able to appreciate the points made on either side.

The Whigs, then, were right to believe that historians should make value judgments, and should make the best value judgments they could, which inevitably would incorporate all the insights available to them in their own time. Where they erred was in thinking that their own age was necessarily right, and earlier ages correspondingly wrong. To reach a just understanding we need to remember both that Wilberforce and Huxley were arguing in 1860, when many relevant facts and considerations had not yet come to light, and that our timeless judgment on the cogency of their arguments, although believed by us to be correct, could turn out to be wrong. Although I think the main lines of the theory of evolution have been established beyond reasonable doubt, I could be mistaken, and if so my judgment will be as wrong as that of the late Victorians. I am not passing a definitive 1970s judgment but attempting a judgment *sub specie aeternitatis* on the intellectual merits of the arguments; only, being myself a time-bound creature, I cannot actually take up a timeless stand-point, and my time-bound judgments always may fail to achieve timeless validity.

The case with practical and moral judgments is the same. We must remember that people in the past lived in different situations, factual, social, intellectual, emotional and moral, and must see the situation in which they acted as they saw it, and not simply as we would. But having appreciated their situation as they saw it, we must assess their response to it as best we can, and say whether it was reasonable, prudent, honest, fair, just, meaningful or generous. These are the common concepts of human action, concepts which people in the past applied, and concepts which we must be prepared to apply ourselves if we are to share a common humanity with them and if we are to make sense of their actions. To take Collingwood's example of Caesar crossing the Rubicon (Collingwood, 1946, pp.213–16) we must attempt to enter into Caesar's situation *vis à vis* the senate, and see the situation as he saw it. But in doing this we cannot help but ask whether it was legal, prudent, reasonable or moral for a general in that position to defy the legally constituted authority of the state. We may not be able to answer the question – people in past ages were as often ambivalent as we are ourselves – but we cannot disallow it, any more than we can disallow questions on the cogency of the arguments adduced in 1860, without disengaging from the human activity in question, and regarding it no longer as human activity, but only as hominid behaviour.

Having reconstructed, as far as I could, what actually had happened, having overturned a false judgment and replaced it by others I believed to be true, I had achieved my main purpose. There were, however, further questions that troubled me. Why had the false account gained currency? Why had it not been countered by Wilberforce's many friends and admirers? The first half of the twentieth century had been highly critical of everything Victorian – why had no historian debunked this Victorian myth? And why had I, not nearly as sceptical as most of my contemporaries, been led to doubt it. As I sought to answer these questions, I became aware of further facets of what the historian is trying to do.

The received account was chiefly due to Huxley, and was emotionally true for him. For him the British Association had not been a great success, and he had almost gone away before the Saturday meeting. For him the conflict between science and religion was very real, and for him Wilberforce was pre-eminently a bishop, and not an ornithologist or a Vice-President of the British Association. Moreover Wilberforce was a notable public speaker, and Huxley was relatively unknown. It required great courage to beard the bishop, and to have done so was no mean achievement. In J. R. Searle's *The Campus War* I found a striking analogy in the immense significance placed by some timid don on his speaking out against the university authorities on some matter of student discipline. At College Gaudies old members often regale me with vivid accounts of how they put me or one of my colleagues down with crushing repartee, but I can scarcely remember the incident. I have a very clear memory of my own entrance interviews and various dialectical encounters with my tutors, but a dimmer and soberer one of the interviews and tutorials I have conducted. History is not just biography, and an incident that looms large in one man's experience may seem quite different and much less significant to a dispassionate observer.

It is not only individuals who distort and dramatise. The Darwinians, who were a small minority in 1860, triumphed over the next twenty years, and with the benefit of hindsight saw Huxley's attack on Wilberforce as an important stage on the path to victory. We cherish our histories not only from a disinterested love of knowledge about the past but as telling us about ourselves, who we are and how we came to be as we are. We turn to our own history to give us a sense of our own identity and our own significance, and therefore endow it with a thematic unity and a significance that might elude those who saw the same events from other standpoints or with other interests. Even if we are outsiders, we are naturally impelled to take an inside view. In order to understand actions as actions we need to see them from the agents' point of view, and once we do that, we see them not only as responses to situations but as achievements. History tends to be not merely the record of what happened, but of *res gestae*, and, in the absence of other axes of interest, acquires a first-personal perspective, either individual or corporate, which gives dramatic edge to the narrative. It is a commonplace that the histories of different nations, French and English, British and American,

Dutch and Flemings, are very different, each full of victories few of which are remembered as defeats by the other side. But this should not be seen as a defect of history, which the emancipated historian should altogether avoid. Although the truth is that Huxley did not triumph over Wilberforce on 30 June 1860, it is not the whole truth. The whole truth has to include the fact that for Huxley it was a triumph, and for the Darwinians generally it came to be one.

History is fertile in legends, but that does not by itself explain why one legend rather than another is deemed meet to be written down. Huxley's *riposte* to Wilberforce was improved and remembered because it made a good story, like the many undergraduate stories which circulate today. But there were other factors at work, which I tried to discern but largely failed to identify. People tell stories largely for fun, but often also to make some other point, and the points they want to make depend on all sorts of currents flowing through the minds of speakers and bearers. Huxley was a prophet. Many of the problems he saw and spoke out about were problems that beset many late Victorians. They saw in evolution a challenge by Science to Religion, and were ready to believe in the simple truthfulness of the one, and obscurantist dishonesty of the other. The legend expressed in dramatic form a confrontation that was real in their own lives. So too in every age some stories circulate whereas others die out. But the general way in which different climates of opinion allow different legends to flourish is an aspect of historical understanding which eludes me still.

None of Wilberforce's friends set the record straight. At the time there seemed to be no need. He had carried the day, and although Professor Huxley had been rude, Professor Huxley was often rude, and was in the habit of thinking he had scored victories in argument which were invisible to other men's eyes. Nobody rushed to Wilberforce's defence because he did not seem to need defending. Later, when geological evidence for evolution mounted up – as Wilberforce had allowed that it might – the debate on the other difficulties he had raised continued among professional biologists, but, quite naturally, without reference to him. At the time of writing Wilberforce's *Life* in 1881, his family could still look back with pride on the part he had played at the British Association in 1860 (Wilberforce, 1881, pp.450–1). How many bishops today could lead a discussion at the British Association on a new scientific theory? The need to defend Wilberforce arose only in the 1880s and 1890s, as Darwinism became the established orthodoxy, and Huxley's view of the encounter gained currency. Hooker supplied for Darwin's biography in 1888 an account substantially different from the account he had given Darwin himself the following day (Darwin, 1888, pp. 320–3; cf. Huxley, 1918, pp.525–7). In 1887 two canons of Durham, T. S. Evans and A. S. Farrar, did spend an evening discussing what happened, but did not write it up then. When he was writing his father's biography in 1899, Leonard Huxley sent his account to Canon Farrar for his comments, and published some of Farrar's reply. An article in *Macmillan's Magazine* in

1898 gave the legend in its classical form, and might have occasioned a rejoinder, but there must have been by then few people alive with undimmed memories of exactly what was said thirty-eight years earlier. Perhaps if Wilberforce had not met an untimely end, the need to set the record straight would have been apparent by the time his biography came to be written; if Canon Evans and Canon Farrar had published their account in 1887, it might have elicited most of the relevant facts. But I suspect that there were other influences at work which would have made it difficult for truth to prevail. Scientists were becoming more isolated in late Victorian England, and churchmen were more and more on the defensive. Under Jowett's influence, Oxford was schooling itself to produce rulers for Britain and the Empire, and the scientifically inclined clergyman was a dying breed. Scientists began to feel themselves an oppressed minority, and ready to treasure the memory of an occasion when they had humbled the Establishment, and few churchmen gave themselves – perhaps dared give themselves – sufficiently wholeheartedly to scientific enquiries to be able to understand all the subtleties of the Darwinian debates. The general, widely educated public of the mid-Victorian era was disappearing, and England was moving towards the Two Cultures delineated by Lord Snow.

Certain philosophical conclusions follow from the previous two paragraphs. Relatively little history just gets written. Most history, and most historical records arise from someone's wanting to tell someone else what happened for some special purpose. Typically, although not always, it is to recount the experiences and achievements of one's own life or own society. But it depends very much on circumstances and occasion whether there is anyone who wants to relate what happened or anyone to relate it to, and what sort of understanding can be sought or achieved. Huxley needed to make a story out of the incident: Wilberforce did not. The Darwinian biologists had reason to cherish it, the non-Darwinian biologists were gradually dispersed and absorbed. Superannuated politicians write their memoirs to make sure history has their point of view, but Wilberforce was never superannuated and always had better things to do than write about himself. There was no natural occasion, as it happened, for him or any of his friends to give a full account of the course of the debate, nor anyone to tell it to, certainly not anyone capable of following the intricacies of the argument. And so there was no enquiry, while witnesses were still available and memories fresh, into the exact course and significance of the debate. And in the twentieth century the received account fitted prevailing prejudices and was readily accepted, all the more so because few historians knew anough about evolution to recognise the real import of the points being made.

My final question was about myself. Why had I come to disbelieve the legend? Partly it was a matter of half-forgotten clues. While writing a draft, I remembered an incident when Disraeli came to Oxford in 1864, and alluded to the incident in Wilberforce's presence, which I must have read in Monypenny and Buckle when I was sixteen, and must have left me half aware that the legend cannot have been current at that date. Colleaguely loyalty led me to read G. S. Carter's *A Hundred Years of Evolution*, and later Sir Alister Hardy's *The Living Stream*, and so to recognise both the difficulties scientists had had in accepting Darwin's theory, and the extent to which it had been modified subsequently. A conversation with Maurice Cowling at a Septcentenary Dinner in 1964 about the climate of religious opinion before 1859 had shown me how little the crisis of faith among the Victorians was due to the conflict between religion and science. More important, I suspect, was the changing perspective with the passage of time. Religion and science both look different in the last third of the twentieth century from what they did previously, and the suggestion of total conflict or total separateness seemed implausible. I had been grappling with questions about the nature of mind and different sorts of explanation. I was aware, although unable to articulate it clearly, of the difference between the sort of question biology has answered and the sort it has not, and of the different demands we make of an explanation before we will accept it as satisfactory. The legend jarred. It was too *simpliste* and did not fit what seemed to me to be the real issue. And so I was led to look at the legend afresh and engage in history myself. And in that sense Croce's dictum that all history is contemporary history proved true.

REFERENCES

The Athenaeum (1860), July, nos.1706 & 1707.
Collingwood,R.G. (1946) *The Idea of History*. Oxford, Clarendon Press.
Darwin,F. (1888) *Life and Letters of Charles Darwin*, vol.II. London.
Dray,W.H. (1980) *Perspectives on History*, London, Routledge and Kegan Paul.
Dummett,M.A.E. (1975) Wang's Paradox *Synthese*, 30, 301–24; reprinted (1978) *Truth and Other Enigmas*, pp.248–68. London, Duckworth.
Huxley,L. (1918) *Life and Letters of Sir Joseph Dalton Hooker*, vol.I. London.
Jackson's Oxford Journal (1860) 7 July, p.2, col.6.
Tuckwell,W. (1900) *Reminiscences of Oxford*. London.
Wilberforce,R.G. (1881) *Life of Bishop Wilberforce*, vol.II. London.
Wilberforce,S. (1860) *The Quarterly Review* LVIII, July, 225–64.
Walsh,W.H. (1951) *An Introduction to Philosophy of History*. London, Hutchinson.
Wright,C.J. (1975) On the Coherence of Vague Predicates *Synthese*, 30, 325–65.

11. History as Patterns of Thought and Action

P.H.NOWELL-SMITH

I

In the course of replying to J.H. Hexter's review of his *Analytical Philosophy of History*, Arthur Danto undertook to explain to the unsympathetic and, as he thinks, misguided historian just what, as a philosopher, he was trying to do. His reply merits careful attention because Danto's book is, apart from its exceptional length and thoroughness, a typical example of what analytical philosophers write when they try to come to terms with history as a form of intellectual inquiry aspiring to truth. 'When concerned at all with history', wrote Danto, '(philosophy) is so in terms of the illumination which (history), may bring upon the most general features of that conceptual scheme which it is the chief task of philosophy to analyse. It is the location of history in *the general conceptual economy* which alone makes it of the least philosophical interest, however otherwise interesting it may be'. He went on to explain that he was concerned to 'confront certain skeptical impediments to the achievement of what I consider the "minimal historical aim", namely, to make true statements about the past. . . . I was attempting *an analysis of cognitive success as such*' (Danto, 1967, emphasis added).

Danto is surely right in suggesting that it is the traditional business of philosophy to be synoptic, to try and devise an abstract structure in terms of which all experience can be accommodated, a conceptual economy that is truly general. Historians make claims to knowledge and it is the business of philosophers to inquire what cognitive successes they have achieved. But Danto's approach is bound to provoke such questions as 'How is the general conceptual economy to be constructed?', 'Are there any general conditions of cognitive success?', and 'If so, how are they to be discovered?' The approach to these questions that has, on the whole, found most favour with analytic philosophers is to start with some outstanding, paradigmatic examples of cognitive success – something about which we want to say that, if we have any knowledge at all, surely this is knowledge. From these paradigmatic cases we abstract the necessary and sufficient conditions of their cognitive success, and we then use these to assess the legitimacy of claims to knowledge in other fields. If this approach is itself legitimate, philosophers may safely ignore Hexter's complaint that for twenty-five years they have 'investigated history without ever once subjecting to close and detailed scrutiny a single complete piece of historical writing by a competent historian in order to discover how it works' (Hexter, 1967).

The paradigms chosen by the philosophers have been mathematics itself and the most highly mathematised of the natural sciences, and from these examples three things stand out. First, their propositions are universal; secondly, their arguments are deductive; finally, both propositions and arguments are expressed in a symbolic notation that has come to be known as 'canonical form'. If these three features are taken to be necessary conditions of cognitive success as such, then either historians are not to be credited with any cognitive successes or what they write must somehow be shown to satisfy the conditions.

On the face of it, none of the requirements is satisfied by what historians write. They eschew generalisations and sometimes go out of their way to tell us that, when they explain a particular event, they are not committed to saying anything at all about other events of a broadly similar character. Their discursive prose seldom contains immediately recognisable deductive arguments and is manifestly far from being expressed in any canonical form; and this poses a problem for any philosopher who wishes to say that, in spite of appearances, historians do sometimes achieve cognitive success. What such a philosopher has to do is to show that the historian's prose can be analysed in a way which exhibits it as composed of a 'skeleton' of truth-bearing content expressible in canonical form 'fleshed out' with mere rhetoric which, from the epistemological point of view, must be dismissed as irrelevant. In the course of this enterprise the philosophers have fastened on two features of much, but not all historical writing that can be expressed in something at least approaching canonical form. These are the particular past tense sentence of the form '*a* happened at time *t*' and the universal generalisation of the form 'whenever *X* happens, *Y* happens'. Any piece of historical prose in which the author undertakes to explain why something happened or how a certain state of affairs came to be what it was can, it is suggested, be recast into the form of an 'explanatory narrative' of which the skeleton is composed solely of sentences of these two forms.

This reduction of cognitive content to what can be expressed in canonical form has the advantage that historical explanations can be immediately seen to satisfy the deducibility and generalisation requirements. The first requires that the statement that event *E* occurred must be entailed by whatever the historian offers by way of explaining why it occurred, and the rationale for this requirement is clear. If the *explanans* does not entail the *explanandum*, it is compatible with the non-occurrence of *E*, so that the historian has not explained why *E* occurred rather than something else (Donagan, 1964). The second requirement is often stated in the form that the *explanans* must contain at least one universal law (Hempel, 1942). The rationale underlying this requirement is not so clear, but what its proponents have in mind might be expressed as follows: granted that each historical event is unique, that the conditions of its occurrence will never be repeated, it has not been explained if the alleged explanation is entirely *ad hoc*. If Newton's theory of gravity explained nothing but the fall of the apple on his head, it would explain nothing at all – not even the fall of the apple on his head. In the same way, if an historian explains the outbreak of a revolution as being due, in part, to the miserable condition of the peasantry or to the frustrations of a bourgeoisie excluded from political power, his explanation would be unconvincing if he were able to point to no other instances of revolutions in which these factors played a part.

Yet the thesis that historical explanation must take the form of a narrative of which the skeleton is expressible in canonical form is not without its difficulties. First, not all writings claimed by their authors to be explanatory are couched in narrative form. For example, in the preface to the first English translation of *The Waning of the Middle Ages*, Huizinga wrote that the thesis of the book 'presented itself to the author ... whilst endeavouring to arrive at a genuine understanding of the art of the brothers van Eyck and their contemporaries, that is to say, to grasp its meaning by seeing it in connexion with the entire life of their times' (Huizinga, 1955, p.7). Clearly Huizinga thought of himself as giving an explanation of how something came to be as it was, but the book is just as clearly not cast in narrative form. Yet it would be arbitrary in the worst sense to conclude that Huizinga's book is either not explanatory or not history. Further, the idea of a skeletal explanatory narrative fleshed out with material inessential to the historian's argument will not fit even those examples of historical writing that could be called explanatory narratives for reasons cogently presented by Mandelbaum (1967, p.417).

Expressibility in canonical form is enticing precisely because canonical forms, of which the most important from our point of view are class membership and class inclusion, can most readily exhibit the fulfilment of the deducibility and generalisation requirements. Yet the history of the idea of canonical form itself must lead us to ask whether these requirements can only be fulfilled by its use. The idea can be traced back to Aristotle's *Prior Analytics*, but we need to trace it no further than to Whitehead and Russell's *Principia Mathematica* (1910–13). At the very beginning of that work the authors tell us that Part I was 'constructed under the guidance of three different purposes. In the first place it aims at effecting the greatest possible analysis of the ideas with which it deals. ... In the second place, it is framed with a view to the perfectly precise expression, in its symbols, of mathematical propositions' (Whitehead and Russell, 1910–13, p.1). On the next page we are told that the ideas with which it deals are 'the ideas and steps in reasoning employed in mathematics'. The authors of *Principia Mathematica*, then, had no intention of contributing to any topic other than an analysis of *mathematical* reasoning and, though it is entirely possible that their ideas and methods might be usefully employed elsewhere, it has been assumed rather than argued that expressibility in canonical form can, indeed *must* be employed wherever claims to cognitive success are made. The purpose of this essay is to inquire whether patterns of explanation in fact used by historians can be allowed such content without expressibility in canonical form. It is not contended that explanations reducible to canonical form are never to be found in history or that reliance on generalisations must be excluded on *a priori* grounds as Collingwood (1946) contended. Rather the case to be made is that the patterns of explanation sketched below satisfy the deducibility and generalisation requirements in a non-rigorous way appropriate to the open texture of the natural language used by historians and that these explanations cannot be expressed in the limited lexical and syntactic forms known as cononical.

Each of the patterns to be sketched is used to explain why someone did what he did, how a particular event came about, or how a particular state of affairs came to be what it was. The explanation offered is 'general' in two ways. First the pattern invoked as explanatory colligates the item to be explained with other items of the same or different kinds, and the colligation must not be fortuitous or arbitrary. This much is implied by calling it a *pattern*. Secondly, the pattern invoked must be one which is found frequently in human history or at least characteristic of the relevant culture or period. The deducibility requirement is satisfied because the item to be explained is subsumed under some wider concept; these subsumptive relations are different in the case of each different pattern, and none of them can be identified with the relations of class membership or class inclusion allowed by canonical form.

II

Rule-governed Activity

An historian who tells us that something happened 'because' such and such was the case is committed to saying that it would not have happened, or would not have happened when and how it did, if such and such had not been the case. Notoriously against his inclinations, he is in fact committed to counterfactual suppositions and predictions, and his unease can be attributed to a disinclination to subscribe to universal generalisations which, he fears, commitment to counterfactuals might require. Murray G. Murphey goes far to alleviate such doubts by allowing to socio-cultural generalisations, limited in place and time, an explanatory role similar to that of universal laws (Murphey, 1973). In any society or sub-society such as a church, a university, or a trade union, there are rules and roles that, in some sense, determine the behaviour of individuals. We explain why a car was driven on the right side of a street by referring to the rule of the road and why Professor X met his class last Monday in terms of his role in the university (Murphey, 1973, pp.78–9). Murphey tries to cash out the concepts of rule and role empirically in terms of behaviour expected by others and enforced by sanctions. But this is just the old Hobbes/Austin theory of obligation and, as Herbert Hart (1961) has shown, it simply will not do. To say that Professor X has an obligation to meet his classes is not just to say that others expect him to do so and that he is afraid of being fired if he does not. Nor is it to say, in Austin's words that there is a 'chance or likelihood' of his suffering. We do not treat a red light as a *sign that* drivers will in fact stop; we treat it as a *signal to* drivers *to* stop, and to fail to see it in this way is to misunderstand the behaviour of drivers. Normative language cannot be reduced to descriptive.

So the question before us is whether explanations of particular actions by reference to rule- and role-governed patterns of behaviour can satisfy the generalisation and deducibility requirements. The generalisation requirement is satisfied because rules are inherently general; they specify what is to be done, not by this or that individual, but by any professor, policeman, prime minister, and so on. And they satisfy the deducibility requirement since, from the premises that it belongs to the office of a professor to meet classes and X is a professor, it follows that it belong to X's office to meet classes. To this the standard reply is that, to explain why Professor X met a class yesterday or predict that he will do so tomorrow, we need additional empirical information as to his being a conscientious individual or afraid of being fired. It is not clear that this objection is sound, but to argue the point would require too lengthy an analysis of the concept of the existence of a rule. What at least is clear is that if most of the more important rules governing the role of professor were frequently flouted, being a professor would no longer be a rule-governed role. The point of insisting on the importance of role- and rule-governed institutions is that the real explanatory work undertaken by historians frequently consists in discovering just what these rules and roles were; and if, for formal completeness, it is necessary to add empirical premises about an individual, the addition will often be trivial. It may be of interest to discover why a certain individual did what his role required of him on a certain occasion; but very frequently it is not, and the information that he was a member of a certain (formal or informal) group together with a grasp of the patterns of thought and action typical of that group provide all the explanation that can be required. It may be very difficult for an historian to discover what the rules, practices, conventions, and institutions of the society he is studying were – especially if they differ widely from our own; but once he has done that he is justified in saying that he now knows why so and so did what he did.

Plans and Policies

Sometimes a chess move can be explained as strictly rule-governed – for example, if it is the only move that will get the player out of check; but more often the rules permit any one of a number of moves; and then the particular move made is explained as implementing a general policy or strategy. This type of explanation is often used by historians when their problem is to make sense of what was done by some powerful individual or group. If, for example, he is puzzled by something that Napoleon did, he will attribute to Napoleon some general plan or policy such that, if he did have that plan or

L

policy, the particular action can be seen as a way of implementing it. Explanations of this type satisfy the generalisation requirement in that they show particular actions to be implementations of a general plan, but actions which implement a plan are neither instances nor species of the plan, so that the relation of *explanans* to *explanandum* is not one that is allowed by canonical form. As to deducibility, the fact that someone has a plan certainly does not *entail* that he will make a particular move even if that move is the only one that implements the plan. He might fail to see the move or change his mind or die; but if we know that he did in fact make the move, it is preferable to suppose that he made it *because* he saw it as a way of carrying out a plan, the preference being dictated by economy of hypothesis.

Motive and Character

The same holds for the relation between statements about particular actions and statements about the motives or character of the agent. Consider, for example, the statement that during and after the French Revolution the bulk of the peasantry 'remained attached to their altars and their priests' (Markham, 1966, p.92). This is a generalisation, limited in time and place, of a kind often used to explain the behaviour of individuals; and the evidence to support it is taken from accounts of individual behaviour. One peasant is found sheltering a non-juring priest from the police; another refuses to seek absolution from a constitutional priest; a third hides the silver candlesticks so that the local Jacobins cannot seize them for melting into bullion. A sufficient number of such actions – and there are no rules as to what constitutes sufficiency – combined with a paucity of actions of an opposite tendency constitute solid grounds for accepting the general statement about the peasantry. Yet the predicates ascribed to each of the three peasants are *different* predicates. So the relation between the statements about individual peasants and the motivational characteristic ascribed to the peasants (attachment to altars and priests) cannot be one of instance to universal law or even instance to law of high statistical probability.

The historian's thought could be roughly schematised as follows:

1. A large number of peasants did *A*, a large number did *B*, a large number did *C*.
2. Anyone who does *A* or *B* or *C* is attached to his religion.
3. Therefore a large number of peasants were attached to their religion.

Assuming that 1 could be established in the ordinary way of evidence, the trouble clearly arises over 2. Expressed in canonical form, 2 becomes (x) (if x is a peasant and Ax or Bx or Cx, then Zx) where Z is the predicate 'attached to religion' and A, B, C are specific action-predicates. But this manoeuvre is open to several objections. First, however long we make our A, B, C list there are likely to be some types of action manifesting attachment to religion that we have missed out; so to make 2 in its canonical form at all plausible we should have to add 'etc.'; but no such symbol is available in canonical form. Secondly, 2 in canonical form is supposed to express a universal, but contingent relation between observable predicates; but the predicate 'being attached to one's religion' is not contingently related to the different action-descriptions and, indeed, is not observable at all without them: it is a higher-order motivational predicate whose presence manifests itself in and by those actions. From the established facts that Jacques Bonhomme sheltered a non-juring priest, cold-shouldered a constitutional priest and hid the candlesticks we are entitled to infer that he was attached to his religion – especially if, in so doing, he risked his life. But in making this inference we are not inferring from the presence of three predicates to a fourth connected to the three by a contingent universal law. Motivational predicates are 'general' in the sense that they function as ways of organising detailed information about the diverse activities of a person or group of people – in this case the French peasantry. To be sure, such predicates are loose and open-textured; we cannot say in advance just what types of conduct manifest and thereby constitute evidence for attachment to one's religion. The Aztecs manifested their attachment to their religion by killing prisoners taken in battle; we do not; so we are bound to harbour an initial scepticism when told that that was one of their ways of exhibiting religious faith. But the doubt is removed when we learn more about the manner and circumstances in which they killed their prisoners and above all by what they themselves said about this custom. All this is admittedly loose and untidy, and the standard positivist reply is that if historians use the sort of patterns of interpretation I suggest they use, then historiography is *unscientific*. But what does this reply amount to? If the positivist only means that, in certain very important ways, history is not like theoretical physics, we have no quarrel. But if he means that, because open-textured predicates about motives, character, plans and policies cannot be subjected to the strait-jacket of canonical form, explanations of human action which use them are inferior, unacceptable, and lacking in cognitive content, he simply begs the question.

The Spirit of the Age

'*Qui n'a pas l'esprit de son age . . .*' (Voltaire). Explanations in terms of the Spirit of the Age can easily become the last refuge of the intellectually slothful. Indeed, simply to say that Byron wrote, Schumann composed and Delacroix painted as each did because each embodies or reflected in his art the Spirit of the Romantic Age is clearly to explain nothing. But historians who invoke this concept are not necessarily condemned to vacuity. What they have in mind is that these artists share characteristics which are other than those of – say – Dryden, Handel and Poussin, and that this is not an accident. Anyone who uses a phrase such as 'The Romantic Movement' as a principle for organising a history of the arts can be challenged to tell us just what these characteristics are; and only then can we profitably raise the question why these characteristics emerged just when they did.

The Waning of the Middle Ages is a book which, in spite of a title which suggests that it is a narrative history, tries to make clear to us what happened in an almost totally non-chronological way. Books with overtly non-narrative titles have been written in increasing numbers since the 1930s. One could instance Paul Hazard's *The European Mind 1690–1715* and Perry Miller's *The New England Mind*; but the book to be used as an example is W.J. Cash's *The Mind of the South*, written in 1939. This book is an attempt to explain certain features of contemporary southern culture which differentiated the South from other regions in the United States. It is a work of explanatory history rather than of descriptive sociology, since Cash's task was to explain how these differential features of the South came to be what they were. Yet it is not a narrative in the sense in which Carlyle's *French Revolution* or Prescott's *Conquest of Mexico* or, indeed, most historical works written before 1930 are narratives. There are hardly any dated events, and the names of such prominent individuals as Calhoun and Jefferson Davies, who would have to be mentioned in any narrative history, do not appear at all. Instead, the *dramatis personae* are types such as planter, preacher and politician, and in so far as the book has a hero at all, an entity whose story it is, the hero is the pattern itself – the mind of the South.

This entity was a certain pattern of thought and action which, if what Cash writes is true, distinguished white Southerners from other inhabitants of the United States. The pattern was an amalgam of individualism, paternalism, romanticism, hedonism and puritan evangelical fervour. That this particular pattern ever existed anywhere is something that should occasion some surprise, since one would not expect extreme individualists to have accepted the paternalistic rule of the greater planters or expect hedonism and evangelical fervour to flourish in the same breasts. But Cash explains in a convincing way both the intelligibility of the pattern – how these apparently incompatible traits could go together – and how it came to exist, its historical origins.

The epistemological problem raised by Cash's thesis is, as often, a blend of the conceptual and the empirical. On the conceptual side we need to ask what specific patterns of behaviour constitute evidence for saying that the Southerners were, for example, romantic. On this Cash offers such facts as the relative popularity in the South of the novels of Sir Walter Scott, the vogue of the word 'chivalry', the tendency of the newly rich planters to imitate the style of the old Virginian aristocracy, the belief that anyone who had money was a gentleman, and the zest for fabricating genealogies tracing one's descent from Brian Boru, a companion of William the Conqueror or at least a highland chief. And on the empirical side, Cash must convince us that these things were, typically, done by Southerners more than by Northerners or Westerners. As in the example of the French peasants and their attachment to religion, the relation between specific acts and the predicate 'romantic' is not one of instance to universal but of manifestation to generic trait of character. The second, and more interesting, move is to relate these traits of character to each other. Of this I shall only give one example – the relation between romanticism and what Cash calls 'a childish tendency to unrealism'.

Once the pattern of romanticism is firmly grasped, this move hardly needs to be made, because every ingredient in the pattern of romanticism entails, in a most obvious way, a habit of mind to which realism and a regard for truth are alien. Cash makes the connection in the following way. First he tells us that the people he is writing about had, for one reason or another, cut themselves adrift from their ancestral background of European culture and that the land they tilled was poor. These are empirical assertions, and if they were shown to be false, Cash's thesis would be destroyed. He adds that the sheer business of filling their bellies prevented them from developing a new culture. That is a causal generalisation; but I doubt if we should need a Ford Foundation grant to establish it. Let what happened when, in the course of time, life became a little easier, be told in Cash's own words:

> Relax that drive a little, let him escape a little from this struggle, and the true tenor of his nature promptly appears; he stands before us, has always stood before us in such circumstances as a romantic and a hedonist. ... To say that he is simple is to say in effect that he necessarily lacks the complexity of mind, the knowledge, and, above all, the habit of skepticism essential to any generally realistic attitude. It is to say that he is inevitably driven back on imagination, that his world-construction is bound to be mainly a product of fantasy, and that his credulity is limited only by his capacity for conjuring up the unbelievable. And it is to say also that he is the child-man, that primitive stuff of humanity lies very close to the surface in him, that he likes naively to play, to expand his ego, his senses, his emotions, that he will accept what pleases him and reject what does not, and that in general he will prefer the extravagant, the flashing, the brightly colored – in a word that he displays the whole catalogue of qualities we mean by romanticism and hedonism. (Cash, 1941, p.45)

Any philosopher who would draw a sharp distinction between the *a priori* or conceptual and the contingent or empirical or who insists on the necessity of canonical form as a condition of cognitive success will have a hard time analysing that passage, and a successful analysis would add nothing to its cogency.

Nevertheless, in spite of the difficulty of sorting out the empirical from the conceptual elements in a rhetoric of this type, it seems clear that Cash's thesis satisfies both the generalisation and the deducibility requirements, provided that we are willing to slacken those requirements in a manner appropriate to the open texture of the concepts involved. It is general in two ways. First, Cash claims that what he says is true of the Southerners is true of uncultured people on whom the pressures of mere survival have been relaxed a little everywhere; and this is subject to empirical check. Secondly, he claims that it is true of a large number of Southern whites during the period about which he is writing. This number is finite, but unknown. We do not need to know it since, if we know it to be true at all, we know this in the same kind of way that Murphey claims to know how North American professors and motorists behave – that is not by exhaustive enumeration. Cash's generalisation supports counter-factuals. For the actual evidence on which his account is based relates, as often in history, to a very small proportion of the total population. For example, after quoting one touchingly naive genealogy, he tells us that it is typical of 'hundreds' of others. But the population is to be numbered, not in hundreds, but in hundreds of thousands. So if, *per impossibile*, we had exhaustive evidence about every member of this population and if this evidence showed that, in fact, only a few hundred went in for fabricating genealogies, Cash's thesis would be seriously weakened.

It also satisfies the deducibility requirement in the following way. Suppose we are puzzled by the extraordinary conduct of the Southern soldiers at Gettysburg or by the steady growth of evangelical religion in the South at the expense of a more high-toned Anglicanism, the pattern which Cash has built up solves the problems because we can clearly see that if that pattern is indeed true of white Southerners these initially puzzling facts fall into place; they are precisely what we would expect of people whose temper of mind conforms to the pattern. Here is part of Cash's description of the Southerner as Romantic:

> Despite the unquestionable harshness of the life he led, the Southern pioneer (like his congeners elsewhere on the American frontier and in every new country) early began to exhibit a kind of mounting exultancy, which issued in a tendency to frisk and cavort, to posture, to play the slashing hell of a fellow – a notable expansion of the ego testifying at once to his rising individualism and the burgeoning of the romantic and hedonistic spirit. . . . To stand on his head in a bar, to toss down a pint of raw whisky at a gulp, to fiddle and dance all night, to bite off the nose or gouge out the eye of a favourite enemy, to fight harder and love harder than the next man, to be known eventually as a hell of a fellow – such would be his focus. (Cash, 1941, pp.46–50)

How would you expect such men to behave on the field of battle in a hopeless cause? Let Cash continue:

> Allow what you will for *esprit de corps*, for this or for that, the thing that sent him swinging up the slope at Gettysburg on that celebrated, gallant afternoon was before all else nothing more or less than the thing that elsewhere accounted for his violence – was nothing more or less than his conviction, the conviction of every farmer among what was essentially only a band of farmers, that nothing living could cross him and get away with it. (Cash, 1941, p.44)

To summarise the argument of this essay, the patterns of thought and action here sketched are among those frequently used by historians to explain why some individual did what he did, why the members of certain groups behaved as they did, or how some state of affairs came to be what it was. They satisfy, in non-rigorous ways appropriate to historical discourse, both the generalisation and the deducibility requirements, but they are not reducible to canonical form since, in each case, the relation between the *explanandum* and that part of the *explanans* which supplies the required element of generality is neither class membership nor class inclusion. It is, of course, open to us to try to reduce the characteristic rhetoric of historical prose to symbolic notation by inventing new canonical forms, and the fact that such a reduction would deprive historical works of literary merit would be irrelevant from a purely epistemological point of view. But there seems to be no reason to suppose that until such a reduction has been shown to be possible historical writings must be denied either cognitive content or cognitive success.

REFERENCES

Cash, W. J. (1941) *The Mind of the South*. New York, Alfred A. Knopf.

Collingwood, R. G. (1946) *The Idea of History*. Oxford, Clarendon Press.

Danto, A. C. (1967) *New York Review of Books*, May 18.

Donagan, A. (1964) The Popper-Hempel Theory Reconsidered, *History and Theory* IV, No.1.

Hart, H. L. A. (1961) *The Concept of Law*. Oxford, The Clarendon Press.

Hempel, C. G. (1942) The Function of General Laws in History, *J. Phil* XXXIX, N3.1.

Hexter, J. H. (1967) *New York Review of Books*, February 9.

Huizinga, J. (1955) *The Waning of the Middle Ages*. London, Penguin Books.

Mandelbaum, M. (1967) A note on history as narrative, *History and Theory*, VI, No.3.

Markham, F. (1966) *Napoleon*. New York, Mentor Books.

Murphey, M. G. (1973) *Our Knowledge of the Historical Past*. Indianapolis/New York, Bobbs-Merrill.

Whitehead, A. N. and Russell, B. (1910–13) *Principia Mathematica*. Cambridge, Cambridge University Press.

12. Colligation Under Appropriate Conceptions

W.H.DRAY

I

W.H.Walsh's 'greatest contribution to analytical philosophy of history', opines C.B.McCullagh, may have been 'the identification of colligatory terms and the investigation of their function in historical writing' (McCullagh, 1978, p.276). If this is so – and the judgment is, at any rate, a plausible one – Walsh's contentions in this connection have scarcely yet received the critical attention they deserve. Only McCullagh himself and L.B.Cebic (1969) among philosophers, and D.Thompson (1967) among historians, have discussed his account of colligation at any length. Others, like Morton White (1965, pp.252–4), D.C.Williams (1963, pp.388–90), J.W.N. Watkins (1953, p. 733) and the present writer (Dray, 1959, pp. 407–8), have picked up and used the notion of colligation without offering much analysis of it. Marvin Levich made brief but stimulating comments on it in reviewing the work of some other authors (Levich, 1965, pp.338–41); but the reviewers of Walsh's own *An Introduction to Philosophy of History*, in which his claims about colligation are given their best known formulation, scarcely noticed it. Walsh in fact adumbrated his central idea as early as 1942 in an article entitled 'The Intelligibility of History', and he adverted to it in a number of other writings before offering an extensive reconsideration and elaboration of his views in his 'Colligatory Concepts in History' of 1967. In the present paper I propose to review some of the things he has had to say about historical colligation at various times, to attempt certain clarifications, and to consider some difficulties which the notion may seem to raise.

Walsh came to formulate his account of colligation as a fundamental historical procedure in response to an apparent need to choose between positivist and idealist theories of historical understanding. Completely satisfied neither with the claim of scientistic philosophers that historical events, like natural occurrences, must be explained by subsuming them under general laws, nor with the view propounded by Collingwood that, since the events in question were the actions of human beings, they should be understood from the 'inside' as expressions of the agents' thoughts, Walsh pointed to a common historical procedure which, he held, conforms strictly to neither of these alternatives, although affording understanding of a sort especially appropriate in history. At its simplest, this is the placing of events in their context by tracing a myriad of connections between them and other events with a view to discovering and characterising the larger historical wholes which they jointly composed. Walsh's paradigm case in his introductory book (Walsh, 1967a, p.59) is the understanding of Hitler's re-occupation of the Rhineland as a stage in the implementation of an overall policy of German self-assertion and expansion, of which others were the withdrawal from the League of Nations, the absorption of Austria, and so on. Borrowing a term from the nineteenth-century logician, William Whewell, Walsh called this 'colligating' events under 'appropriate conceptions'. Other examples of familiar colligatory conceptions to which he drew attention are 'the rise of the gentry', 'the Romantic movement', 'the age of reform', 'the evolution of Parliament', 'the Enlightenment', 'the Industrial Revolution'.

Walsh's account of how historians make the past intelligible has obvious affinities with the view of Michael Oakeshott (whose writings he often mentions with respect) that historical inquiry aims at bringing into focus large-scale 'historical individuals' (Oakeshott, 1933, pp. 120–2). It has affinities, too, with Hegel's notion of historical thinking as discerning the 'concrete universal'; and it is of interest that, although in his original statement of his theory, Walsh warned against making too much of the latter similarity, in his most recent account (Walsh, 1967b, p.82) he makes it plain that he regards his colligated wholes as very much what Hegel had in mind. Despite his criticism of some of Collingwood's doctrines, his theory is also more Collingwoodian than his various descriptions of it might lead one to believe. It seems plainly prefigured, for example, in that author's contention that, when an historian sets out to understand a given event, he does not typically, like the natural scientist, try to relate it to other events of the same kind; he tries rather to see its connections with other events of the same period (Collingwood, 1946, p.250). Thus an historian studying the Hundred Years War, Collingwood maintains, is more likely to be in the first stage of a general inquiry into the Middle Ages than a general inquiry into war. Of course, colligation goes well beyond the narrower conception of the historian's task most often attributed to Collingwood: the mere re-thinking of the thoughts expressed in *discrete* actions of the past. Walsh, however, is prepared to concede this much even to the latter view: that the individual connections traced out in colligating historical events are more often of the 'internal' kind envisaged by Collingwood than mere 'external' relations of cause and effect. For this reason, he tends to represent his own account, in the end, more as a revision of the idealist view than as an alternative to it.

The emphasis Walsh places on the importance of the part/whole relation for historical understanding aligns his approach also with that of a number of recent analytical writers such as Maurice Mandelbaum and Louis Mink. Like them, he uses the notion of 'part' somewhat loosely to include 'phase', 'aspect', 'symptom', 'manifestation', etc.; and possible differences between colligatory accounts applying such similar but not identical notions might ultimately require some attention. Another potential point of difficulty concerns what it is precisely that colligation is supposed to make intelligible. In different places Walsh appears to say somewhat different things (McCullagh is similarly ambivalent—see 1978, pp.276,277). In the Hitler example, for instance, what Walsh represents as colligated seems to be an initially isolated event: what the historian makes more intelligible is the re-occupation of the Rhineland, and doing this consists in discovering its multifarious connections with other events (see also Walsh's treatment of the British General Strike in 1967a, p.24). In other cases, the implication seems rather to be that what is colligated is a whole collection of events, these being conceived first as just a collection and then later as constituting a unity of an appropriate kind. Thus a vast number of things that happened in Europe in the fifteenth and sixteenth centuries may be said to be made more comprehensible by being seen as together constituting 'the Renaissance' (see also Walsh's reference to the historian's use of 'pervasive themes' in 1967b, p.75).

Perhaps the difference between these two sorts of case will not seem very important. Corresponding to it, however, are two very different kinds of inquiry that historians might be thought to undertake: inquiry into happenings and inquiry into periods; and this difference is one that needs to be borne in mind when considering some of the criticisms the idea of colligation has received. Walsh's initial presentation of the notion (Walsh, 1942) clearly envisaged inquiry of the period-delineating kind. Engaged in the task of deflating a full-blown hegelian approach to the problem of meaning in history, he contended that the most historians can hope to do is find meaning in some rather arbitrarily limited stretch of historical space and time – this by seeking out 'dominant trends' and 'leading ideas' displayed by the most important events to be found in them. It is colligation so conceived that Morton White must have in mind when he asks about the degree of objectivity to which this procedure can aspire, since his main worry is how the events worth colligating within a selected period are to be determined, and how much the task of determining them will involve the historian in value-judgment (White, 1965, pp.252–3).

Cebic (1969, p.49) and McCullagh (1978, pp.277 ff.) are presumably thinking of colligation in the same way when they ask whether it is a species of classification. For (as McCullagh makes clear) there is no question of contributory *individual* events being classified by a procedure which brings a number of them together under concepts like 'renaissance' or 'revolution'; if anything is classified in such cases, it is the totality which these conceptions designate and which colligatory thinking has collected. On the other hand, when Levich questions the propriety of regarding colligation as a distinctive type of explanation in history, and especially as a type to be contrasted with explanation by subsumption under law, what concerns him seems rather to be how an individual event is to be understood (Levich, 1965, pp.340–1). Levich claims that Walsh's theory of colligation raises no problem for the positivist account of historical explanation; but at least part of the interest of this contention would disappear if the object of colligatory understanding were taken to be, not individual events but periods. For Levich's point is that colligation and covering law explanation respond to different questions about the same thing (How should it be regarded? Why did it occur?). The positivist theory, however, offers no account at all of how periods are to be understood, some of its supporters apparently believing, indeed, that the very attempt to study a period, as such, lands an investigator in a hopeless pseudo-problem.

For some purposes, however, a resolution of the ambiguity may not be necessary, provided one is aware of it. This appears to be the case with regard to the main questions about Walsh's theory that I now want to go on to consider. All are questions which Walsh himself has raised; all direct attention to features which have been seen as making colligation a distinctive and especially important historiographical procedure. The first is the extent to which, and the sense in which, colligation in history must be said to be teleological. The second is how far the colligatory procedure can be regarded as a means of expressing the supposed concern of historians with the concrete and the unique. The third is what follows for the choice of 'appropriate' colligatory conceptions from the retrospective nature of historical inquiry – a feature of it which Walsh's various formulations have increasingly stressed.

II

To a casual reader, Walsh may sometimes give the impression that he considers the colligation of events under appropriate conceptions to be, as such, an exercise of teleological thinking. That this can hardly be his real view is suggested by his having derived the very idea of colligation from an account of theory-construction in the natural sciences. Understanding natural events, too, sometimes involves seeing them as together constituting larger wholes – for example, a cold front or the solar system – although presumably not by virtue of the 'inner' connections so much emphasised by Collingwoodians in the case of human actions. What Walsh must be taken as asserting is only that colligation *in history* is necessarily teleological.

As long as Hitler's re-occupation of the Rhineland is taken as a paradigm case of historical colligation, it is easy to see why he might want to make the latter claim. As he puts it himself, seeing an event as a stage in the realisation of some overall aim necessarily involves assigning a *common* teleological explanation to it and all the other events with which it is colligated, this providing the 'whole' with its principle of unity. The paradigm case, in fact, expresses a conspiracy theory of historical change. Since conspiracies, as Walsh points out (Walsh, 1967a, p.61), do play a role in history, it is none the worse for that provided the way other cases may deviate acceptably from the paradigm is made clear. Walsh offers no analysis of teleological explanation itself beyond remarking, a bit mysteriously, that, in a teleologically related series of actions, there is reciprocal determination, the earlier being explicable by reference to the later as well as the later by reference to the earlier (Walsh, 1942, pp.132,136; 1967a, p.69; 1967b, pp.72–3). Since this is generally softened to the claim that what determines earlier events is only later events *as envisaged* (and thus not really the later events at all), perhaps no problem need arise out of this potentially puzzling turn of phrase. What is literally true (and may perhaps lie behind Walsh's way of putting it) is that later events in such a series (for example, the series implementing Hitler's plan to re-assert German power), 'determine' the whole that colligation brings into view quite as much as earlier ones do. They do this, however, only in what might be called a 'constitutive' sense, not a causal or reason-affording one: that is, they contribute quite as much as do the later to making it the kind of whole it is.

Walsh in fact recognises from the first that, in most cases, colligable series of actions will deviate from the conspiracy paradigm in a variety of ways. For example, historians will be able to discern governing purposes and goals in cases where the agents concerned did not *deliberately* seek to realise them, let alone *plan* to bring them about by stages. People act with ideas 'in mind' as well as with ideas 'before their minds'. As an example, Walsh cites the way a 'sense of imperial mission' throws light on much that happened in the political history of Great Britain in the late nineteenth century, although few of the agents concerned ever articulated such an idea to themselves (he concedes that some did, but it could surely have been otherwise). Colligations depending upon the idea of unconscious motivation in this way Walsh calls 'semi-teleological' (Walsh, 1967a, p.61). In the revised statement of his position, he also lays considerable emphasis on deviations from a straightforwardly teleological paradigm by reason of the intervention of chance occurrences or other unintended consequences in most historical endeavours. Even when agents are pursuing plans and policies, he observes, the latter may often have to be adjusted because of changing circumstances, especially those resulting from the uncontrollable actions of others. Teleologically comprehensible series can also, to a degree, accommodate gaps – periods of inactivity with respect to some long-term goal pursued.

However, many of the cases of colligation that Walsh himself admits, fit an overall goal-seeking model rather badly even when unconscious motivation and unintended consequences are taken into account. As Cebic has pointed out, a renaissance has no final state or end-result (not even one unconsciously desired) that gives directional sense to what leads up to it (Cebic, 1978, p.19). What makes it a 'whole', a colligable unity, is more the similarity or complementarity of the ideas, principles and values expressed by the activities of the many agents involved in it. And a revolution, although perhaps always a movement towards some crucial point, some fundamental change in a process studied, may not only be unplanned but even unexpected or undesired (like the English Revolution of the seventeenth century, which, on some interpretations at least, occurred almost by accident). In considering cases of this kind, a distinction drawn by McCullagh between 'formal' and 'dispositional' colligatory concepts is useful (McCullagh, 1978, pp.272 ff). McCullagh calls 'revolution' a formal concept because its

applicability depends, not on the general nature of the aims and motives of
the participating agents, but on the general nature of the change their
actions bring about (other such concepts are 'evolution', 'decline', 'polaris-
ation'). If such cases are teleological, they are surely so only in a rather
attenuated sense. To recognise an historical change as revolutionary, since
it will be a change in a process made up of human actions, will certainly
require an understanding of many of its constituent actions as goal-directed
in various ways. However, the overall pattern indicated by the colligatory
concept itself need not be teleological (or even semi-teleological) in any
sense explicitly recognised by Walsh.

Colligation by means of what McCullagh calls 'dispositional' concepts,
unlike that by means of formal ones, directs attention to wholes the nature
of which directly depends on the nature of ideas shared by the many agents
concerned. Both Walsh's paradigm case and his semi-teleological approxi-
mations to it would fall into this category; but so would those, like 'renaissance', in which the shared ideas furnish an overall (if extremely general)
teleological explanation of the activities colligated even in the absence of
any linear purpose of achieving some end-result. In the case mentioned, this
might be something like a general desire to revive the style and values of
classical civilisation. A problem about such cases on which neither Walsh nor
McCullagh shed sufficient light is whether mere similarity or complementarity of the expressed ideas would be enough to make the actions
expressing them colligable. Walsh has insisted that colligation is concerned
only with the relations of expressed ideas themselves, all causal or quasi-
causal questions about origins lying beyond its purview. This leads him to
concede – for example, in contrasting his own position with a hegelian view of
history – that, at best, this technique ascribes a 'surface rationality' to
historical processes (Walsh, 1967a, p. 62). Yet if what is envisaged is the
recognition of the sort of thing sometimes called a 'climate of opinion', it is
hard to see how questions about origins and influences could be entirely
excluded. Historians would surely not want to represent as a significant
unity expressions of ideas, however similar or complementary, that simply
happened to be juxtaposed in time and space – although, as Walsh observes,
they would doubtless fight shy of looking for anything behind them resembling a hegelian 'cunning of reason'.

For its full development, a theory of the nature and role of colligatory
concepts in history clearly needs a fairly explicit account of the logic of social
as opposed to individual concepts. In his attempt to revise and develop his
position in 1967, Walsh acknowledged, on looking back at earlier formulations of it, that he had somewhat neglected the social dimension of historical understanding. Rather than policies of individual agents and their
implementation, he said, the idea of social process should have been taken as
primary. The account he then gave of the way individual actions constitute
social processes nevertheless suggests a continuing influence of the original
overtly teleological and directional paradigm. Just as the same aim may

show itself in successive actions of the same agent, Walsh points out, so it may show itself in successive actions of different agents. People 'take up each other's work', and when they do, historians can, in a sense, ignore the individuals and work at higher levels of abstraction (Walsh, 1967b, p.74). But such considerations are clearly more helpful for the analysis of directional teleological processes than for the kind of social unities indicated by terms like 'renaissance'; and they are applicable only marginally to what historians call 'the Industrial Revolution' or 'the decline of the Roman Empire'. Walsh does to some extent clarify his position on the question of the relation of the individual and the social when he insists that, while at some level men 'make their own history', social processes cannot be *reduced* to independent human actions. However, the sense in which he intends thus to deny independence to individual actions appears to be an exclusively causal (or, at any rate, explanatory) one; what he means is that no human action is unaffected by the agent's social (or, indeed, natural) environment. The further question that needs consideration is whether social processes can be *logically* reduced to congeries of individual actions, each with its own teleological explanation, or whether (to use McCullagh's language) the social wholes which colligatory terms often designate are 'greater than their parts' (McCullagh, 1978, p.279) in some sense which excludes this possibility.

I have noted departures from Walsh's original 'conspiracy' paradigm of historical colligation as account is taken of the way unconscious motives, unintended consequences and other interventions, purely formal properties of social change, similar or complementary ideas not constituting terminal goals, and (perhaps) ideas that are apparently purposive but not attributable distributively to participating individuals all find a legitimate place in the recognition of understandable historical wholes. The question arises how far such an attenuation of meaning can go while still retaining the claim that, in some residual sense at least, colligation in history *must* be teleological. Walsh explicitly draws the line at purely natural processes: a spell of bad weather, he says, would lack the appropriate kind of unity, since it is a purely 'mechanical' phenomenon (Walsh, 1967b, p.73). He is nevertheless prepared to admit that physical terms like 'desiccation' may sometimes be colligatory in history (Walsh, 1967b, p.68). It may seem that, in doing so, he at any rate remains true to his doctrine that historical colligation will be 'of processes which can be initiated, forwarded or impeded by human effort' (Walsh, 1968, p.12). Is it so clear, however, that a humanly *un*controllable desiccation, with its attendant human suffering and perhaps its stimulus to actions other than successful attempts to alter it, would be beyond the historian's purview? Perhaps the most we can say is that natural processes will find a justifiable place in historical inquiry only through their relations to actual or possible human action and experience. But if that is sufficient to warrant the claim that historical colligation must be (rather than just characteristically is) teleological, the relevant sense of 'teleological' turns out in the end to be rather thin.

III

Walsh's characterisation of colligation in history as teleological is in part an attempt to do justice to the emphasis that idealists like Collingwood placed upon understanding past human activities from the 'inside'. As he generally frames it, it is also an application of another doctrine characteristic of idealist philosophers of history: that historical inquiry is 'idiographic' – concerned with the past in its concreteness and uniqueness. What colligatory expressions like 'Hitler's expansionist policy' or 'the rise of the English gentry' bring into view, Walsh maintains, are unique concatenations of events and conditions: complex particulars with 'a temporal and also a spatial spread' – or, in hegelian language, 'concrete universals' (Walsh, 1967b, p.81). This emphasis remains strong in all of his formulations of his doctrine.

As McCullagh has pointed out, such an emphasis needs at any rate to be somewhat qualified. For to conceive events as 'complex particulars' apparently means not to bring them (jointly) under a general or classificatory concept. But some of Walsh's own examples do precisely this. Historians, Walsh observes at one point, colligate events by means of such notions as 'a widespread shift of allegiance, a continuing crisis of confidence, a prolonged struggle for political independence . . . '(Walsh, 1967, p.81). If they do, then, as the use of the indefinite article suggests, they surely regard them (jointly) as events of a certain *kind*. The real question is not whether historians *ever* colligate by assigning things to their class, but whether they ever do, or can do, otherwise. McCullagh has argued, in support of Walsh, that at least *some* historical colligations are of events viewed jointly as unique, citing as a relevant case his example of Hitler and the Rhineland. Here the event to be made intelligible is related to the particular plan of a particular person to aggrandise a particular historical society – hardly a class of things other instances of which it would make sense to look for at other places and times. It might be argued too that when historians use uniquely referring expressions such as 'the Renaissance' or 'the Romantic movement', they do not classify. What they do rather is designate particular and probably unique processes or states of affairs.

There is important truth in this qualified defence of Walsh's theory; but McCullagh's position seems to me also to require some qualification. For although historians clearly do sometimes make events intelligible through the use of uniquely referring expressions, these expressions typically contain general terms – for example, 'movement' or 'plan of conquest'. And this is surely not accidental. For unless they did so, it is hard to see how they could perform their colligatory function. As McCullagh puts it himself, colligated wholes must be seen to be more than mere *collections* of events and conditions compendiously referred to: they must be seen to form a *unity*, and presumably a unity of a certain *kind*. A mere name would not colligate as such: only one that was to some extent also descriptive. McCullagh does concede that, since even uniquely referring colligatory terms often contain general concepts, they *may* to some extent classify (the French Revolution, for example, has to be *a* revolution) (McCullagh, 1978, p. 279). But that concession is surely not enough; for it seems that they *must* classify. This is not to deny that colligation, as Walsh perhaps overemphasised, may be achieved through singular as well as through general terms. Nor is it to ignore the fact that, although singular terms like 'the Renaissance' use classificatory concepts and are descriptive as well as referential, they at the same time indicate that there is in fact only one concatenation of events or circumstances to which the description in question truly applies, as the employment of general terms like 'a widespread shift of allegiance' would not do.

It is necessary to take issue also with the way McCullagh, in trying to reconcile Walsh's generalised examples with his claim that colligation is of the unique, represents the not uncommon *replacement* of singular terms by corresponding general ones as historical inquiry develops. Two fundamentally different kinds of colligatory terms must be recognised, McCullagh maintains: but terms that begin their historiographical career as singular may become general – or, as he puts it, may be 'found' to be general (McCullagh 1978, p.278). The use of the term 'renaissance' by historians is offered as an example. This term was first introduced by Michelet to designate a particular historical configuration in fourteenth- to sixteenth-century Italian cultural history and, when introduced, was not itself a general term since it did not refer to a class of conditions believed to recur. But later, McCullagh avers, the term was 'discovered' to be general after all, as historians found reason to speak of renaissances occurring in other periods and even other civilisations, this development being signalised by the substitution of a common for a proper noun.

Now the kind of discovery to which McCullagh draws attention here is obviously genuine and important in historiography; but it is surely misleading to characterise it as the discovery that a colligatory term originally thought to be singular is general after all. When renaissances other than the Italian one are eventually discovered, the expression 'the Renaissance' remains as singular as it ever was. *It* has not been found to be applicable to other cases, any more than 'Hitler's plan of conquest' can be found to be applicable to the plans of conquest of other people. On the other hand, when the term 'renaissance' was applied only to events in fourteenth- to sixteenth-century Italian history it was as general as it ever later became. Indeed, as was contended above, if it had not been general from the start, it would have failed to colligate in the sense of making clear an appropriate sort of unity. Confusion on this point may perhaps be traceable to some extent to an ambiguity in the word 'can' when a general term is said by McCullagh to be one that 'can describe more than one historical whole' (McCullagh, 1978, p.277). It is true that the term 'renaissance' cannot *in fact* be applied to other cases as long as historians know of no other configurations sufficiently like 'the Renaissance' in relevant respects. What makes it general, however, is not its in fact applying to such cases, but its being logically of a nature to apply to them, as a uniquely referring expression taken *in toto* is not. In the kind of case McCullagh has in mind, something is certainly discovered; but this is about the course of history, not about the nature of a certain colligatory term.

In this connection, it may be worth my repeating a point I made some years ago in a paper (Dray, 1959, p.407) which, as Cebic and McCullagh correctly observe, envisaged a kind of intelligibility in history very like what Walsh calls colligation (although the emphasis was somewhat different). This is that, when an historian believes himself to discern a certain kind of unity in his materials, he will often find no term in the current vocabulary of social description that will adequately capture it, making it necessary for him to coin a new one, this often requiring his reaching for a metaphor. Historians' use of the term 'renaissance' is surely a case in point. This term (we may assume) had no accepted social or historical meaning before Michelet's employment of it, although it has a sense in more general contexts. The latter's use of it *established* such a meaning, even if the criteria for applying the term were left somewhat vague – more shown than defined: indeed, if such criteria had been entirely lacking, it would have been impossible for later historians to discover that other cases were sufficiently like the original one to warrant the term's further application. Of course, not all uniquely referring expressions employed in historical colligation display such conceptual inventiveness. An historian who colligates events under 'Hitler's plan of conquest' clearly draws upon the ordinary language of social description.

What has been said so far about the presence of general terms even in the colligation of events as unique accepts without question Walsh's own characterisation of the activity he has in view: the colligation of events *under appropriate conceptions*. Since Walsh is the one who introduced the term 'colligation' into critical philosophy of history, he is, of course, free to mean what he likes by it. But before leaving the question of the relation of colligation to general terms and classification, it may be worth asking whether something like colligation as Walsh describes it does not play an important part in historical inquiry even in the absence of 'appropriate conceptions', whether singular or general, especially when historians attempt to render understandable what is regarded as unique. Walsh himself seems to hint at such a possibility in comparing the way a map makes a multitude of details intelligible, i.e., simply by setting them forth in their right relationships to each other (Walsh, 1967b, p.78). Maps organise and unify, but without articulating the achieved organisation or unity conceptually. It is surely characteristic of good historical accounts to do the same.

Whether Walsh himself would, in the end, accept such an extension of his notion of colligation is not entirely clear to me: his remark about an analogy with mapping was made only in passing. Of all the writers who have recently urged more attention to the part/whole relation in historical thinking, only Mink has explicitly held that tracing out a configuration is itself (i.e., even

M

in the absence of an interpretive concept or description) a mode of understanding (Mink, 1970). The most important conclusions historians reach, Mink has maintained, are 'undetachable' from the works that formulate them (Mink, 1966, pp. 180–1); for the conclusions *are* the details in their complicated inter-relationships. Any attempt to summarise them – for example, in the title of a book (one of the vehicles for colligatory expressions noted by Walsh [1947, p.57]) – would yield no more than a device for recalling the real thing. Clearly, in 'colligation' of such a *trans-conceptual* sort (if this extension of the term may be allowed), the alleged idiographic concerns of historians would get their fullest recognition. I see no reason why Walsh should not accept some further development of his theory along these lines.

IV

When Walsh came to reconsider and elaborate his earlier views in his 1967 article, one of the main questions he raised was the extent to which the essential retrospectivity of historical investigation ought to be allowed to affect the choice of colligatory concepts by historians (Walsh, 1967, pp. 75 ff.). A recurring claim about historical inquiry – and one that must obviously, in some sense or other, be correct – is that its aim is to recover the past *as it actually was.* Some philosophers, influenced by writers like Collingwood, and some historians too, characteristically interpret this claim to mean that the historian's task is to discover what it was like to live through earlier periods and circumstances: to 'revive' the past as it was experienced. Since Walsh represents himself as, on the whole, rather friendly to idealist theories of history, the question arises whether 'appropriate' colligatory conceptions, when employed, should not be limited to those which the original agents themselves employed, or at any rate would have understood. For otherwise, will they not be somehow imposed on the past; will they not constitute a projection of the present upon the past rather than an attempt to take it for what it was and to study it for its own sake?

Of course, in admitting the legitimacy of colligating past actions by reference to unconscious as well as conscious motivation and by means of collective or social as well as individual concepts, it has already been conceded that the past can be made intelligible through concepts that the original agents did not in fact possess – at least explicitly. But some concepts used by historians to organise or synthesise the past appear to be such that the original agents not only *did not*, but *could not* have had them. In some cases, this may be simply because they lacked the knowledge required to apply them; they may have lacked relevant evidence, perhaps, of which historians often have much more at their disposal than any contemporary had. But they may also have lacked the theoretical sophistication required to formulate them. Men could hardly have understood their own activities by means of Marxist notions, for example, before Marx performed the creative act of inventing them: there is no way of anticipating the future of inquiry.

Equally clearly – and for present purposes it does not much matter whether this is because history is unpredictable in fact or in principle – they cannot anticipate the longer-term consequences of their actions; and without knowledge of these they cannot make adequate judgments of relative importance. The need for retrospection in making judgments of the latter sort, so much emphasised by philosophers like Arthur Danto, puts in question any claims by contemporaries to colligate a given episode of their own experience as, for example, the initiation of a fateful policy or the end of a period of advance or decline. Walsh sometimes describes colligation as the relating of past actions to the (often large-scale) ideas which they *expressed*; but it seems odd, at least, to suggest that such actions could have expressed, say, the idea of bringing about a bourgeois revolution when the very conception of such a thing was beyond the imaginations of the agents concerned, or the idea of leading to the demise of the monarchy when this was a future consequence of what was being done of which the agents knew and could know nothing.

Under what conditions, if any, then, is it legitimate for historians to colligate by means of concepts which are applicable only retrospectively? In considering this question, Walsh responds sympathetically, but ultimately critically, to the warnings of philosophers like Oakeshott against 'reading the past backwards' (Walsh, 1967b, p.76; 1968, pp.5–18). According to Oakeshott, to give an account of the past from the standpoint of the present in any sense other than regarding it as what present evidence obliges us to believe, is to engage in a practical, not a theoretical activity. It is to elaborate a 'practical' and not an 'historical' past – a past for the sake of the present, not for its own sake. Walsh agrees, to the extent that 'reading the past backwards' means looking for what is of practical value in the present, or seeing it as culminating in (or, at any rate, as explaining) the present. Searching out the 'useful' past, although not, as such, that debasement of history we call propaganda, is at any rate not history itself. And looking for the past that led to the present, although a theoretical activity, is still historical knowledge put to a certain use, and cannot, due to the kind of selectivity it involves, claim even to *aim* at representing the past 'as it actually was'. But retrospective colligation, Walsh points out, need not be 'presentist' in either of these senses. It obviously need not be so in the first sense, since the choice of what to colligate, or what colligatory concepts to use, may be decided without reference to any present utility other than thorough and coherent synthesis of what is presently known about the past. And it need not be so in the second sense either, since the later point of time at which an earlier event is seen as having a colligable 'outcome' need not be that of the historian himself.

When is it justifiable, then, to interpret past actions in terms of ideas their agents not only did not have, but could not have had? Walsh surely gives the correct answer when he replies: when it makes them intelligible *to us* (Walsh, 1967b, pp.79–80). Whether parliamentarians had the idea of the evolution of parliament or not (and they seem to have thought of themselves in altogether different terms in the crucially important seventeenth century at least: much more static, even backward-looking ones), *we* can see important relations between their actions over time by means of this idea. As Walsh puts it, the application of colligatory concepts, like all serious historical work, must do justice to the evidence; historians may not choose such concepts arbitrarily. But colligations must also do justice to the interests and knowledge of those to whom they are addressed; and this may require the application of concepts not devised until after the event. This is not to justify *anachronism*, the deformation of the past by falsely twisting it into a likeness to the present. In fact, the rule for avoiding anachronism follows from the two principles just noted. Thus Namier avoided it, as Walsh points out, by refusing to colligate eighteenth century English politics as a series of 'party rivalries'; but his reason for doing this was not that the agents concerned applied no concept of 'party' to themselves; it was that their activities fail to conform to *our* idea of what a political party is (Walsh, 1967b, p.80). Similar considerations would forbid our characterising the English Revolution as 'bourgeois' (at any rate, according to much recent historical writing on the subject). McCullagh's notion of formal colligatory terms is perhaps especially useful here. If a past movement takes a form which can be discerned only retrospectively, then by all means let historians capture it, when it becomes discernible, by retrospective colligation.

The general thrust of Walsh's account of retrospective colligation thus appears satisfactory. A caveat might nevertheless be entered on two points of detail. The first is his tendency, after having repudiated the view that we must always and only understand the past from the standpoint of the agents, to slip back, at times, into what looks very much like a version of the rejected view. For example, against Oakeshott's contention that, if the historian uses purposive language at all, he identifies with particular persons and adopts their own practical orientation, Walsh argues only that it is possible to speak from a point of view without oneself embracing it. His solution to Oakeshott's problem is therefore the historian's adopting a policy of speaking from the standpoint of *many* agents, thereby remaining 'impartial', while giving purpose its due. This sort of strategy, however, is surely indistinguishable from that of the extreme Collingwoodians; it suggests falsely that the historian need never speak about past actions from his own point of view. In fact, colligation, including colligation of actions, must always be undertaken, in the end, from the point of view of the historian, not that of the agent. Opinions of the participants cannot be allowed to determine, for example, whether a movement is correctly called a 'decline' in political morality, or whether a revolution was really a 'bourgeois' one.

The other point of detail – also arising out of Walsh's response to Oakeshott – is a tendency not to distinguish sufficiently between the questions whether colligation should aim at understanding the past *for its own sake* and whether it should deal with it *in its own terms*. Walsh notes (and this is doubtless true) that it is sometimes said that historians should confine themselves to agents' terms *because* history should be a study of the past for its own sake (Walsh, 1967b, p.76). Against this, he argues that historians *cannot* entirely avoid 'reading the past backwards' (mainly because, unlike the agents, they cannot avoid knowing the real future of the past), but that the extent to which they must do this is rather less than a theorist like Oakeshott would seem to imply. But it needs also to be said that studying the past for its own sake (which is really just the negative idea of *not* studying it for the sake of any present purpose other than that of understanding it) implies nothing about whose terms should be used in describing or explaining it. Whether we should use the terms 'Great Rebellion' or 'bourgeois revolution' in colligating events of early seventeenth-century English history is a theoretical historical question to be settled along the lines already indicated. Using *our* terms does not commit us to a practical orientation towards the past, using *theirs* does not protect us against it.

REFERENCES

Cebic, L. B. (1969) Colligation and the Writing of History, *Monist* 53, 40–57.
Cebic, L. B. (1978) *Concepts, Events, and History*. Washington, D.C., University Press of America.
Collingwood, R. G. (1946) *The Idea of History*. Oxford, Clarendon Press.
Dray, W. H. (1959) 'Explaining What' in History. In Gardiner, P. (ed.) *Theories of History*. New York, Free Press.
Levich, M. (1965) Review of Hook, S. (ed.) *Philosophy and History: A Symposium*, in *History and Theory* IV, 328–49.
McCullagh, B. H. (1978) Colligation and Classification in History, *History and Theory* XVII, 267–84.
Mink, L. O. (1966) The Autonomy of Historical Understanding. In Dray, W. H. (ed.) *Philosophical Analysis and History*. New York, Harper & Row.
Mink, L. O. (1970) History and Fiction as Modes of Comprehension, *New Literary History* I, 541–58.
Oakeshott, M. (1933) *Experience and Its Modes*. Cambridge, Cambridge University Press.
Thompson, D. (1967) Colligation and History Teaching. In Burston W. H. and Thompson, D. (eds.) *Studies in the Nature and Teaching of History*. London, Routledge and Kegan Paul.
Walsh, W. H. (1942) The Intelligibility of History, *Philosophy* XVII, 128–43.
Walsh, W. H. (1947) The Character of an Historical Explanation, *Proceedings of the Aristotelian Society*, Supp. Vol. XXI, 51–68.
Walsh, W. H. (1967a) *An Introduction to Philosophy of History*, 3rd ed. London, Hutchinson. (1st ed., 1951.)
Walsh, W. H. (1967b) Colligatory Concepts in History. In Burston, W. H. and Thompson, D. (eds.) *Studies in the Nature and Teaching of History*. London Routledge and Kegan Paul.
Walsh, W. H. (1968) The Practical and the Historical Past. In King, P. and Parekh, B. C. (eds.) *Politics and Experience*. Cambridge, Cambridge University Press.

Watkins, J. W. N. (1953) Ideal Types and Historical Explanation. In Feigl, H. and Brodbeck, M. (eds.) *Readings in the Philosophy of Science.* New York, Appleton-Century-Crofts.

White, M. G. (1965) *Foundations of Historical Knowledge.* New York, Harper & Row.

Williams, D. C. (1963) Essentials in History. In Hook, S. (ed.) *Philosophy and History: A Symposium.* New York, New York University Press.

13. Truth and Fact in History

LEON POMPA

I

It is often held, not least by historians themselves, that the past consists of the totality of events, processes, conditions, causes, states of affairs, changes, developments and so on, which 'have occurred', and that the historical past, if it is to be distinguished from this 'real' past, is simply that subset of these things for the occurrence of which we have evidence. The difference between the two pasts is thus simply that between what occurred and what we know to have occurred. It follows, as part of this view, that since the set of occurrences which constitutes the historical past is a subset of the set which constitutes the real past there is no difference in ontological status between the two pasts. The fact that we know one and not the other has no ontological implications.

Not surprisingly, since it involves the notion of a reality which transcends what can be verified from present experience, idealist philosophers have rejected the distinction as stated. Thus Michael Oakeshott, in the course of expounding an idealist metaphysic, wrote: 'a fixed and finished past, a past divorced from and uninfluenced by the present, is a past divorced from evidence (for evidence is always present) and is consequently nothing and unknowable' (Oakeshott, 1933, p.107). The implication here, that to be is to be knowable, points towards a different conception: the real past is nothing but the past which we know in virtue of our access to present evidence. The seemingly paradoxical consequence of this view, that the past will vary as present evidence varies, was drawn by Oakeshott himself: 'If the historical past be knowable, it must belong to the present world of history.... The fact is, then, that the past in history varies with the present, rests upon the present, is the present. "What really happened" (a fixed and finished course of events, immune from change) as the end in history must, if history is to be rescued from non-entity, be replaced by "what the evidence requires us to believe" ' (ibid., pp.107–8).

It is difficult not to feel that in his anxiety to rescue history from its alleged total non-entity, Oakeshott has given it the paradoxical ontological status of existing only insofar as it is the object of warranted present belief. What is excluded is the notion that the past can have an existence independent of 'what the evidence requires us to believe' and thus exist as a referent which is essentially independent of any present knowledge. And this, indeed, was the position to which Professor W. H.Walsh objected when he first discussed Oakeshott's view: 'When it is said that our knowledge of the past must rest on evidence which is present that is one thing; but when the conclusion is drawn that the past *is* the present, that is quite another. Evidence for the past must no doubt be present in the sense of being presented to us now, but it does not follow that it must *refer* to present time, as it would have to if Mr Oakeshott's conclusion were to be justified. And, indeed, it is a characteristic of the evidence with which historians deal that it refers not to the present but to the past' (Walsh, 1951, p.89). Oakeshott's paradoxical conclusion can thus be avoided by invoking the distinction between a judgment and its reference for, as Walsh went on to argue, although judgments may vary as different evidence becomes available to us, this does not entail that their referents must also vary.

As Walsh remarked in a later essay (Walsh, 1977, p.53), the question of the ontological status of the historical past has been the least discussed of the main questions brought to the fore in his *An Introduction to Philosophy of History*. Recent developments, however, in philosophy and in other disciplines, have raised increasing doubts both about the internal coherence and the methodological utility of the notion of a determinate, verification-transcendent reality, thus tending to support the sort of view Oakeshott advanced and, by implication, to deny the presuppositions upon which Walsh's criticism of it rested. It comes as no surprise, therefore, that the issue should finally come forward again in philosophy of history itself, as it has done through the publication of Leon J. Goldstein's (1976) book, *Historical Knowing*, and of a *Beheift* of *History and Theory* in which Goldstein (1977) Nowell-Smith, (1977), and Walsh (1977) discussed Goldstein's restatement of an idealist conception of the historical past.

A central feature of Goldstein's view, arrived at by discussing long examples of the infra-structure of argument which supports assertions about historical fact, is the claim that there is simply no verificational role for the notion of an independent or real past to play: 'To demand of historical descriptions that they conform to such a past is to demand what cannot be realised. Far from overlooking the distinction between facts and the description of facts . . . in history that distinction does not exist' (Goldstein, 1976, p.xxi). As a result, Goldstein describes the historian as 'constituting' the past, by which he means bringing it into existence as an object of consciousness in the course of historical research. The constructivist nature of Goldstein's view is quite explicit: 'What we know about the historical past we know only through its constitution in historical research – never by acquaintance – never as anything having a status independent of what is constituted in historical research' (*ibid.*). Thus when we attend to the specialised technical skills involved in historical research, we cannot avoid thinking of what historians produce, the historical past, as something which exists only in virtue of being so produced. Goldstein is prepared to concede to the realist that there is nothing incoherent in the notion of there being some other past, the real past, which is different from the historical past, but insists that this concession does nothing to weaken his position, since the notion of such a past is verificationally vacuous with regard to the historical past.

Despite the similarities between his and Oakeshott's view, Goldstein would seem to have safeguarded himself against Walsh's claim that such a theory must be rejected because it mislocates the reference of historical statements. For Goldstein's insistence upon the verificational vacuousness of the real past is the obverse side of his claim that the reference of historical statements is part of what the historian is constructing when he constructs the historical past, a reference which cannot be specified independently of the statements themselves. Goldstein does not take this to commit him to the view that there is no past for 'no one would engage in historical research if he did not believe that a past time in which human events took place had existed' (Goldstein, 1976, p.22), but it is a past which can exist only in relation to, and as a product of, the techniques of historical investigation, a past which can exist only as conditioned by historical thought. This being so, the statements are verified not in virtue of the existence of some independent referents for *historical* statements, but solely in virtue of the techniques of historical research and argument which have been used to construct them.

It is not clear from his discussion of Goldstein's view whether or not Walsh thinks that it is immune from the criticism he advanced against Oakeshott. He does not, at any rate, raise the question of reference in this connection and this suggests that he may think that Goldstein has surmounted this particular difficulty. He does, however, make it clear that he is not persuaded by Goldstein's arguments, asserting, as Hume did of Berkeley's, 'that they admit of no refutation and produce no conviction' (Walsh, 1977, p.62). Yet the only reason which is offered for this is that Goldstein's view clashes with our deeply ingrained belief in an actual past. This is clearly unsatisfactory, however, for philosophy ought to be constrained not by belief, no matter now deeply ingrained, but by argument, and arguments which admit of no refutation ought to be accepted. It may, indeed, be some acceptance of this which explains why, for the larger part of his discussion, Walsh is concerned to show how certain distinctions, grounded in a Kantian theory of judgment, will enable Goldstein to meet the most radical of the objections which Nowell-Smith advances against him. As I shall try to show, I am not convinced that this strategy will suffice to save Goldstein's position. As the same time I am impressed by Goldstein's claim that a realism which depends upon a verificationally vacuous notion of reference simply begs the question and I shall therefore try to show how to understand the correct role of the reference requirement in history.

II

To understand the Kantian theory of judgment which Walsh introduces into the discussion, it is convenient to start from two pairs of difficulties which Nowell-Smith raises, which it is devised to meet. In his account of the methods by which historians reach their conclusions, Goldstein lays great emphasis on the variety of kinds of argument and types of evidence which they use. Conclusions are not arrived at by some single, linear process of reasoning, but by an assessment of evidence from many different directions, including much argument from probability. As a result the historian will come to have an increasing degree of conviction about some hypothesis which may, indeed, have started life as little more than an intelligent guess. This gives rise to the first pair of questions which Nowell-Smith raises: for, if the historian is said to be responsible for the constitution of the historical past, at what point in this process, at what degree of conviction, can he be held to have constituted it and what is to be said of what he has constructed before he reaches the point at which it is deemed to be constituted (Nowell-Smith, 1977, p.21)? Second, although it is true, as Goldstein points out, that there is a remarkable amount of agreement between historians about certain facts, there is also considerable disagreement about others. Where the latter obtains, however, does it not follow, on Goldstein's view, that they have constituted different things in the past, i.e., different historical pasts? And if this is so, what sense is to be made of the notion of disagreement between historians?

The suggestion which Walsh makes to counter these difficulties employs a distinction, which he drew in his book on Kant (1975, pp.49–53), between the judgments which we make as individual thinkers and the ideal impersonal form of judgment, what he calls 'judgment proper', to which we try to make our judgments conform in order that they may be acceptable to, and indeed command the assent of, intelligent persons as such. The product of judgment proper will be a conclusion arrived at by argument without preconceptions, from true and adequate premises and by proper methods (Walsh, 1977, p.63). Historical fact will be constituted when, and only when, historians' actual judgments satisfy these ideal conditions, 'since the notions of *fact* and *true judgment* are internally related' (*ibid.*). Thus, 'what exists in the objective sense, on this way of thinking, is now what is acknowledged or concluded to by any actual thinkers, but what would be acknowledged or concluded to by thought in its ideal form' (Walsh, 1977, p.64). The last sentence must not, of course, be understood counterfactually, otherwise the historical past will never have been, or be, constituted. But if it is allowed that sometimes the conditions specified here are satisfied, a part of the historical past will have been constituted. Walsh does, it is true, later seem to be worried by the thought that, as historical techniques change, a judgment which satisfies these conditions at one time may cease to do so at another, in which case the historical past will come to have a shifting character, out of keeping with what we expect of fact (Walsh, 1977, pp.68–70). But it is equally the case that it may not and the consensus of historians about many propositions may be good grounds for thinking that in some cases these conditions have been met and for not taking the worry seriously. Despite this, however, as I shall argue below, Walsh is right in raising a worry along these lines, but he has misdiagnosed its proper nature: it is not that some judgments which satisfy the standards appropriate to judgment proper may later cease to satisfy them, but that the standards are unsatisfiable in principle within an idealist context.

Before discussing this point, however, it is worth noting how Walsh's theory, if acceptable, would deflect Nowell-Smith's objections: the historical past would be constituted only when judgment has been properly conducted; disagreement between historians would obtain only when one, at least, was arguing in such a way as to fail to satisfy the appropriate standards and such disagreement would therefore not entail that different pasts had been constituted. The possibility that the historian might simply conjure the past into existence, by accident or mistake, as it were, would thus be removed. Finally the theory would go a long way towards clarifying the suggestion that the historian constitutes the past *for consciousness*, by interpreting this to mean that the historical past is the past as it is stated to be by propositions which command a perfect degree of warrant.

The greater the merits of Walsh's suggestion, however, the more important it becomes to see that it cannot be accepted by Goldstein. This can be shown by noting two features of Goldstein's account of the way in which an historical account of, say, some determinate event is built up. The first is his claim that this is never the result of an inference from the evidence. For, as we have seen, evidence of many different kinds, and of varying degrees of strength, may be relevant to the event in question. To allow for the fact that a claim is strengthened by its relation to evidence of many different kinds, evidence moreover which must itself be evaluated, Goldstein stresses that the event is hypothesised in order to make the evidence coherent (Goldstein, 1976, p.127). Second, however, the evidence itself is not given in any hard, that is to say, unrevisable way. Indeed, it is not given *as evidence* at all: it becomes evidence only after it has been subjected to the questions and techniques characteristic of history (Goldstein, 1976, pp.88–9). A useful example here, which Goldstein mentions in another connection (Goldstein, 1976, p.70), is Collingwood's rejection of Suetonius's claim that Nero once invaded Britain: 'I reject his statement, not because any better authority flatly contradicts it, for of course none does; but because my reconstruction of Nero's policy based on Tacitus will not allow me to think that Suetonius is right' (Collingwood, 1961, p.245). Goldstein's point is that not even evidence constitutes 'hard fact', if by this we mean something which is given along with an interpretation or evaluation which cannot conceivably be rejected. It follows, however, that when he talks of any hypothesis being acceptable if it makes sense of, or is coherent with, the evidence, he cannot mean that it is acceptable if it makes sense of something which is antecedently given as evidence. For one is as free to reject Suetonius's statement about Nero as one is to accept an hypothesis which would cohere with it, namely, that Nero invaded Britain. One might, of course, have all sorts of other reasons for refusing to accept this second hypothesis, as, indeed,

Collingwood indicates by his appeal to his reconstruction of Nero's policy based on Tacitus. But if this reconstruction itself simply depends upon further hypotheses which cohere with further 'evidence', we would be equally free to reject them, singly or in groups, and thus be no further forward in our attempt to establish that Nero did or did not invade Britain. The function of an historical hypothesis, on this view, cannot therefore be that of making sense of antecedently known evidence, but of providing us with one of a number of competing ways of converting into evidence what would otherwise be only disconnected and relatively unintelligible data.

This suggests that Goldstein's position is not strengthened by Walsh's proposal that the objective historical past be held to be constituted by assertions which satisfy ideal standards of warrant. For on most accounts of warranted assertion, the evidence which comprises the warrant for the assertion must be established independently of the assertion and we must have reasons independent of the assertion for interpreting the data in such a way that it is evidence for that assertion and not some other. But neither of these conditions could obtain here. We could not establish the evidence independently of the assertion since, as we have seen, we can call the evidence in question on the basis of being unwilling to accept the assertion which it is supported to warrant. Nor is it demonstrable that we must interpret a given body of data in such a way as to convert it into evidence for one assertion rather than another, since we are always free so to interpret the data as to convert it into evidence relating to a wholly different assertion. Goldstein has complained that the 'real past' can never be brought to bear upon the verification of historical statements in a helpful way, but neither, it would seem, if the foregoing is correct, can the historical past.

It now becomes clear why the standards appropriate to judgment proper, as specified by Walsh, are unsatisfiable in principle within an idealist framework. For coherence between assertion and evidence can at best be only a necessary condition of the truth of the assertion. What is needed in addition is what Walsh himself indicates – true premises. But given the idealist's inability to constrain the conversion of data into evidence other than by the demand, all too easily satisfied, that it cohere with some assertion, the notion of a true premise simply cannot be given any content. Thus even if 'fact' is internally connected with 'true judgment' nothing could count as true judgment and there would therefore be no way in which fact could be constituted.

It might be objected that a modified account of the criteria appropriate to judgment proper would evade the foregoing criticism and still allow the concept of judgment proper to provide the necessary distinctions. Two such possibilities come to mind. The first, which Walsh himself mentions (Walsh, 1977, p.68), is that the agreement of historians provides a presumption, but no more than a presumption, that any actual judgment satisfies the standards of judgment proper. Since the standard which is at issue is that to do with true premises, this would mean that agreement about a premise would provide a presumption that the premise was true. But if, as I have argued, we cannot make anything of the notion of a true premise within an idealist framework, neither can we make anything of the idea of a presumption that such a notion has been satisfied. This suggestion must therefore be rejected.

The second possibility is that, rather than providing a presumption that the standard appropriate to a true premise has been satisfied, such agreement would constitute the standard to be satisfied. This suggestion does not suffer from the same incoherence as the first. What is to be noted about it is, rather, that it would fail to deal with the difficulties which the notion of judgment proper was introduced to resolve. For agreement is a matter which admits of degrees, whereas constitution does not. The questions which Nowell-Smith raised about the degree of agreement required to constitute the past would therefore simply reappear. Were we to insist, for example, on agreement by all 'historians' whatever, it would surely be the case that no past was or ever had been constituted. If we were to settle on something less, how could we draw the line in a non-arbitrary way? How, for example, would our decision be affected by the credentials of historians and who, indeed, would 'we' be to be competent to make these decisions? These difficulties would seem to be irresolvable, raising the spectre of an historical past conjured up by accident, prejudice or worse, which could never be laid to rest. The obvious answer to all this is, of course, to point out that agreement is not the same thing as warrant. But once warrant is reintroduced we are faced again with the difficulties which arise for the theory of judgment proper when it cannot allude to the notion of a true premise as one of the standards to be met.

III

It is not hard to see that these difficulties do not arise for the sort of realism which goes no further than claim that historical statements are true only if there occurred in the past those events, states of affairs and so on, to which they refer and that their occurrence is logically independent of our capacity to make statements about them. Such a realism is compatible with a fallibilist theory of knowledge, since the existence of the referents is only a necessary and not a sufficicient condition of knowledge. For the same reason it can allow for changes in historical techniques as historians become interested in things from different theoretical perspectives. Nor is it discomfited by the fact, which Danto has done so much to draw to our attention (Danto, 1965, pp. 143–181), that as historians' temporal vantage-points change, it becomes possible retrospectively to discern things as parts of different temporal wholes, since the emergence of these new wholes is a cognitive and not an ontological matter. Such a realism is, then, wholly compatible with the view that no item of knowledge is absolutely secure. This does not, however, provide any ground for scepticism, which has been a traditional worry of idealists, since, given the assumption that historians are rational beings, changes in historical techniques ought to lead to a strengthening rather than a weakening of the basis of our knowledge of the past.

Formally adequate though it may seem, however, this picture invites a difficulty upon which Goldstein lays great stress and which neither Walsh nor Nowell-Smith meet: that the independence of the referents which constitute the real past from the techniques of historical discovery and argument, deprives them of any verificational role with regard to the historical past. As Goldstein puts it, they would be verificationally vacuous since, in history at least, we have no acccess to them other than through the statements they are supposed to verify. Nowell-Smith's response to this claim is to assert that it is based on a failure to distinguish between that in virtue of which a statement is true – its referent – and the means whereby we find out that it is true (Nowell-Smith, 1977, p.17). But this cannot be wholly correct, since Goldstein is concerned to deny not the distinction itself but its utility in historical practice. What Goldstein is asking for, surely, and what he is failing to receive, is some account of the utility of the appeal to the referent, or to put it otherwise, some explanation of how the obtaining of a condition to which we have no access, other than through the statement it is supposed to make true, can have a part to play in the verification of that statement. It is the inaccessibility, indeed the necessary inaccessibility (Goldstein, 1976, p.27), of the constituents of the real past which leads Goldstein to assert that they cannot have a role to play in the verification of historical statements and this, in turn, lies behind his claim that the states of affairs, events and so on with which historical knowledge is concerned, the constituents of the historical past, emerge as objects of consciousness solely in virtue of the kinds of reasoning which are characteristic of, and peculiar to, historical research. Two crucial claims are evidently involved here: that since we cannot appeal to the referents of historical statements directly or perceptually they can have no part to play in the verification of historical statements; and that the methods of historical verification must be other than those used in areas of research where there is, in principle at least, the possibility of a direct appeal to the referent of a statement as a way of verifying the statement. In what follows I shall discuss both of these claims, largely by an examination of the notion of evidence in relation to historical fact.

IV

As we have seen, one of the most striking things about Goldstein's account of historical method, and one which must surely be correct, is the way in which it stresses the fact that an historical hypothesis is progressively confirmed by its relation to evidence of many different kinds. Some of this evidence may be of a reasonably direct kind, such as, for example, eye-witness accounts of what occurred, although these, of course, need to be authenticated; other evidence may be of a purely circumstantial nature; other again may be relevant to the question of the possibility of the event, if it is an action, by bearing upon the availability of the concepts required for the action; other again may be geographical or geological and so on. In addition Goldstein emphasises the degree to which historians may want to talk about processes which were unobservable, either for temporal or theoretical reasons, to the agents who were involved in them, as, for example, in the case of macrocosmic economic tendencies or changes. It thus seems that an historical hypothesis, which is the basis for an item of historical knowledge, may be such that only historians are in a position to assemble and assess the evidence which could warrant its acceptance.

I do not want to dispute this part of Goldstein's account, which seems to me correct as far as it goes. What I wish to suggest is, however, that it does not go far enough and that in concentrating upon describing historical practice Goldstein has failed to pay sufficient attention to the presuppositions in virtue of which the claims to which that practice leads can constitute a form of knowledge.

With regard to evidence Goldstein (1976, p.58) cites a passage from Collingwood: 'In scientific history anything is evidence which is used as evidence . . . and nothing is evidence except in relation to some definite question'. On the face of it this looks like an assertion of the sufficient and necessary conditions of evidence. Yet this can hardly be accepted. For merely considering something in the light of an enquiry will certainly not suffice to turn it into evidence for something. It is true, of course, that anything may be evidence for something but not that anything may be evidence for anything. The fact that I may be interested in whether or not there was a real King Arthur will not suffice to turn the copy of Schwegler's *History of Philosophy*, which is on my desk, into evidence for or against his existence. The evidence, then, must be relevant evidence. This, of course, is something which Goldstein accepts. What he fails to do, however, is to ask what conditions determine whether or not something is evidence relevant to something else. One suggestion, which will not do, is that there are no conditions and that it is just a matter of what, in practice, we construe to be evidence relevant to something else. For with sufficient ingenuity anything could be construed to be evidence for anything and in this case evidence would lose its constraining power in historical argument. If it were just a matter of human ingenuity, Schwegler's *History of Philosophy* could be construed to be evidence both for and against the existence of King Arthur, as well as that of anyone else we cared to choose. But this would be tantamount to admitting that it was not evidence at all. The evidential status of something cannot therefore be satisfied merely by its relation to a conclusion within an argument. Some further condition must plainly be sought.

It is a feature of Goldstein's account of historical argument, as we noted earlier, that statements about the past are said *never* to be based on inference (Goldstein, 1976, p.127). Rather 'the occurrence is offered hypothetically as what would make best sense of the evidence' (*ibid.*). In denying that inference is ever involved, Goldstein would appear to have what we might call 'strict inference' in mind, i.e., deductive or inductive or causal inference.

On the other hand his view has distinct affinities with Harman's notion of 'inference to the best explanation' (Harman, 1973, Chapter 8), which involves accepting an hypothesis because it provides a better explanation of the evidence than any competing hypothesis. As Thagard (1978, pp.77–85), has argued, an important, though not the sole, criterion for 'the best explanation' would be the capacity of the hypothesis to explain a large variety of different kinds of thing, which is precisely the point which Goldstein makes with regard to the confirmation of the hypotheses which lead to the constitution of the historical past.

It would appear from what I argued above, however, that the notion of inference to the best explanation will still not constrain historical hypotheses sufficiently to allow us to accept them as statements of what occurred, unless somewhere, in the course of our argument, we can relate them to something else which we are prepared to agree exists so that we either are, or take ourselves to be, committed to the existence of the event in question. Failing this even the best hypothesis may remain in the realm of coherent fantasy. One possibility worth pursuing is that the kinds of reasoning involved in inference to the best hypothesis be supported by relevant general knowledge which we are antecedently disposed to accept. We might consider here another example which Goldstein quotes with approval from Collingwood: 'At Silchester a tombstone was found, with an inscription in Ogams containing the name of a certain Ebicatos and written in the Irish, as distinct from the British, form of Celtic. An Irishman who dies in Silchester and left friends able to make him an epitaph in his own language must have been a member of an Irish colony in the town' (Goldstein, 1976, pp.125–6). Here we may say that Collingwood has inferred to the best explanation, but in order to do so he has had to avail himself of all sorts of general knowledge, much of which is not specifically historical at all. Thus we would not be prepared to accept that he has offered the best explanation were we not prepared to admit that tombstones are generally inscribed by friends, that when the inscription is written in a non-native language this is for the benefit of a sub-community of speakers of the language in which it was written, and so on. Were we not independently disposed to accept some general knowledge such as this, we would not accept that Collingwood has, indeed, offered the best explanation.

It is clear, however, that even if the explanation offered thus relates to a wider body of knowledge and is judged the best explanation in the light of this, its being the best explanation would still not show that the event in question occurred, for the fact that an hypothesised event explains other things which we are independently disposed to accept will not suffice to establish its non-hypothetical character. Something further is still required and this, I suggest, is that there be sufficient causal links, of appropriate kinds, between the event hypothesised and our evidence for it. Thus if I say, 'yesterday I saw Caesar murdered' this could not constitute evidence for the occurrence of the event, for there would not be an appropriate causal route

from Caesar's assassination to my assertion of it. If an eye-witness were to have asserted it, however, it would be evidence for it, precisely because there would be an appropriate causal route from the hypothesised event and his hypothesised presence at it to his assertion of it. Of course, it would not suffice that there *could* be an appropriate causal route. We should want to know that each link in the route obtained, and we should want to do so by entrenching it as a common factor in as many independent but mutually compatible causal series as possible. Moreover, if we assume that the eye-witness had written this on a document which we now have, we should want to be assured of the authenticity of the document, which would be a matter of establishing how the document had come down to us, i.e., by further similar causal investigations. The important point here is that since individual occurrences are causally related to many other occurrences – Caesar's death, for example, to his funeral, to eye-witness accounts of his assassination, to the disappearance of his portrait on coins and so on – we should expect there to be many different causal routes from the existence of different items of evidence to a particular historical event which, when traced, would enable us to eliminate other accounts of what occurred.

It might appear that Goldstein would accept this further requirement. But it becomes clear that he could not, as soon as we raise the question how we are to support our accounts of the causal routes by which we reach past fact. For, given that we have no direct access to them, the only way in which we can sustain them, or at least the various links involved in them, is by the use of multiple causal inferences based upon our present knowledge of causes and our possession of particular effects of past occurrences. If this is so, however, it would appear that the task which is presupposed by all else that the historian does, that of establishing that certain things occurred in the past, can be accomplished only on the basis of causal knowledge which we can verify now by methods which are not specifically historical, and which can be applied to trace the connection between present and past phenomena. Causal inferences are thus indispensable for knowledge of what occurred and only such present phenomena as can be subsumed under the relevant causal concepts and thus be taken to be effects of the past, can count as evidence for what occurred in the past.

This point may be clarified by returning to the notion of inference to the best explanation as an account of the use of historical evidence in establishing matters of fact. I do not want for a moment to deny that historical assertions about what occurred are supported in this way. But when they are it is not simply in virtue of the hypothesis' offering the best explanation of the evidence, but of the explanation being the best causal one. Our acceptance of the fact that Caesar died on the Ides of March may be due to a belief that this statement offers the best explanation, but what it explains are the standard causal consequences which such an event would have. We might therefore, of course, infer from each of these consequences to the fact in question, but since effects are usually overdetermined by causes, one such inference would

N

not suffice to establish our claim. On the other hand, given the many different consequences which his death would have, we eliminate other possible hypotheses by showing that they are not compatible with all of the consequences, although to be viable contenders they would have to be with some. Without knowledge of the variety of causal consequences, however, we would never be in a position to argue in this way and never be able to show that he died. When it comes to establishing what occurred, therefore, inference to the best explanation is possible only when construed as inference to the best causal explanation and this comes down to finding the cause which is common to the largest number of independent causal inferences.

It would thus seem that there is nothing peculiarly historical in the reasoning which is here involved. It is precisely the same kind of reasoning as that which we would use to establish anything in our daily lives which we have not witnessed as, for example, that a letter that I received this morning, bearing a certain signature and communicating certain information, was written by a certain person. Similarly, it is the same as that which is used to support statements about the 'non-historical' past: for example, past-entailing statements such as 'this is a scar'. It is true, of course, that the statement 'this is a scar' entails 'this was caused by a wound', but our reason for accepting that it is a scar rather, say, than a blemish of the skin, lie in our belief that such marks are generally caused by wounds. There is thus no kind of reasoning that is peculiarly historical when it comes to matters of fact, hence the distinction between an historical past and a real past cannot be grounded by the claim that the former is a product of a kind of reasoning peculiar to historical fact. Historical reasoning is continuous with our everyday reasoning about matters of fact and were this not so there would be no way in which, when we come to have new causal knowledge, this would have repercussions for our knowledge of past actuality.

V

In the light of these remarks we may now take up Goldstein's second claim, that the realist insists upon the necessity for a referent which is verificationally vacuous. If the claim is, as Goldstein often presents it, that the realist should somehow be able to make a direct comparison between what is stated and what makes the statement true, this demand obviously cannot be met. But that, surely, is because since the past is that of which historical statements are true, the demand is unreasonable and not because the realist ought to be able to satisfy it. If the considerations I have offered above are correct, however, historical verification is possible only on the assumption of a past which is causally related to the present, in virtue of which we can with justification make multiple causal inferences to occurrences in the past. And it is in virtue of this that we are bound to ascribe to it the same ontological status as we do to the present. It follows that since the idealist account disallows the necessary causal connection between historical evidence and the real past, it is defective to the extent that it cannot provide a well

grounded distinction between justified and unjustified ascriptions of actuality that is, between fact and fancy. The difference between realism and idealism in history is therefore to do with the framework of assumptions within which it makes sense to think of the products of a certain mode of enquiry as knowledge of fact. As I have tried to show, in the foregoing discussion, historical investigation of past occurrences is governed by realist assumptions and it is this which allows it to establish what occurred in the past.

It remains here only to note that, whereas I argued earlier that the conditions of Walsh's Kantian theory of judgment could not be satisfied within an idealist framework, they can within a realist one. For the objection was that the idealist was not entitled to the notion of a true premise. On the realist view adduced above, however, the premises are taken to be true statements and since it is so much a part of the way in which we understand the notion of a factual statement that it is typically taken to refer to something other than itself (Putnam, 1975, Vol. II, pp.272–90), there is no difficulty in understanding the conclusion in the same way. Indeed, if the Kantian theory of judgment is acceptable, it is necessary to do so if the validity of the argument is to be preserved.

VI

I should like finally to consider two objections which may be advanced against the above position, one from each side. Since the realist objection is less formidable I shall mention it first. Some realists might hold that my position is not strong enough since, in linking the notion of evidence to that of the present causal consequences of, say, events in the past, it implies that were the events to have had no such consequences we could make no sense of the notion that they had occurred and, hence, no sense of the notion that they had occurred independently of our capacity to know of them. This objection would not seem to be too serious, however, since it is only a necessary condition of evidence, on the above view, that the causal consequences should obtain. A further necessary condition is that we should use these consequences as evidence. It is perfectly coherent to suggest therefore – and, indeed, this is something which most historians accept – that the consequences may obtain without our using them as evidence, and therefore that their causal antecedents could have occurred without our having knowledge of them. The ontological independence of the past from present evidence, which is at the core of the realist's position, is thus not endangered, since although it is a necessary condition of something's being historical evidence that it be linked causally to past occurrences, it is not a necessary condition of past occurrences that they be related to present evidence.

The idealist objection is more serious, since it raises questions to do with the viability of idealism and realism generally. I shall therefore have to content myself with offering the merest sketch of it and the way in which I would try to meet it. The above position, the idealist might maintain, is radically defective because I have simply smuggled in, by claiming that it is

N*

presupposed, the notion of a causal series as an ontological feature of the world, whereas, if we attend to the historian's procedure, we shall find that all that he has to go on is what is available to him in the present and even the notion of a causal series is a judgment warranted by its capacity to render this coherent. Thus if my thesis is duly amended to take this into account, my talk of causal links will be replaced by talk of judgments about causal links and no *independent* notion of reference or truth will be required.

Although this objection raises the wider issue of idealism and realism as general philosophical positions, I shall discuss it primarily through its bearing on history. If we consider the historian's position in the light of the presuppositions of the objection, it would seem to admit of the following description. The historian's claim to produce knowledge must rest, in the last analysis, upon his capacity to appeal to data which can be part of his present experience, for the past itself cannot, under any of the conditions under which the notion of historical knowledge has developed, be an object of experience. Indeed, even were it possible for some parts of it to be such an object, this would be of little avail to the historian, for many of the macrocosmic phenomena, wars, long-term processes, national states of affairs and so on, in which the historian is interested, are such that they can, in principle, never in their entirety be data of experience for anybody. The historical past can therefore only be a construction about what is unavailable to experience, which is justified by its capacity to inject coherence into the data of present experience.

Two points must be made about the position as thus stated. The first is that it could not be sustained if the reference to one's present experience of data were a reference to one's private experience. As Goldstein has emphasised, part of the reason why history is a legitimate branch of knowledge is that the data available to one historian is available also to others. For were historians not to have access to the same data, even though they may choose not to use it, there would be no sense in which they could criticise, accept, reject or improve upon one another's accounts of fact. If it is true that the data must be available for the historian to experience, it is equally true that it must be publicly available.

The second point to note is the ambiguity in the suggestion that the historian is required to provide hypotheses to account for experienceable data. For the word 'data' is ambiguous as between things which are *given* in the sense of being available to present experience, and things which constitute *evidence*. Plainly – and this is the position for which Goldstein has argued – it is only when what is given is also evidence that it has to be explained historically. Equally plainly, however, there are many descriptions under which what is given would not constitute evidence of the sort which would require historical explanation – descriptions such as, say, those of its constitution in chemical or biological terms. What is required, therefore, is an account of the sort of description of the given which would turn it into evidence requiring historical explanation and here, despite Goldstein's attempt to drive a wedge between the real and the historical pasts, the answer must surely be description in the past-entailing terms which are a part of our everyday vocabulary, for what we want to know is what occurrences in the past brought about that object whose description entails that there were such occurrences. Thus taking data, in the sense of present objects, to be historical evidence is possible only if we presuppose that the present existence of the data is a consequence of causal processes in the past.

In this case, however, the description of the historian's position must be radically revised. We can no longer say that he constructs the past on the basis of data which he can experience. On the contrary, he can be confronted by the sort of data which requires historical explanation, i.e., by historical evidence, only on the presupposition that the data is a causal consequence of the past events which he seeks to state. This means that taking what is experienced to be historical evidence presupposes that it have an ontological status which transcends that of merely being part of historians' present experience, i.e., of being given.

These two claims – that something can be historical evidence only if it is public and is a consequence of causal processes which give it a character which transcends that which it has in virtue of being available to present experience – go a long way towards justifying the thesis that realism provides the only philosophical framework which can allow for a coherent notion of historical knowledge. For they amount, in effect, to showing that historical enquiry can be carried out only in a world whose characteristics transcend those of the experience of any given historian or set of historians. Our present experience of things may be a necessary condition of meaningful enquiries about the past, but unless what we experience is accepted as part of a world of experience-transcending processes, states of affairs, events and so on, we shall not find a conceptual framework of sufficient complexity to make historical practice a coherent and self-consistent activity. But since it is accepted on all sides that the practice is coherent, it cannot be correct to think of it as involving the notion of a past which exists only for consciousnesss.

If my account is correct, it would seem that the historical past cannot be just that set of conclusions which present evidence compels us to draw. For the notion of the historical past presupposes that of the real past as what has occurred whether we know it or not. If it is useful to retain the expression 'the historical past', it should be used, I suggest, as a name for that part of the real past which we happen to know.

REFERENCES

Collingwood, R. G. (1961) *The Idea of History*. Oxford, Clarendon Press.
Danto, A. C. (1965) *Analytical Philosophy of History*. Cambridge, Cambridge University Press.

Goldstein, L. J. (1976) *Historical Knowing*. Austin, University of Texas Press.

Goldstein, L. J. (1977) History and the Primacy of Knowing, *History and Theory*, Beiheft 16.

Harman, G. (1973) *Thought*. New Jersey, Princeton University Press.

Nowell-Smith, P. H. (1977) The Constructionist Theory of History, *History and Theory*, Beiheft 16.

Oakeshott, M. (1933) *Experience and Its Modes*. Cambridge, Cambridge University Press.

Putnam, H. (1975) *Mind, Language and Reality. Collected Papers* Vol. 2. Cambridge, Cambridge University Press.

Thagard, P. R. (1978) The Best Explanation: Criteria for Theory of Choice, *The Journal of Philosophy* LXXV, No. 2.

Walsh, W. H. (1951) *An Introduction to Philosophy of History*. London, Hutchinson.

Walsh, W. H. (1975) *Kant's Criticism of Metaphysics*. Edinburgh, Edinburgh University Press.

Walsh, W. H. (1977) Truth and Fact in History Reconsidered, *History and Theory*, Beiheft 16.

Bibliography of Published Writings
of W. H. Walsh

1939
Review of *A Short Commentary on Kant's 'Critique of Pure Reason'*
(A. C. Ewing), *Philosophy* **14**, 215–7.
Kant's criticism of metaphysics (I), *Philosophy* **14**, 313–25.
Kant's criticism of metaphysics (II), *Philosophy* **14**, 434–48.
Review of *The Kantian Philosophy of Space* (C. B. Garnett),
Philosophy **14**, 496–8.

1940
Two functions of the intellect, *Mind* **49**, 224–7.
Kant's conception of scientific knowledge, *Mind* **49**, 445–50.

1942
The intelligibility of history, *Philosophy* **17**, 128–43.

1943
The need for a philosophy of democracy (letter), *Philosophy* **18**, 285–7.

1944
Review of *Freedom Forgotten and Remembered* (H. Kuhn),
Philosophy **19**, 184–7.

1945
Review of *World Hypotheses: a Study in Evidence* (S. C. Pepper),
Philosophy **20**, 86–9.

1946
Hegel and intellectual intuition, *Mind* **55**, 49–63.
F. H. Bradley, Centenary article, *The Times Literary Supplement*
(unsigned), 2 February, p.54.
Review of *Introduction to Kant's 'Critique of Pure Reason'*
(T. D. Weldon), *Philosophy* **21**, 177–8.

1947
Reason and Experience. Oxford, Clarendon Press.
The character of a historical explanation, *Proceedings of the Aristotelian
Society* supp. vol.21, 51–68.
R. G. Collingwood's philosophy of history, *Philosophy* **22**, 153–60.

1948
Review of *Logical Studies* (H.H.Joachim), *Mind* 57, 524–7.

1949
Review of *The Life of Reason* (W.G.deBurgh), *Philosophy* 24, 376–9.

1950
Review of *Kant : Essai pour introduire en Philosophie le Concept de Grandeur négative* (R.Kempf), *The Philosophical Quarterly* 1, 77.

1951
An Introduction to Philosophy of History. London, Hutchinson. 2nd ed. (minor changes), 1958; 3rd ed. (revised with additional essays), 1967. American paperback as *Philosophy of History, an Introduction*, New York, Harper & Row, 1960. Hardback edition, original title: Atlantic Highlands, N.J., Humanities Press, 1976. Translated into Spanish, Hindi, Greek, Portuguese, Japanese.

1952
A note on truth, *Mind* 61, 72–4.
Review of *The Conditions of Knowing* (W.A.Sinclair), *The Philosophical Quarterly* 2, 267–8.

1953
On the philosophy of Hegel, *Philosophy* 28, 207–28.
A survey of work on Kant, 1945–51, *The Philosophical Quarterly* 3, 257–70.
A survey of work on Hegel, 1945–52, *The Philosophical Quarterly* 3, 352–61.
Review of *The Theory of Universals* (R.I.Aaron), *The Philosophical Quarterly* 3, 372–3.
Review of *Ethics and the History of Philosophy* (C.D.Broad), *Mind* 62, 570–1.

1954
Analytic-synthetic, *Proceedings of the Aristotelian Society* 54, 77–96.
Categories, *Kantstudien* 45, 274–85.
Review of *A Study of History* vols.VII–X (A.J.Toynbee), *The Times*, 14 October.
Review of *New Studies in the Philosophy of Descartes* and *Descartes' Philosophical Writings* (N.Kemp Smith), *Nature* 173, 416.

1955
The philosophy of Kant and his successors. In Levine,I. (ed.) *Philosophy – Man's Search for Reality*. London, Odhams Press.

1956

Bradley, Francis Herbert. Green, Thomas Hill. Kant, Immanuel.
Philosophy, history of (modern section). In *Encyclopaedia
Britannica*, 14th ed., revised version.
Review of *Reason and Revolution: Hegel and the Rise of Social Theory*
(2nd ed., H. Marcuse), *Philosophy* **31**, 267–8.

1957

The autonomy of ethics, *The Philosophical Quarterly* **7**, 1–14.
Schematism, *Kantstudien* **49**, 95–106.

1958

'Plain' and 'significant' narrative in history, *Journal of Philosophy* **55**,
479–84.

1959

'Meaning' in history. In Gardiner, P. (ed.) *Theories of History*.
New York, The Free Press; London, Collier-Macmillan.
True and false in metaphysics, *Filosofia* **10**, 715–32.
Review of *The Nature of Metaphysics* (D. F. Pears, ed.), *Philosophy* **34**,
53–4.

1960

Scepticism about morals and scepticism about knowledge, *Philosophy* **35**,
218–33.
Bradley et la métaphysique, *Les Études philosophiques* **15**, 29–50.
Review of *Hegel: A Re-Examination* (J. N. Findlay), *Philosophy* **35**,
138–45.
Review of *The Poverty of Historicism* (K. R. Popper), *Philosophy* **35**,
357–8.

1961

The limits of scientific history. In Hogan, J. (ed.) *Historical Studies III*.
London, Bowes and Bowes; Cork, Cork University Press.

1962

Plato and the philosophy of history: history and theory in the *Republic*,
History and Theory **2**, 3–16.
History and theory, *Encounter* **18**, June, 50–4.

1963

Metaphysics. London, Hutchinson. U.S. paperback edition: New York,
Harcourt, Brace.
Historical causation, *Proceedings of the Aristotelian Society* **63**, 217–36.
Toynbee reconsidered, *Philosophy* **38**, 71–8.

Kant's moral theology (Dawes Hicks Lecture on Philosophy),
  Proceedings of the British Academy **49**, 263–89.

1964
F. H. Bradley. In O'Connor, D. J. (ed.) *A Critical History of Western
  Philosophy.* New York, The Free Press; London, Collier-Macmillan.
  English original of item from *Les Études philosophiques* listed under
  1960.

1965
Moral authority and moral choice (The Presidential Address),
  Proceedings of the Aristotelian Society **65**, 1–23.
Hegel on the history of philosophy, *History and Theory*, Beiheft **5**;
  The Historiography of the History of Philosophy, 67–82.
Review of *The Concept of a Person* (A. J. Ayer), *The Philosophical
  Quarterly* **15**, 76–8.
Review of *Philosophy and History, a Symposium* (S. Hook, ed.),
  Mind **74**, 434–8.
Review of *The Later Philosophy of R. G. Collingwood* (A. Donagan),
  The Philosophical Review **74**, 119–22.

1966
Philosophy and psychology in Kant's *Critique*. In Heidemann, I. and
  Specht, E. K. (eds.) *Einheit und Sein : Gottfried Martin zum 65.
  Geburtstag.* Koln, Kolner Universitätsverlag.
Review of *Foundations of Historical Knowledge* (M. G. White),
  Political Science Quarterly **81**, 331–2.
Review of *Philosophy and the Historical Understanding* (W. B. Gallie),
  English Historical Review **81**, 220–1.
Review of *Philosophy of History* (W. H. Dray), *History and Theory* **5**,
  186–91.
Review of *The Philosophy of Hegel* (G. R. G. Mure), *Philosophical
  Books* **7**, no.2, 20–1.

1967
Colligatory concepts in history. In Burston, W. H. and Thompson, D.
  (eds.) *Studies in the Nature and Teaching of History.* London,
  Routledge and Kegan Paul; New York, Humanities Press.
Kant on the perception of time, *The Monist* **51**, 376–96.
Green, Thomas Hill. Kant, Immanuel. Metaphysics, Nature of. In
  Edwards, P. (ed.) *The Encyclopaedia of Philosophy*, New York,
  The Macmillan Co and The Free Press; London, Collier-Macmillan.
Review of *Francis Herbert Bradley* : '*les Présupposés de l'Histoire critique :
  étude et traduction* (P. Fruchon), *Mind* **76**, 602–3.
Review of *Hegel* (W. Kaufmann), *The Philosophical Review* **76**, 238–41.

Review of *The Bounds of Sense* (P. F. Strawson), *Philosophical Books* **8**, no.2, 29–31.
Review of *Analytical Philosophy of History* (A. C. Danto), *English Historical Review* **82**, 220–1.

1968
The practical and the historical past. In King, P. and Parekh, B. C. (eds.) *Politics and Experience.* Cambridge, Cambridge University Press.
Metaphysics. In Hirst, R. J. (ed.) *Philosophy : an Outline for the Intending Student.* London, Routledge and Kegan Paul.

1969
Hegelian Ethics. London, Macmillan. Also in Hudson, W. D. (ed.) *New Studies in Ethics,* vol.1. London, Macmillan, 1974. Translated into Spanish and Japanese.
The notion of an historical event, *Proceedings of the Aristotelian Society* supp. vol.**43**, 153–64.
Was Hegel a Great Philosopher? *The Times Literary Supplement* (unsigned), 19 June, 649–51.
Review of *The Credibility of Divine Existence : the Collected Papers of Norman Kemp Smith* (A. J. D. Porteous, R. D. Maclennan and G. E. Davie, eds.), *Philosophy* **44**, 70–1.
Review of *Kant's Analytic* (J. Bennett), *Ratio* **11**, 159–64.

1970
Pride, shame and responsibility, *The Philosophical Quarterly* **20**, 1–13.
Herbert James Paton, *Proceedings of the British Academy* **56**, 293–308.
H. J. Paton, 1887–1969, *Kantstudien* **61**, 27–32.

1971
Knowledge in its social setting, *Mind* **80**, 321–36.
Principle and prejudice in Hegel's philosophy of history. In Pelczynski, Z. A. (ed.) *Hegel's Political Philosophy : Problems and Perspectives.* New York, Cambridge University Press.
Social and personal factors in morality, *Idealistic Studies* **1**, 183–200.
Kant en het synthetische a priori (trans. W. J. van der Dussen), *Wisgerig perspectief op maatschappij en wetenschap* **11**, 168–77.
Review of *Bradley's Metaphysics and the Self* (G. L. Vander Veer), *The Philosophical Quarterly* **21**, 374–5.
Review of *A Behavioural Approach to Historical Analysis* (R. F. Berkhofer) *History and Theory* **10**, 241–6.

1972
Open and closed morality. In Parekh, B. and Berki, R. N. (eds.) *The Morality of Politics.* London, George Allen & Unwin.

Hume's concept of truth. In *Reason and Reality : Royal Institute of Philosophy Lectures, vol.*5, 1970–71. London, Macmillan.
Collingwood and metaphysical neutralism. In Krausz,M. (ed.) *Critical Essays on the Philosophy of R.G.Collingwood.* Oxford, Clarendon Press.
Review of *Early German Philosophy* (L.W.Beck), *Ratio* 14, 205–9.

1973
History as science and history as more than science, *Virginia Quarterly Review* 49, 196–212.
Review of *The Religious Dimension in Hegel's Thought* (E.L.Fackenheim), *The Philosophical Quarterly* 23, 77–9.
Review of *The Ascent to the Absolute* (J.N.Findlay), *Mind* 82, 300–3.
Review of *History as Applied Science; a Philosophical Study* (W.L.Todd), *Clio* 3, 84–6.

1974
Kant's concept of practical reason. In Körner,S. (ed.) *Practical Reason.* Oxford, Basil Blackwell.
Metaphysics. In *Encyclopaedia Britannica*, 15th ed.
Review of *Langage et Métaphysique dans la philosophie anglaise contemporaine* (P.Dubois), *Erasmus* 26, 193–5.

1975
Kant's Criticism of Metaphysics. Edinburgh, Edinburgh University Press. U.S. paperback edition: Chicago, Chicago University Press, 1976.
Intuition, judgment, appearance. In *Akten des 4. Kant-Kongresses* (Mainz, 6th-10th April, 1974, Teil III). Berlin, Walter de Gruyter.
The causation of ideas, *History and Theory* 14, 186–99.
Review of *Experiential Realism* (A.H.Johnson), *Mind* 84, 628–30.
Review of *Kant on History and Religion* (M.Despland), *Philosophical Books* 16, no.3, 20–2.
Review of *La Théologie kantienne précritique* (P.Laberge), *Canadian Journal of Philosophy* 4, 723–9.
Review of *Lectures on the Philosophy of World History, Introduction* (Hegel, trans. H.B.Nisbet) and of *Hegel on Reason and History* (G.D.O'Brien), *The Owl of Minerva* 7, 2–5.

1976
The logical status of Vico's ideal eternal history. In Tagliacozzo,G. and Verene,D.P. (eds.) *Giambattista Vico's Science of Humanity.* Baltimore, The Johns Hopkins University Press.
The constancy of human nature. In Lewis,H.D. (ed.) *Contemporary British Philosophy*, Fourth Series. London, George Allen & Unwin.
Kant and metaphysics, *Kantstudien* 67, 372–84.

The structure of Kant's antinomies. In *Proceedings of the Ottawa Congress on Kant*. Ottawa, University of Ottawa Press.

Review of *The Problem of Metaphysics* (D. M. Mackinnon), *Mind* **85**, 136–8.

Review of *Hegel* (C. Taylor), *Canadian Journal of Philosophy* **6**, 785–96.

1977

Truth and fact in history reconsidered, *History and Theory*, Beiheft **16**; *The Constitution of the Historical Past*, 53–71.

Review of *Kant and the Problem of History* (W. A. Galston), *History and Theory* **16**, 196–204.

1978

Review of *Vico and Herder: Two Studies in the History of Ideas* (I. Berlin), *Mind* **87**, 284–6.

1979

Review of *The Anatomy of Historical Knowledge* (M. Mandelbaum), *English Historical Review* **94**, 365–7.

Review of *Historical Explanation* (R. Martin), *Mind* **88**, 607–10.

Author Index

Subject Index